Economics today

for

Rebecca and Mark

Economics today

A Christian critique

Donald A. Hay

Fellow and Tutor in Economics,
Jesus College, Oxford

WILLIAM B. EERDMANS PUBLISHING COMPANY
GRAND RAPIDS, MICHIGAN

APOLLOS is an imprint of Inter-Varsity Press
38 De Montfort Street, Leicester LE1 7GP, England

First published 1989

British Library Cataloguing in Publication Data

Hay, Donald A. (Donald Andrew), *1944–*
Economics today
1. Economics. Christian viewpoints
I. Title.
261.8'5

ISBN 0-85110-797-4

Set in Linotron Baskerville

Typeset in Great Britain by Parker Typesetting Service, Leicester
Printed in Great Britain by
Billing & Sons Ltd, Worcester

Contents

Acknowledgments

Chapters Four to Seven are, in part, substantially revised versions of previously published materials. I am grateful to the following publishers for permission to use this material:

Chapters Four and Five are derived respectively from *A Christian Critique of Capitalism* and *A Christian Critique of Socialism* (Grove Booklets on Ethics, Nos 5(a) and 5(b), Nottingham, 1975 and 1982).

Chapter Six (especially section 4) appeared in *Perspectives on Economics* (CIO Publishing, 1984, for General Synod Board for Social Responsibility), Chapter 4, and is reproduced by permission of the Central Board of Finance of the Church of England.

Chapter Seven draws on R. Sider (ed.), *Lifestyle in the Eighties* (Paternoster Press, Exeter, 1982), Chapter 5, and J. Stott (ed.), *The Year 2000 AD* (Marshalls, Basingstoke, 1982), Chapter 3.

Chapter Eight (sections 3 to 6) was presented to the 1986 Au Sable Conference at Mancelona, Michigan, under the title 'Biblical Economics and the Long Term Future of Creation'.

Readers are asked to note that in the process of revision I have made substantial changes to my evaluation of particular economic issues. This book replaces the previous publications.

Many friends have been extremely helpful in reading various drafts: David Atkinson, Nigel Biggar, Paul Collier, Andrew Dilnot, Andy Hartropp, Dieter Helm, Oliver O'Donovan, A.G. Pouncy and George Yarrow. Andy Hartropp gave me access to unpublished material from his doctoral dissertation. Andrew Dilnot read an entire draft typescript and provided detailed comments, which were a great help in preparing the final version. Oliver O'Donovan has been a wise mentor for many years. His sustained encouragement and criticism have greatly improved the arguments of the book. These friends are not, however, to be held responsible for any deficiencies which remain.

Betty Ho Sang and Sue Chilton deciphered my handwriting and cheerfully produced typescripts of successive drafts.

The idea for this book was conceived about ten years ago. It has taken a long time to come to fruition, but I hope it is a better book in consequence. But for the encouragement of my wife, Elizabeth, it might never have appeared (Proverbs 31:29).

Donald Hay
Oxford
May 1988

Preface

The purpose of this book is to bring a Christian mind to bear on the discipline of economics. I am both a Christian and an academic economist. The content therefore represents a personal intellectual pilgrimage. It is not, of course, the first time that such a task has been attempted. However, on reading other books and papers on the subject I found myself very dissatisfied. At the risk of some caricature, books on Christianity and economics may be said to fall into two groups. Some books are written by theologians and ethicists. Almost invariably they are deficient in their understanding of economic analysis, and far too respectful of it. There is also a marked reluctance actually to apply theological insights in any substantial manner. Other books are written by economists. Not surprisingly the economic analysis tends to determine the shape of these works, with the theology appearing more or less as an afterthought, or, less commendably, as a prop to a pre-determined polemic.

Being an economist rather than a theologian, I have tried very hard not to fall into the latter trap. This explains why the book opens, in Chapter One, with a sustained presentation of biblical material relevant to our theme, leading in Chapter Two to the derivation of principles for economic life which are subsequently applied. But theological understanding needs to be matched by an appreciation of the methodological principles which underlie secular economic analysis. This is the content of Chapter Three, which develops a critique of economic methodology in the light of a Christian understanding of truth. The subsequent chapters of the book are studies which take the arguments of the first three chapters and apply them to particular areas of economic analysis. Most of the application is quite abstract, looking at general principles rather than specific cases. This is deliberate. The purpose is to equip the reader with arguments and principles that can continue to be applied as the nature of the economic problems confronting us changes.

In writing the book, I had in mind a university student with some training in economics. But the style is not, I hope, that of an economics text, through which a student has to work laboriously. On the contrary I hope they will find it a readable stimulus to thinking a bit harder about what they are being taught. I hope that the book is also accessible to intelligent non-economists, who are prepared to make some effort to read it. They may however find Chapter Three and the latter part of Chapter Eight rather hard going. Unfortunately, I believe Chapter Three is essential to a proper understanding not only of academic economics as it is practised in the West, but also to an understanding of the presuppositions of economists when they pronounce on public policy.

The scope of this book is so extensive that I have frequently trespassed into areas where my knowledge is minimal. Despite the advice of kind colleagues, I am only too well aware that my reading is insufficient and my understanding inadequate for what I am trying to do. I hope therefore that the book will be regarded as a stimulus to others, better qualified than I, to improve on what is written here. For myself, I shall keep on trying to improve my understanding, in obedience to Jesus' words: 'Love the Lord your God with all your heart and with all your soul *and with all your mind* and with all your strength' (Mark 12:30).

CHAPTER ONE
Christianity and economics: biblical foundations

1. Christianity and economics: an introduction to method

Few people would deny that economic issues remain high on the political agenda of the modern world. Choices between market and planned solutions in the allocation of resources, problems of unemployment and inflation, economic relationships between rich countries and poor countries, and sustainability of economic growth in the face of pollution and limited resources pose major questions to which answers are being sought. This search involves not just technical economic analysis; a wide range of ethical judgments is also required. What is the proper relationship between man and his environment? Can the holding of private property be morally justified? Is work no more than a necessary evil, or is the experience of work important to human fulfilment? Is it right that some should enjoy wealth and comfort, while others live in poverty and squalor? These, and similar questions, confront any sensitive economic analyst as soon as he looks up from his preoccupation with technical matters. Indeed the ethical issues may be an important determinant in his choice of economic problems for detailed analysis.

The thesis of this book is that Christianity has much to contribute to the analysis of these major economic issues. This is by no means a new thesis. Ever since mediaeval theologians debated the question of the Just Wage,

Christians of diverse theological persuasions have made their contribution.[1] This book is differentiated from previous works in two respects. The first is that the precise nature of economic problems tends to vary from one period to another. So each generation of Christian analysts has to bring theological insight to bear on a new set of issues. The second is that in establishing a Christian framework for analysis, this book will perhaps make more explicit use of biblical material than its predecessors. Even a cursory examination of the Scriptures reveals many passages with apparent relevance to our theme. Our objective is to see how these can be utilized to develop a distinctively biblical framework.

Given that we ascribe importance to the biblical witness, we are still faced with the problem of how to interpret it. Although the material is not lacking in self-interpretation, particularly in some of the New Testament epistles, it cannot be treated like a treatise or a textbook. Answers to questions cannot be obtained by turning to particular verses. This difficulty of interpretation is compounded by the fact that the biblical revelation is set in an historical context which is remote from our own. Our method of grappling with these difficulties is to rely on a systematic theology. This theology seeks to relate the elements of the biblical revelation in such a way that the significance and weight attached to each element can be more readily understood in the context of the whole. The possibility of constructing such a theology relies on a presumption that the biblical witness is itself consistent, a faithful record of the revelation of a consistent God. Our belief is that God does not act capriciously or arbitrarily, so that by reading of his dealings with man, we can discern consistent patterns in the relationships of God, man and the created order.

There are two dangers in any theological system. The first is that the system itself begins to become autonomous, obscuring rather than facilitating our understanding of the relationship between God and man. The second danger is that the *provisional* nature of a theological system is easily forgotten. It is derived from the primary material, by a process which involves both deduction and imagination.

But the theologian is himself subject to error in his thought. This suggests that the theological task needs to be conducted in the context of the community of faith. We shall be more secure in what we assert if a proposition is one which has received widespread assent in the history of the church, and which is accepted by the Christian community. Even then it will be provisional in the sense that it must remain open to modification or restatement in the light of the biblical revelation.

We see this as an interactive process. The theological system develops from the biblical material. Part of that system will involve principles for interpreting the material. But it is important to note that any tensions between the system and the biblical data must be resolved by adjusting the former, rather than discounting the latter. The Bible controls doctrine rather than the other way round.

The method outlined can help us with the two hermeneutical problems mentioned above. First, the system itself may suggest principles of interpretation. A particular narrative or element of teaching in the biblical materials will be examined for its significance within the theological system, paying regard to the biblical context and any interpretation given by the writers themselves. Second, it deals with the problem of cultural distance. We are looking for the universal principles of God's dealings with man. The death of Christ, for example, was a concrete event in a particular historical and cultural context. But it has a significance for all men in every generation, as the means by which man can be reconciled to God.

A consequence of adopting this method is that our treatment of the biblical material is *thematic* rather than strictly exegetical. For this reason we will not be particularly concerned with critical questions concerning the composition of different books. Our objective is to understand the elements of the biblical world-view, rather than to understand the process by which that world-view was formed and written down. In reaching that understanding we will not hesitate to follow a particular theme through different biblical literatures, and even from the Old Testament to the New.

We now sketch the theological themes which form the

reference point for the biblical analysis which follows. A complete articulation of a theological system lies outside the scope of this book. Since our concern is with social and economic life, it is the relation of the theological themes to that area which we stress. The main themes are creation, fall and judgment, and the people of God. This structure has the advantage that it is faithful to the biblical sequence, and to the biblical understanding of history.

The creation theme is prominent in the first two chapters of Genesis, though the idea of God as the creator and sustainer of the universe is a recurring theme throughout the Bible. The main elements are the sovereignty of God in creating an earth which is good, and the creation of man as part of, yet distinct from, the rest of the created order. The distinctiveness of man arises in part from his capacity to enter into relationship with God, and hence to have relationships with his fellow human beings. It also arises from his rôle as God's steward for creation. He is given dominion over the created order to care for it, and to use it to sustain his existence. This theme is further explored in section 2 of this chapter.

The second theme, that of the fall and judgment, is explored in section 3. Despite his high calling to relationship with God, and obedience to him, man chose to rebel against God, and to assert his independence from God. The consequences are dramatic. Man becomes subject to physical decay and death. Evil becomes an established feature of human life and human society. Human relationships are disrupted. Work becomes toil, and man's dominion over nature becomes harsh and exploitative. Furthermore, driven out from the presence of God in the Garden of Eden, man begins to construct his own security apart from God, and this is symbolized by the building of cities. The fall, and the consequent growth of evil, result in God's judgment.

This theme is established first in the story of the flood, where God demonstrates that evil cannot and will not be tolerated for ever. However, instead of immediate and total destruction, God shows his forbearance by saving a remnant, the family of Noah, which begins life again. This life is now regulated by a covenant described in more detail in section 4. This covenant is a framework for relationships between God and man, which takes account of the fallen nature of man. The open relationship for which man was created is no longer possible. Something altogether more formal is required. God states what he is prepared to do for man, and his purposes in so doing. Man's obligations in response to this gracious initiative from God are then stipulated.

The third theme is that of the people of God, and is the concern of sections 5 and 6. God has chosen to redeem, not to destroy. His method is the redemption of individuals in the world, creating a new redeemed community. In the Old Testament he calls Abraham, and his descendants, to form the community of Israel. They are to be a model people, a light to the nations and a vehicle and pattern of God's redemption. This is made clear in the events of the exodus, and the giving of a covenant at Sinai. That covenant spells out, in far greater detail than the previous covenants with Abraham, what God purposes to accomplish in his chosen people, and what he expects from them.

This covenant with Israel is however only a fore-shadowing of the new covenant which is disclosed in Christ. In the incarnation God shows, by sending his own Son, to what lengths he is prepared to go to redeem mankind. Jesus proclaimed the commencement of a new age, the kingdom of God. By his teaching and his ministry he made it clear that the kingdom demands of its adherents a radically new life. This life involves a new relationship with God, and a relationship with our fellow men based on self-giving love. Within this covenant, God offers the means to attain both of these. The death of Jesus on the cross, and his resurrection, dealt once and for all with the problem of human sin. The power of evil is broken, and the path back to God is open. On those who accept the new covenant God then has a further gift to bestow, the presence and power of the indwelling Holy Spirit to enable the believer to deal with his sinful nature and to lead the new life of the kingdom. The New Testament goes on from the gospels to detail the growth and development of the new covenant community, the church. The vision of the kingdom is translated into the concrete form of worshipping communities, not only in Palestine, but more widely in the Eastern Mediterranean.

The exposition of these biblical theological themes leaves unresolved how we are to make the move to universal principles which may be applied generally to economic life. Reactions to that question have varied from a denial that the exercise is possible to assertions that the biblical material can be applied directly. Our conclusion, in Chapter Two, is that the exercise is possible, but needs considerable care, and that the results can at best be provisional judgments. The method we adopt is to derive a set of principles for economic life which are universal in their application.

The content of these principles is set out in section 2 of Chapter Two. It may help the reader to follow the biblical analysis if a brief outline is given here. The organizing concept is that of stewardship. Our personal talents, and the natural resources with which we work, are God's provision for us. They are entrusted to us, and we will have to give account to God for the use we have made of them. We exercise our stewardship particularly in work. The fruits of our work are goods and services, which enable man to live in a way which respects his dignity. Since we are stewards working on God's behalf with the resources he has provided, there is an obligation on those who have much to provide for those who have little. The rich must help the poor. While these ideas are elaborated in more detail in Chapter Two, they remain in essence quite simple. However we hope to show in the rest of the book that they are powerful in application to economic problems.

A final section of Chapter Two deals with the biblical view of the political authorities in their God-given role of dealing with injustice in a fallen world. The involvement of governments in economic life is a major issue in debates about economic policy so an analysis of the political authorities is an essential complement to the derivation of economic principles.

2. Creation

The major biblical source for the doctrine of creation is found in the first two chapters of Genesis,[2] though it is a theme that recurs, particularly in the Old Testament. There are many references to creation in the Psalms (24:1–2; 33:6–7; generally in Psalms 95–98, and in 104), and in the prophetic writings (for example Isaiah 45:18). The stress in these passages is on God himself. Thus in Genesis 1, God is referred to no less than thirty-two times in thirty-one verses. The whole of creation begins with God, and is an expression of his will and purpose.

The word 'creator' from verse 1 is only used of God in the Old Testament. It means to bring something into existence from *nothing*, and without an intermediary. Furthermore, once it is brought to existence, it is sustained and perfected by his word of power (Hebrews 1:3).

The means of creation is also notable: God speaks. There is a recurring refrain, '. . . and God said', in Genesis 1:3, 6, 9, and so on. This point is stressed by the prologue to John's Gospel: 'In the beginning was the Word . . .'. The interpretation is that the universe is not the clockwork mechanism of the deists. A closer analogy would be that of the playwright and the play. God is not remote from his creation. He is the God who knows when a sparrow dies, and who counts the number of hairs on our heads.

The doctrine of creation has three implications. First, it makes objective knowledge of the physical world possible. God's character is consistent, so is the world that he has made. Second, the doctrine reminds us that it is God's world, not ours. He controls it by his word. But it is a part of the tragedy of man that he does not acknowledge God's sovereignty, and desires to take the created order for himself. Third, our worship should be directed to the creator and not the creation. A materialistic creed, or even materialism itself, allows the created order to usurp the creator in our affections and spiritual strivings.

We now turn to what it is that God creates. In Genesis 1:2 we learn that 'the earth was formless and empty'. God acts in creation to provide form— a stage— in the first three days of creation. Light and dark, sea and sky, and then a fertile earth are the stage. On days four and five, the actors begin to assemble: the lights of the night and the day, the creatures of water and air, and then the creatures of the land. God puts all these in their places: the creation is ordered and consistent, not haphazard and chaotic. So at each stage God reflects on his work, and says that it is good. It has purpose and value, in and of itself.

This account must exclude a universe that is self-existent and random. Jacques Monod in *Chance and Necessity*[3] has written: 'Chance alone is at the source of all creation in the biosphere. Pure chance, absolutely free but blind, is at the very root of the stupendous edifice of evolution'. But for all Monod's scientific prestige as a Nobel prize winner, this statement is utterly misleading.[4] In the physical sciences, 'chance' refers to lack of predictability (that is, unpredictable by us), not to having no determining causes. There is nothing in Genesis 1 either to confirm or disprove the scientific theory of evolution. A very different story is being told, and its unequivocal meaning is that our world was formed as God intended.

The stage has been set, the cast has assembled. There has been an ascending order of creation from the inanimate to the animate. Now the major character, man, appears on the stage. We note that his existence is continuous with nature. He is created on the same day as the animals. In Genesis 2 he is formed from the dust, explaining his continuity with the physical creation. But there is also discontinuity. This is emphasized by the threefold repetition of the word 'create' in 1:27, to indicate something quite new.

In verse 26 we are told that man is made in the image and likeness of God. In the ancient Near East, a king would often erect an image of himself in a territory as a symbol of his sovereignty. Something of the same idea may underlie the creation of man in God's image. But there is also the implication that man shows something of the attributes of God. In the context, that of God's purposeful activity in creation, the obvious attributes are those of creativity, purpose and discernment of values. Further, in verse 26, man is given 'dominion' over the created order. The word is a strong one, and implies that man is God's vice-gerent, and steward of the created order, with an important role to fulfil. The writer of Genesis sharpens this point by the device of encompassing the whole creation narrative in six days. Contrast the evidence from geology which suggests that the age of the earth runs into millions of years, and human history occupies only the last tiny fraction of that time. To the writer of Genesis creation is only important as a backdrop to human history: so it is accomplished in a *week*.

The nature of man's dominion and stewardship is spelt out in 1:28–30, and in 2:15. Man is enjoined to be fruitful and multiply. He is to exercise his dominion by filling and subduing the earth. The model is that of Adam in the Garden. He is to till it and to keep it. He is also, with the beasts and the birds, to sustain himself from the seeds and the fruits of the green plants. There is no mention, at this stage, of the eating of animals as food.

There is a paradox in the language. The description of man's dominion is in terms of subduing nature and controlling it. But this is offset by language which speaks of respect for nature, and an obligation to care for it. Thus the action of Adam in naming the animals in Genesis 2:19–20 suggests a desire to respect each animal for what it is. Similarly the activity of keeping and tilling a garden suggests care rather than exploitation.

We should particularly note that man's dominion over nature is characterized by work. He is made in the image of God who is himself described as resting from all his work (Genesis 2:3). Man's role in creation is not passive, but involves tilling and keeping the garden. The naming of the animals may suggest some element of intellectual effort and scientific endeavour, as man seeks to understand, and to differentiate, the various elements of the creation.

C. J. H. Wright has summarized[5] the creation structure as a triangle with God at the apex, and man and the earth at the other two vertices. The sides of the triangle represent the relationships involved. God relates to man personally, since man is made in God's image and is capable of relationship with him. God relates to his creation by sustaining and

upholding it. Man relates to the creation by exercising
dominion and caring for the creation, which in turn is
fruitful and supplies an environment within which man can
enjoy his existence.

3. The fall and judgment

The contrast between Genesis 2 and Genesis 3 is dramatic.
The narrative passes from life that is good and fruitful to a
sombre pattern of evil, pain and death. The story of the fall
is descriptive rather than explanatory. We are told *what*
happened: but its explanation has been the source of a
great deal of philosophical and theological discussion ever
since.[6] It would be inappropriate to detail these discussions
here. But we should note that the story insists that Adam
had a real choice, and that the nature of his offence was
disobedience to God. The story of temptation by the ser-
pent makes it clear that the appeal was to human pride: the
desire to establish autonomy and independence from God.
Bonhoeffer[7] stressed the subtle transition from being in the
'likeness' of God (Genesis 1:26) to being 'like God' (Genesis
3:5). Man in the image of God is obedient to the word of
God, and is God-like in his existence for his neighbour, and
his dominion over nature. Man 'like God' stresses his autonomy. His is the knowledge of good and evil; his actions are
no longer bound by obedience to the word of God. His
glory, being made in the image of God, is perverted to
become a fatal flaw as he takes upon himself the right to
exercise the powers that his nature implies, but without
restraint. Three consequences follow, affecting the relationships between God, man and earth which were outlined
in the previous section.

   We consider first the relationship between man and
nature. Man is driven out of Eden, and a curse is laid on his
dominion over creation. '. . . Cursed is the ground because
of you; through painful toil you will eat of it all the days of
your life. It will produce thorns and thistles for you, and
you will eat the plants of the field. By the sweat of your brow
you will eat your food until you return to the ground . . .'

(Genesis 3:17–19). Cain is told: 'When you work the ground, it will no longer yield its crops for you . . .' (4:12).

The significance of this curse is that the earth no longer provides a responsive environment for man. The breakdown in relationship has effects in both directions. From the fall onwards it is evident that man is killing animals for food. Working the land now involves an element of struggle and domination. It is a sharp contrast to the creation picture of man caring for a garden, and naming the animals. In this lies the seed of the ruthless exploitation of nature which is characteristic of modern man.

In the other direction, from the earth to man, there is a consistent emphasis in the Old Testament on the occurrence of natural disasters as a consequence of man's sinfulness. In the early chapters of Genesis, the paradigm of natural disaster as a judgment on sin is the flood. The consequences of the fall are the growth and spread of evil. 'The LORD saw how great man's wickedness on the earth had become, and that every inclination of the thoughts of his heart was only evil all the time' (Genesis 6:5). 'Now the earth was corrupt in God's sight and was full of violence. God saw how corrupt the earth had become, for all the people on earth had corrupted their ways' (6:11–12). This is the same created order of which it was written in Genesis 1:31, 'God saw all that he had made, and it was very good.' It is not surprising therefore that God regrets his creation, and grieves over the evil state to which it has fallen. He determines therefore to 'put an end to all people . . . I am . . . going to destroy both them and the earth' (6:13).

In the aftermath of the flood God makes a covenant which includes the promise not to destroy the whole created order. However that promise does not rule out the possibility that fallen man will find the earth a more difficult environment, and that God can use natural disasters to discipline evil men and nations. The latter is evident from a number of Old Testament passages. There are the plagues on Egypt prior to the exodus of the children of Israel (Exodus 7 and following). The people of Israel are also warned that one of the consequences of disobedience is that the land will 'vomit' them out (Leviticus 20:22), which is

presumably a reference to the revulsion of the created
order against a people that abuses its God-given privileges.
The curses of Leviticus 26 include references to natural
disasters such as plague and wild beasts. 1 Kings 17 seems to
imply that the drought which afflicted Israel in the reign of
Ahab was a consequence of the wickedness of the king.
Jeremiah is given a 'word of the LORD . . . concerning the
drought' in Judah, which is set in the context of a judgment
on a disobedient people (Jeremiah 14). Ezekiel prophesies
famine and desolation on a land which has deserted God
(Ezekiel 14), and the prophet Joel refers to a plague of
locusts as God's instrument of judgment on a disobedient
people (Joel 1:2–4).

Second, man's relationship with his fellow man suffered
grievous disorder. The curse pronounced on the woman in
Genesis 3:16 indicates that desire and power will become
symptomatic of the marriage relationship, replacing the
mutuality and delight that characterizes the creation of
woman for man in Genesis 2:18–25. The nakedness of 2:25,
implying openness to one another, is replaced by the clothing of 3:21 symbolizing self-regarding shame. At the beginning of Genesis 4, the jealousy between Cain and Abel
erupts into murder. Cain becomes a fugitive, and God puts
his mark on him with the words, 'If anyone kills Cain, he
will suffer vengeance seven times over' (Genesis 4:15). Lam-
ech boasts that he has killed a man for wounding him, and a
young man for injuring him (4:23). The implication is that
violence, and the exercise of brute strength, are now significant in human society.

The third relationship is that between God and man. At
the fall the relationship is broken by man's disobedience
and his assertion of his autonomy. Man is cut off from God,
is incapable of leading a life which is pleasing to God, and
his destiny is death and judgment. God's gracious initiative
in dealing with this radical problem is the major theme of
the biblical story. However for our purposes we need to
consider one particular aspect of the consequence of the
fall, the building of cities, which has been much emphasized
by Ellul,[8] who evidently draws his inspiration from
Augustine.

After the murder of Abel, Cain is cursed by God: '. . . You will be a restless wanderer on the earth . . .' (Genesis 4:12). In response, '. . . Cain went out from the LORD's presence and lived in the land of Nod, east of Eden'. Nod means 'wandering'. Cain wanders, seeking to regain Eden, to find a way back to God. In Nod, Cain does two things (Genesis 4:17). First, he knows his wife, who bears a son, Enoch. Second, he builds a 'city', which he also calls Enoch. Enoch can signify initiation or inauguration, as opposed to creation. In these acts Cain symbolizes two concerns of man without God. The first is to perpetuate his life in the life of a child. He procreates life, in pale imitation of God's creation and sustaining of life. The second is the search for security. For the Eden of God, man substitutes his own constructed environment. He constructs a new, relatively secure, world. He realizes man's wisdom in material form, bending natural materials to his own ends.[9]

The role of the city emerges even more strongly in the description of the work of Nimrod in Genesis 10:6–12. Nimrod is a descendant of Ham, on whom a curse has been laid that he will be a servant and a slave (9:25–27). Nimrod reacts to the curse by seeking power in the building of cities. He responds to God's judgment by determining to take care of his problems on his own. He is described as a 'mighty hunter before the LORD'. But he is better understood as a conqueror and plunderer. The city is the centre from which he wages war. He is 'before the LORD', since even though he is in rebellion against God he cannot escape God's watchful eye. Among the cities he builds is Babel (Babylon).

Since Babylon plays such an important part in biblical history and imagery, it is worth examining its significance in some detail. We note, for example, that the writer locates Babel in Shinar, which is the land of sin, a place of noise and destruction. Thus in Zechariah 5, Shinar is the place to which all wickedness is consigned. Further insights as to the significance of Babel are given by Genesis 11:1–9. Once again the context is that of migration and wandering. The people come together to provide security for themselves, and to 'make' a name, lest they be scattered again. The theological significance of the story lies in the stress on the action of the builders in creating their own secure environment, and their desire for domination and power as epitomized by the building of the tower. It is not just security, but also power that they are seeking. It is this that explains the action of God. He perceives in the collective action of man, with a will for power and fame apart from God, the potential for immense evil (11:6). So his action is preventive. He destroys their unity of purpose by breaking down the communication between them, and once again they are scattered.

The importance of Babylon in biblical history is that it epitomizes *the* city, in rebellion against God. It is the embodiment of sinful arrogance (Isaiah 13:19; 14:13; Jeremiah 51:6 and following). So God's judgment in these passages falls on the city itself, not on its individual inhabitants. Thus in the judgment on Babylon in Revelation 14:6–12 is incorporated a judgment on all cities (Revelation 16:18–19). It is a judgment on all she represents. In Isaiah 14, Babylon is the maker of war. She is the centre of commerce in Revelation 18, a passage which is transposed from the condemnation of the prosperous commercial city of Tyre in Ezekiel 28 and Isaiah 23. In that condemnation there is a strong association drawn between commerce and idolatry. The link perhaps lies in the greed for material things that the biblical writers associate with trade and commerce. In the absence of God, man makes his idols from those things which give him security and power. In Revelation 17 and 18, Babylon is revealed as the city with the capacity to seduce and control political and economic forces. Yet in so doing, man becomes mere merchandise, a slave to the city.

But Revelation speaks of a judgment on the city which is yet to be consummated. In the meantime even the people of God must live in the city, and seek its welfare. Thus Babylon is the place of captivity for the people of God, yet Jeremiah encourages them to '... seek the peace and prosperity of the city' and to 'pray to the LORD for it' (Jeremiah 29:4–7). Indeed the presence of the righteous in the city may be its guarantee of survival, as the story of Abraham's intercession for Sodom suggests (Genesis 18:16–33). Judgment will come, and the people of God will be told to leave (see Jeremiah 50:2, 8; Revelation 18:2–4). Their last act before leaving will be to pronounce God's judgment.

We can now summarize the significance of the theme of the fall and judgment for our subsequent analysis of economic issues. First, the curse on man's relationship with the land can explain the perception of work as toil, and the way in which the natural environment is exploited by man. Second, the interpretation of the building of cities as man's response to judgment helps us to understand the nature of the human enterprise apart from God, including all aspects of economic and political life. It is a warning to us to be suspicious of political and economic programmes that claim they can bring solutions to problems of human need. It is also a warning concerning the dangers of concentrations of political and economic power. Third, the fact of the fallen nature of man must be taken into account when we move from the stating of ethical principles to their application to particular human circumstances. This point is taken up in Chapter Two below.

4. The covenant with Noah

Despite the growth of evil and its consequences, it seems that God has graciously decided to stay his hand in executing judgment. The clue to understanding this lies in the covenant made with Noah after the flood.[10] We will argue that this covenant implies mechanisms which check the growth of evil and therefore defer its necessary destruction by God. These mechanisms allow time and space for God's gracious initiative of salvation to come to fruition. Evil is restrained so that man and the created order may eventually be renewed.

God's dealings with Noah after the flood involve a renewal of the creation ordinances, but in a modified form, linked to the making of a covenant. We will look at the covenant first, since this records the promises of God. Specifically God makes a covenant with the whole created order, beginning with Noah and his family, but including

all the living creatures that had gone with Noah into the
ark. In this covenant, God promises that he will never again
bring a flood to destroy 'all flesh' on the earth. For all future
generations the natural cycle of the seasons will continue. It
does not exclude, as we saw above, natural disasters limited
in time and place, possibly linked to judgment on particular
nations or peoples. This covenant is then sealed with the
sign of the rainbow, which is described as a reminder to *God*
of the promise which he has made.

Echoes of this promise to sustain the natural order can be
found elsewhere in the biblical record. Thus the psalmist
extols God: 'The LORD is good to all; he has compassion on
all he has made' (Psalm 145:9); 'The eyes of all look to you,
and you give them their food at the proper time' (Psalm
145:15). Jesus speaks of the Father who '... causes his sun
to rise on the evil and the good, and sends rain on the
righteous and the unrighteous' (Matthew 5:45). The same
thought is part of Paul's appeal to the Athenians in Acts
14:17.

It is only in the context of this covenant promise that the
renewal of the creation ordinances to Noah makes sense
(Genesis 9:1–7). But the ordinances are greatly modified.
Noah and his family are enjoined to be fruitful and multiply, and to fill the earth. The living creatures are delivered
into the hand of man, together with the rest of creation. But
the relationship is no longer one of harmony between man
and the created order. On the contrary, 'The fear and
dread of you will fall upon all the beasts of the earth and all
the birds of the air ...' (9:2). The living creatures are now
ordained as food for man. But God is well aware that to
leave man without restraints is to permit evil and corruption
to grow again. So he makes two stipulations. The first is that
the life of the animal is to be respected. The blood, which
symbolizes the life of the animal, is not to be eaten with the
flesh. In taking the life of the animal to provide food, man is
reminded that that life is not to be taken wantonly or
wastefully. The second stipulation is that man's life is to be
protected. God states a law, that man's life is not to be taken,
and a principle of justice, that the shedding of blood must
be paid for by the life of the one who did the killing. This

particular case exemplifies the two aspects of God's provision of law for sinful mankind. The law states the standard that God requires. The stipulated punishment is no more than is necessary to restrain the spread of evil.

God's provisions for restraint of evil are essential if man is to be able to live out his life. God's purpose is to give man time to repent, and to turn to God, and to give space for his scheme of salvation to be worked out in the people of God. These restraints, together with the continuation of the cycles of the natural order, are sometimes described as providence or 'common grace'.[11] This grace is common in the sense that it extends to all mankind, regardless of their spiritual standing before God.

There are various aspects to providence. One, already mentioned, is the stability of the natural order of creation. A second is the operation of conscience in the life of man. Paul sums it up in Romans 2:14–15 as follows: 'Indeed, when Gentiles, who do not have the law, do by nature things required by the law, they are a law for themselves, even though they do not have the law, since they show that the requirements of the law are written on their hearts . . .'. The point is that the image of God in man is marred but not destroyed by the fall. Man without God is capable of acts of kindness; he is capable of showing love; and he is capable of refraining from acts of violence.

A third aspect of providence is the revelation of God's law, in the first place to Moses and the prophets, and later in the teaching of Jesus. This law comes to be embodied in the institutional life of God's people, and it is the quality of that life which is a light to the heathen. Thus Abraham is promised that through him and his descendants all mankind will be blessed. Israel is described as a 'light for the Gentiles' in Isaiah 42:6 and 49:6. The same ideal recurs in the Sermon on the Mount, where Jesus challenges the people of God to be 'the light of the world' and 'the salt of the earth'. He goes on to say, 'Let your light shine before men, that they may see your good deeds and praise your Father in heaven' (Matthew 5:13–16). In the scheme of salvation, the people of God are a light not only to remind others of their spiritual state, but also as an example of how to live.

The fourth aspect of God's common grace or providence is the existence of authorities in society. This is discussed most explicitly in Romans 13:1–7. In this passage Paul is continuing with the theme of God's sovereignty in human affairs, which he has expounded in relation to sin and salvation in the first eleven chapters. The question in chapter 13 is how the Christian should relate to the state. The answer is to see it as one aspect of God's providence, moral rule and ordering of the world. There is a definite parallel with the teaching about conscience in Romans 2. Paul writes: 'For rulers hold no terror for those who do right, but for those who do wrong . . . he is God's servant, an agent of wrath to bring punishment on the wrongdoer. Therefore, it is necessary to submit to the authorities, not only because of possible punishment but also because of conscience. This is also why you pay taxes, for the authorities are God's servants, who give their full time to governing' (Romans 13:3–6). The authorities, then, if they fulfil their God-given role in society, are to restrain the growth of evil and violence, and to provide an environment in which the individual and the family can lead a relatively peaceful life. This is a theme to which we return later in the chapter.

The relevance of the covenant with Noah for our later discussion is evident. First, the created order is itself preserved by God, and despite man's fallen nature the creation mandate to man as steward of the created order is restated. The pattern and purpose of economic activity enshrined in creation are thereby continued, albeit in modified form. Second, God's final judgment on evil is postponed, and the growth of evil is restrained by the operation of conscience, by the revelation of God's law, and by the institution of authorities in society.

But God is not only concerned with making life tolerable for his creatures. He is also reaching out in love to call man to himself, to redeem him from the consequences of sin and death. He does this by creating communities of people, the people of God. They are to be a witness to the love of God, and a witness to how he requires man to live. With his people God makes a covenant which details the nature and content of God's gracious promise, and the response that he demands in terms of faith and obedience to him. It is these covenant communities, Israel and the church, to which we now turn.

5. The people of God: the children of Israel

The story of the people of God in the Old Testament begins at the call of Abraham in Genesis 12 with the promise that God will make of Abraham's descendants a great nation, through whom all the families of the earth will be blessed. It is notable that this passage follows the story of Babel with the scattering of peoples, and that Abraham himself is called to leave the city of Haran and become a wanderer. It is only outside the environment of the city, with its pagan influences arising from man's will for power, that God can meet with the man he has chosen, and that that man can respond in faith and obedience.

The promise to Abraham is renewed in Genesis 13, after Abraham has parted from his nephew Lot, but this time it is associated with the promise not only of a great nation, but also of a land in which to dwell.

> 'Lift up your eyes from where you are and look north and south, east and west. All the land that you see I will give to you and your offspring for ever. . . . Go, walk through the length and breadth of the land, for I am giving it to you' (Genesis 13:14–17).

The fulfilment of these promises to Abraham is the subject of the Pentateuch. God acts in history to bring the children of Israel out of slavery in Egypt. He bears with their rebellion in the wilderness, and for forty years they are condemned to wandering before they finally enter the promised land under the leadership of Joshua.

However our interest is not in the history *per se*, but in the covenant which God makes with the people of Israel at Sinai, a covenant which is renewed and applied in the book of Deuteronomy prior to the entry into the land. The significance of this covenant is that it deals with the restoration of the 'triangular' relationship between God, man and earth which was broken by the fall.[12] The restored pattern relates God, his chosen people and their land.

The covenant at Sinai, inaugurated through Moses, contains three characteristic elements. First, God reminds the people of what he has done for them in bringing them out of Egypt (Exodus 19:4). Second, God calls on the people to obey him and to keep the covenant (verse 5). Third, God makes a promise, which is conditional on the people fulfilling their part of the covenant: '... if you obey me fully and keep my covenant, then out of all nations you will be my treasured possession. Although the whole earth is mine, you will be for me a kingdom of priests and a holy nation' (verses 5–6).

The Law or *torah* is the substance of the second part of the covenant pattern: it spells out what God requires of his people. It is summed up in the covenant rule: 'Be holy because I, the LORD your God, am holy' (Leviticus 19:2). To be 'holy' requires the covenant people both to '... love the LORD your God with all your heart and with all your soul and with all your strength' (Deuteronomy 6:5) and to '... love your neighbour as yourself' (Leviticus 19:18). These two aspects are clearly present in the Decalogue, which begins with a man's duty towards God and particularly with the injunction to avoid idolatry, and then goes on to the prohibitions relating to a man's relationship with his fellow men. The two aspects are also characteristic of the Book of the Covenant, Exodus 20:22–23:19, to be considered in more detail below, where they are interwoven rather than separated out. The implication is that for the covenant people love for God and love for one's neighbour cannot be separated or divided. Both are appropriate to a holy life.

The means of expressing the covenant relationship with God is spelt out in the Holiness Code of Leviticus 17–26, which follows the detailed explanation of the construction of the Tabernacle. The sacrificial system and the rituals associated with it are designed to remind the Israelites of God's requirements, that they should be holy, that their wrongdoing deserves death (for which the death of sacrificial animals makes symbolic atonement), and that they need to rely wholly on the mercy of God. However, that aspect of the Law is not a primary focus of this book, since we are more concerned with the social and economic aspects of the life of the covenant people. But we need to remember that these aspects cannot and should not be divorced from the total structure of the covenant. We shall consider later how this will affect the use of the covenant material relating to social and economic life in drawing ethical conclusions.

The teaching of the Law concerning economic and social life can be found in three places. The first is in the Book of the Covenant in Exodus 20:22–23:19. The ostensible setting is of a Bronze Age nomadic people. So while there are some references to land and to crops, more consideration is given to the use of animals, and disputes about them. There are also many detailed regulations with respect to social relationships and the administration of justice.

The second passage is in Leviticus 25, and forms part of the Holiness Code, which is primarily concerned with sacrificial and priestly ritual. It extends the sabbatical principle to the use of the land, introduces the notable institution of the Jubilee and makes provision for support for a fellow Israelite who has fallen on hard times and lost his land. This passage is evidently applicable to the context after the settlement of the promised land. In some ways, its inclusion in the Holiness Code is puzzling. But it probably bears witness to the point we have already made: that a right relationship with God, righteousness in respect of the use of the land, and love of neighbour, are inextricably linked in the requirement that the covenant people be holy.

The third group of passages is found in Deuteronomy. The context is that of the people poised ready to enter the promised land, and the book is presented as Moses' last address to the people before his death. It has the standard content of a covenant. The history of God's dealings with the people is remembered. The people are reminded of God's requirements of obedience to his law. The consequences of obedience and disobedience— blessings and curses— are spelt out. The Law is expounded in chapters 5

to 26, beginning with a restatement of the Decalogue and
going on to detailed commands, which are broadly divided
between those relating to worship and ritual purity, and
those relating to social and economic relationships. Once
again the various aspects are interwoven, suggesting that it
needs to be looked at as a whole. Not surprisingly the laws
are more appropriate to a settled people, rather than a
nomadic one: for example there is provision for cities of
refuge (19:1–13), land boundaries are to be respected
(19:14), and there is reference to local administration of
justice (16:18–20).

Within this body of law it is possible to discern the main
features of the social and economic organization envisaged,
and the provisions for the administration of justice.[13] This
organization represented an ideal for the people of God as
they settled in the land. We shall see subsequently that the
reality was somewhat different.

(a) The social structure

The main elements of the social structure were the tribe,
the clan and the family. As we shall see below, these units
were fundamental in the allocation of the land. In the
conquest of the land, military organization was by tribes.
Once the land had been settled, the tribe became less
important. A clan, consisting of several families related by
ancestry, would settle in a small 'town' or village, possibly
for mutual security. Such an organization is implicit, for
example, in the story of Gideon in Judges 6.

The family was represented by people with close blood
ties. Within the extended family, obligations for mutual
support were very important. These even extended to an
obligation on a brother to take as his wife his brother's
widow (Deuteronomy 25:5–10). There is also considerable
stress on the basic family unit. This is indicated by the
injunction in the Decalogue to honour parents, and by the
prohibitions on adultery and coveting another man's
spouse. These injunctions and prohibitions are spelt out in
subsequent passages of the Law. For examples we may take
the terrible punishments to be meted out to a rebellious son
in Deuteronomy 21:18–21, or the regulation of divorce in

Deuteronomy 24:1–4. On a happier note there is the requirement that a newly married man is to be absolved from military service for a year: 'he is to be free to stay at home and bring happiness to the wife he has married' (Deuteronomy 24:5).

(b) The division of the land

Underpinning this social structure was the system of land-holding, which determined the economic structure of the community. In the ancient Near East, the feudal system of a fief was widespread: a family or individual would be made a grant of land by the ruler in return for the obligation to perform specified services. The service was tied to the land, so it was inherited or sold with it. This system never applied in Israel, but the same idea existed transposed to the theological plane. Yahweh is the Lord of Israel, so he is the Lord of the land too. This is categorically expressed in Leviticus 25:23: 'The land must not be sold permanently, because the land is mine . . .'. The fact that the land is given to Israel as an inheritance (Deuteronomy 4:38) emphasizes the theological dimension of their occupation of the land: it is an indication of Israel's sonship, a sign of the covenant relationship, and a fulfilment of the promises to Abraham. The land to the Israelites symbolized their spiritual heritage: it was a witness to the fact that God had chosen them.

The status of the Israelites in respect of the land is made clear by the continuation of Leviticus 25:23, the first part of which was quoted above: '. . . because the land is mine and you are but aliens and my tenants'. The words for 'aliens' and 'tenants' ('strangers' and 'sojourners', RSV) are precisely those which are used elsewhere in the law for those who live in the land but are not ethnic Israelites, and therefore have no security or inheritance. The dependence of the Israelites on God for their land could scarcely be more forcefully stated.

The fact of God's ownership limits the rights of the human occupants. They are required to leave the gleanings for the poor (Leviticus 19:9–10; 23:22; Deuteronomy 24:19–21). A passer-by has the right to satisfy his hunger when passing through a field or vineyard (Deuteronomy

23:24–25). A tithe is to be given to God each year (Leviticus 27:30–32), and an additional tithe to the poor every third year (Deuteronomy 14:28–29; 26:12). The land itself is to be allowed the rest of a sabbatical year (Leviticus 25:2–7).

The actual division of the land between the families of Israel is prescribed in Numbers 26:55–56 and 33:54. The land is first divided by tribes, and then within tribes it is allocated by casting lots. Joshua 13–19 describes how this worked out in the actual occupation of the land. Numbers 26:52 implies equality of landholdings by families: '. . . The land is to be allotted to them as an inheritance based on the number of names . . .' in the tribe. The drawing of lots to allocate the land avoids the invidious question of how to distinguish good and poor lands that will arise in any administrative allocation. The only tribe not to be allocated land was the Levites. They were to be set aside dwelling-places in the towns.

The allocation of land to each family was strongly defended. We have already drawn attention to the injunctions against the moving of boundary stones (Deuteronomy 19:14; 27:17). In addition, land could not be alienated permanently from the family. Leviticus 25:8–13 provides for the institution of Jubilees every fifty years, when land is to be returned to the family to which it was originally allocated. If an Israelite is forced to sell his land due to poverty or misfortune, the price is to be reckoned on the basis of the number of years to the Jubilee when it will be returned to him (25:13–17). It is also incumbent on the next-of-kin, if there is one of sufficient means, to come to his rescue by redeeming the property for him (25:25–28). The reluctance of Naboth to sell his family land to Ahab in 1 Kings 21 is certainly explicable by these provisons of the Law.

(c) The pattern of work

The normal pattern envisaged in the Law is work on the family land. Hence, if the allocation of land by families is protected there should be no lack of work opportunities for the individual. If, however, an Israelite falls on hard times, and loses possession of his land, then his brother is to take care of him (Leviticus 25:25). He is to be maintained, and to be treated as a hired servant (25:39–40). Those who by definition do not possess any land— the aliens and the tenants— are also to be given work. All wage labourers are protected by the provision that they are to be well treated and to be paid immediately on the day that they earn their wage (Deuteronomy 24:14–15).

These provisions were also designed to prevent slavery of Israelites: if one becomes a slave, by falling into debt to a stranger, then a near kinsman is enjoined to buy him out of it (Leviticus 25:47–55). However the same prohibition of slavery does not apply to non-Israelite slaves[14] (Leviticus 25:44–46). But there is a general injunction in this case: 'Do not oppress an alien; you yourselves know how it feels to be aliens, because you were aliens in Egypt' (Exodus 23:9). Furthermore a fugitive slave is not to be restored to his master: he is to be allowed to choose where he will dwell in one of the towns (Deuteronomy 23:15–16).

The only section of the people who fell outside these provisions for work were the Levites. Holding no land, they were in no position to work to support themselves. Hence the requirement that other tribes should pay a tithe for their support (Numbers 18:21–24), and the right given to the Levites to retain a portion of sacrificial victims for their own consumption.

(d) Lending and borrowing

The provisions concerning lending and borrowing also make a distinction between transactions between Israelites and transactions with foreigners.

> Do not charge your brother interest, whether on money or food or anything else that may earn interest. You may charge a foreigner interest, but not a brother Israelite; so that the LORD your God may bless you in everything you put your hand to in the land . . . (Deuteronomy 23:19–20).

> If one of your countrymen becomes poor . . ., help him . . . Do not take interest of any kind from

him ... You must not lend him money at interest
or sell him food at a profit (Leviticus 25:35–37).

The reason for this prohibition on interest is presumably
that a fellow Israelite who is in need is to be treated as one
who needs to be helped, rather than as an opportunity for
financial gain. But normal financial transactions with
foreigners are acceptable,[15] though even here the general
requirement not to oppress strangers could act as a break
on usurious greed. The problem with banning interest on
loans between Israelites is that there is no financial incentive
to lend to a poor brother, particularly if the seventh year,
the year of release from debt, is near (Deuteronomy
15:7–11). So the injunction follows: '... I command you to
be open-handed towards your brothers and towards the
poor and needy in your land' (verse 11).

(e) Markets

The Law has nothing to say directly about the regulation of
markets, though the existence of markets can be inferred
from the references to the use of money. For example in
Deuteronomy 14:22–27, those living too far from the
shrine to bring their tithes in kind are enjoined to turn the
produce into money, go up to the shrine and purchase
produce there. There is also an injunction to use fair
weights and measures: 'The LORD your God detests anyone
who does these things, anyone who deals dishonestly' (Deuteronomy 25:13–16). But even this passage makes no direct
mention of markets.

The reason for this silence about markets is possibly that
the market economy under the economic structures
envisaged by the Law would be very small. Each family
would have its own farm. The produce of that farm would
provide for subsistence of the family, and for the tithes,
which frequently could be made in kind. As we have seen,
the system of wage labour was for emergency only, and
even these payments could be in terms of subsistence,
rather than a money wage. The absence of any financial
markets (no money-lenders evidently) implied that a
family's prosperity depended entirely on the success or

otherwise of its farming enterprise. Each family had to decide how much effort to put into that enterprise. The returns are returns to the whole enterprise and accrue to the family: there is no division between wages and profits. In terms of modern economic analysis, the system approximated to the kind of subsistence farming which characterizes much of the rural economy in the third world, and would be characterized as 'primitive'.

(f) The problem of poverty

Although the primary economic organization is that of the family farm, which provides a livelihood for the men of the population, the range of mechanisms to deal with poverty is very remarkable. For those without family land for any reason, the stranger, the fatherless and the widow, there is the right to glean in fields and vineyards, the farmer being exhorted not to harvest too carefully (Deuteronomy 24:19–22). If they are involved in wage labour, then wages are to be paid immediately on the day, and not held back (Deuteronomy 24:14–15). If a farmer falls into poverty, for example through the failure of a harvest, then the extended family is required to maintain him by making a loan (Leviticus 25:35–38). This loan, as we have seen, is to be made without interest. A millstone, essential for preparing food, is not to be taken as collateral, and if a cloak is so taken it must be returned to the owner at night for him to sleep in (Deuteronomy 24:6, 10–13). All debts are to be cancelled at the end of every seven years (Deuteronomy 15:1–3). If a family falls into poverty *and* loses its land, then there is an obligation on members of the extended family to help them out. If they can, they are to redeem the family land (Leviticus 25:47–55). If this is not possible, then the poor man is to be taken on as a hired servant, until his land is returned to him at the Jubilee (25:39–41). The Jubilee means that a family will not be alienated from its land for ever.

(g) The administration of justice

We complete our review of the Law in respect of the organization of economic life with a consideration of the administration of justice, and of government.

The primary administrative unit was the village or 'town', and authority lay with the elders. It is probable that the elders were the heads of all the families represented in the village. Their responsibilities are not spelt out in the Law, but are alluded to, mainly in judicial functions. Thus they are required to deal with unsolved murders (Deuteronomy 21:1–2), disobedient sons (21:18–20) and the fulfilment of family obligations (25:7–9). The Book of Ruth gives an example of the elders acting in this last respect (Ruth 4:1–12).

The Law also provides for the appointment of specialists in judicial functions in each town (Deuteronomy 16:18–20). These are described as 'judges and officials', and very high standards were required of them: 'Do not pervert justice or show partiality. Do not accept a bribe, for a bribe blinds the eyes of the wise and twists the words of the righteous. Follow justice and justice alone . . .' It is not clear how these judges related to the system of elders previously described. One possibility is that the judges actually made the decisions, but in the presence of the elders, who were then responsible, as witnesses to the decisions, for seeing that they were complied with.

The Law also makes reference to a king in Deuteronomy 17:14–20. The main responsibility of a king would be the co-ordination of national defence, though this is not spelt out. The Deuteronomic Law is more concerned to put limits on the power of a king, perhaps having in mind the despotic and tyrannical tendencies of most kings in the ancient Near East. He is not to accumulate horses, which is perhaps a warning against a standing army under his control. Nor is he to amass great wealth, or a great harem. More positively, he is to be subject to the Law in every respect. He is to write out his own copy of the Law, which he is to study and to act upon continually, as an antidote to any personal aggrandizement. He must learn to fear the Lord, and to be the servant of his people.

That concludes our sketch of the ideal pattern of economic life embodied in the Law. Our exposition of the ideal does not in any way depend on any specific conclusions as to the date of composition and authorship of the various books of the Law. But the material we have discussed, with its focus on a 'primitive' economy and social system, fits well with the context of the period of occupation of the promised land. If the Law were a composition from later in Israel's history one might expect much greater reference to the more sophisticated economy, and the urban context of that economy, which characterized the later Israel, *e.g.* under Omri and Ahab.[16] We have, for example, already noted the absence of laws relating to the regulation of markets and trade, and the behaviour of traders. Furthermore there are no obvious references to the specialist craftsmen and artisans who populated the cities of Israel at a later date. The fact is that the Law must have appeared quite irrelevant to the more developed economy that emerged in Israel from the time of the monarchy onwards.

The failure to observe the Law in its social and economic aspects is an important theme in the proclamation of the prophets from the eighth century onwards. We look at their sayings first, before examining the process by which the economy and political system had developed from that envisaged in the Law. The prophetic message concentrates on three elements which are frequently linked: the accumulation of wealth by the rich, the oppression of the poor and the failure to help them, and the perversion of justice.[17]

Accumulation of land and property by the rich is condemned by the prophets. 'Woe to you who add house to house and join field to field . . .' (Isaiah 5:8); 'Woe to those who plan iniquity . . . They covet fields and seize them, and houses, and take them. They defraud a man of his home, a fellow man of his inheritance' (Micah 2:1–2). This is coupled with a denunciation of their lifestyle. Sometimes this is related to their indifference to the calamitous state of the nation, as in Amos 6:4–7, where the rich are portrayed as engaged in revelry and luxury, but will be the first to go into exile. More commonly, it is related to the failure of the rich to consider the needs of the poor, or their active oppression of the poor, particularly through the perversion of justice. Thus Isaiah describes 'a fast, a day acceptable to the LORD' in these terms: 'Is it not to share your food with the hungry and to provide the poor wanderer with shelter— when you see the naked to clothe him, and not to turn away from your own flesh and blood?' (Isaiah 58:7).

More seriously the prophets describe the oppression of the poor. Isaiah 3:14–15 refers to the elders and leaders taking 'plunder from the poor' and 'grinding the faces of the poor'. Amos 8:4–14 condemns trading practices which exploit the poor, particularly by the use of false weights and measures. Finally, the rulers of Israel are condemned for denying justice to the poor. Thus Isaiah pronounces: 'Woe to those who make unjust laws, to those who issue oppressive decrees, to deprive the poor of their rights and withhold justice from the oppressed of my people, making widows their prey and robbing the fatherless' (Isaiah 10:1–2). So too Jeremiah calls on the king of Judah to establish justice for the poor and needy (Jeremiah 22). In the light of these and other references, one writer[18] has commented that the primary cause of poverty in the Old Testament is oppression and injustice, with natural disasters and sloth (particularly in Proverbs) much less significant.

What then is the explanation of this startling disparity between the ideal for the people of God as revealed in the Law, and the reality as perceived by the prophets? The answer must be sought positively in the associated phenomena of the growth in power and influence of the monarchy and the court, the development of cities, and general economic development. Negatively, of course, the explanation is the decline of spiritual life and the failure to observe the Law.

The change in the economic structure generally has been described by de Vaux,[19] drawing on archaeological evidence as well as what can be gathered from the biblical text. An early victim of change was the system of landholding. In warning the people of Israel against a king, Samuel predicts that a king will accumulate land for himself, and will require forced labour to work it. The description of the king's officers in 1 Chronicles 27:25–31 includes a list of stewards of the king's farms. Nor was accumulation of land restricted to the king, as the passages from Isaiah and Micah, cited above, show.

Such accumulation was in direct contradiction to the Law of Jubilee, which has led some to believe that this Law is a post-exilic invention.[20] This theory is supported by the general silence of the prophets on the topic, except for an apparent reference in Ezekiel 46:16–18. However, it is equally possible that it is not referred to because it was irrelevant from the time of Solomon onwards. The Law of Jubilee required lands to be restored to their families, but the disturbances already suffered by the people meant that many were landless. They had no inheritance to which they could be restored. One of the effects of accumulations of land by some, and the growth of a landless class, was increasing inequality. According to de Vaux, archaeological evidence from the tenth century suggests little disparity in house sizes. But by the eighth century there is a marked disparity.

The second feature of economic development was the growth of larger 'towns' and 'cities'. By modern standards these were small: the towns that have been excavated from this period must ordinarily have had a population of 400 to 650, with the largest as large as 3,000. At their peak the major cities, Samaria and Jerusalem, cannot have exceeded 30,000 inhabitants. The towns were associated with markets and craft industries. For example, 1 Chronicles 4:21, 23 refer to families of linen workers and potters. These people were presumably landless and made their living by selling products in the local markets. The cities were associated with the growth of the royal courts of Judah and Israel. Part of the population would be officers of the king, both in the army and in civil administration. The great building projects of Solomon required a body of skilled labour in Jerusalem, as well as the levies that were sent to Lebanon to collect timber and to the hill country to cut stones (1 Kings 5:13–18; 9:15–22).

International trade was also a monopoly of the king, at least in Solomon's reign (1 Kings 9:26–28), and this must have generated considerable commercial activity in Jerusalem and other major settlements. The ordinary Israelite

did not however usually engage in such commerce, which
was left to outside traders, in particular the Phoenicians,
who attract the attention of the prophets in Isaiah 23 and
Ezekiel 27. The latter passage is particularly interesting.
The word of the Lord comes to Ezekiel telling him to 'take
up a lament concerning Tyre'. There follows a detailed
description of the wide geographical extent of Tyre's trading links all over the Western Mediterranean and the Near
East. But then the mood changes to describe commercial
and financial ruin. The explanation is given in Ezekiel 28.
The prosperity and success of Tyre have led to false pride
and security. The pursuit of wealth has become a god, and
it is because of this idolatry that judgment has been visited
upon them (verses 1–7).

Although Tyre was not in Israel this passage is important
for the way it illuminates the reaction of a prophet, who was
much concerned with the Law, to the unbridled operations
of markets in the pursuit of wealth. The prophets were not
likely to welcome uncritically the commercial prosperity
which came to the cities of Israel and Judah through
engaging in trade (as, for example, in the reigns of Omri
and Ahab).

Ellul[21] has suggested that the Old Testament evaluation
of the growth of cities is decidedly unfavourable. At the
occupation of the land, the people of Israel do not build
cities, they take them over. Even when David seeks a capital
for his kingdom, he takes over an existing city from the
Jebusites rather than constructing one (2 Samuel 5:6–10),
though he does undertake some new construction. But the
major builder is Solomon, as we saw above. Not only is he
unfaithful to the Law in that he uses forced labour from the
people, but his building project on the Millo under the
direction of Jeroboam is linked, coincidentally at least, to a
prophecy by Ahijah that his kingdom will be divided on his
death (1 Kings 11:26–40). Furthermore, in his other building projects, recorded in 2 Chronicles 8, the towns are given
names of foreign gods. The Chronicler apparently wishes
to indicate a consequence of Solomon's apostasy in his
reliance on foreign alliances, and his willingness to tolerate
pagan religious practices by his wives and their retinues.

Exactly the same feature is recorded of the military strategy of his successor Rehoboam, who built cities for the defence of his kingdom. However Ellul's point should not be pushed too hard. As he admits, Asa and Jehoshaphat are both builders of cities *and* good kings (2 Chronicles 14:7). And the Psalmist makes it clear that if the work of building is *under* God, then his blessing can be expected (Psalms 69:35; 127:1). This does not, however, negate the general point that the city can easily be, or become, a symbol of man's independence from God.

The significance of this Old Testament material for our later discussion of economic issues is, in one sense, obvious. It is immensely valuable to have spelt out, in the Law, a set of regulations for the economic life of the covenant community. The concept of stewardship through work is given a concrete form in the division of the land between families. The rules concerning the alleviation of poverty encapsulate a concern that the rich should help the poor. However the evidence that this ideal pattern proved difficult to maintain (or even establish) in the face of national apostasy and economic development should make us sensitive to the difficulties of 'applying' the Law to economic life in communities that are in no sense the people of God. How far we may go in this respect is taken up in Chapter Two below.

6. The people of God: the church

The discussion in this section will parallel that in the previous section which dealt with the people of Israel. We shall focus first on the new covenant, which is based on the ministry, death and resurrection of Jesus. This will include his distinctive teaching concerning the kingdom of God; in Matthew's Gospel this is presented in the Sermon on the Mount in a conscious parallel to the giving of the Law at Sinai. We shall then trace the application of that teaching in the life of the early church, the community which emerged subsequent to the resurrection, and which was envisaged by Jesus in his teaching.[22] Naturally our main focus is on those elements which are relevant to the theme of this book. But, as in the covenant with Israel, we shall insist that these cannot be divorced from the whole structure of the new covenant.

Even a cursory reading of the synoptic gospels indicates the prominence of two elements. The first is the focus of Jesus' ministry on the proclamation of the kingdom of God. The second is the apparently disproportionate space given to the events leading to the passion and resurrection of Christ. We must look briefly at the theological significance of these two elements before we concentrate attention on Jesus' teaching.

(a) The kingdom of God

In the account in Matthew and Mark, Jesus' proclamation of the kingdom of God follows immediately after his baptism and temptation in the wilderness, at the outset of his ministry: '... Jesus went into Galilee, proclaiming the good news of God. "The time has come," he said. "The kingdom of God is near. Repent and believe the good news!"' (Mark 1:14–15). The translation 'kingdom of God' is somewhat misleading, since it gives the impression of a domain over which the king reigns. A more accurate rendering would be 'the reign of God'. The concept is dynamic and active. The nature of the reign is summed up in the petition of the Lord's prayer: 'Your kingdom come, your will be done on earth as it is in heaven' (Matthew 6:10).

The announcement of the kingdom is to alert listeners to a manifestation of God's sovereign activity. Its content can be judged from the incident at Nazareth recorded in Luke 4:14–30 immediately after the initiation of Jesus' teaching ministry. Jesus comes to Nazareth and goes into the synagogue on the Sabbath. He is invited to read the scriptures, and he turns to Isaiah 61:1–2:

> The Spirit of the Lord is on me, because he has anointed me to preach good news to the poor. He has sent me to proclaim freedom for the prisoners and recovery of sight for the blind, to release the oppressed, to proclaim the year of the LORD's favour.

Having read, and returned the book to the attendant, Jesus declares: 'Today this scripture is fulfilled in your hearing.'

This declaration has been the subject of considerable scholarly debate. Thus Yoder[23] has pointed out that 'the year of the Lord's favour' refers to the Old Testament Jubilee. He then goes on to argue that the Jubilee and sabbatical year concepts illuminate other elements in Jesus' teaching. His contention is that this teaching would have been *understood* as referring to a literal Jubilee by his hearers. So we should not discount the idea that the kingdom is to be understood in social and political terms. This is consistent with the conclusion that Jesus rejected the Zealot option of revolt against the Roman authorities, since the nature of the kingdom is God acting for his people, not the people of God taking history into their own hands.

However there are some weighty considerations to be set against Yoder's view. If Jesus had wished to proclaim a Jubilee, then Leviticus 25 would surely have been a prominent element in his teaching. In fact, he uses the prophetic utterance of Isaiah 61. A Jubilee would not have been feasible in the first century AD, since a major element would be a return of families to their land. But by that stage in the history of Israel, the allocation of land to particular families had been completely lost. In addition, proclamation of a Jubilee would indeed have been regarded as tantamount to a revolution, and there is no evidence to suggest that Jesus desired that interpretation of his ministry. It seems better therefore to presume that in announcing the kingdom, Jesus simply made use of Jubilee concepts which would have been familiar to his hearers. So his adoption of Isaiah 61:1–2 was intended as a literal description of his ministry, which did indeed involve preaching to the poor, healings including blind people, and releasing people from demonic forces. The linking of these last two aspects is apparent, for example, in the healing of the blind and dumb demoniac recorded in Matthew 12:22–32. In response to the criticism of the Pharisees, Jesus explains that his kingdom is engaged in spiritual warfare with the kingdom of Satan.

Another important aspect of the kingdom is that it challenges people to join in. That Jesus sought a response from his hearers is evident from the gospel narratives. But the parable of the sower shows that he had no illusions about the impact of the message. In some hearers the message would meet with no response, and in others an immediate response would be choked by other cares and concerns (Matthew 13:1–23). The nature of the response he sought was primarily commitment to him. This requires a quality of trust and obedience that is childlike (Mark 10:13–16), totally single-minded to the extent of valuing it more highly than family and wealth (Matthew 10:37; Luke 18:18–30) and ready to accept personal sacrifice even to the extent of death (Matthew 16:24–25).

(b) The new covenant

But there is a problem in all this. If we take the Beatitudes (Matthew 5:3–10) as indicative of the qualities required of those who join in the kingdom, then some will protest that the standard is impossible for fallen man. It is said that the Beatitudes can scarcely be interpreted seriously as pre-requisites. This immediately brings us to another aspect of Jesus' ministry, his passion and resurrection. The problem posed by the fall, the spiritual separation of God and man, is dealt with by Jesus' death on the cross and his resurrection. This is certainly the most important theme in the whole of New Testament theology. We emphasize this, even though our treatment of the theme will be very brief, as it is not directly relevant. But its indirect relevance is immense. If our reading of the New Testament is correct, then all the teaching about the quality of life required of those who participate in the kingdom is subordinated to a solution to the fundamental spiritual problem of man. That quality of life is literally *impossible* to the man for whom the sacrifice of Jesus on the cross has not become a reality applied in his own life. Just as we saw that the old covenant was indivisible in its aspects, so too is the new covenant which Jesus inaugurated.

The synoptics depict Jesus as gradually making known to his disciples the fact that his life was to be sacrificed. The first occasion is after Peter's confession at Caesarea Philippi (Matthew 16:13–23). That confession is the climax of Jesus' ministry and teaching. His disciples have come to the point where they recognize him both as the Messiah, and as the Son of God. That recognition must have been linked to expectations as to what Jesus would do next, including no doubt a solution to the problems of the Jewish people living under the Roman occupation. It is no surprise therefore that Peter protests vehemently when Jesus '... began to explain to his disciples that he must go to Jerusalem and suffer many things at the hands of the elders, chief priests and teachers of the law, and that he must be killed, and on the third day be raised to life' (verse 21).

Jesus repeats the same prediction after the transfiguration (Matthew 17:22–23), and again meets with a distressed response from his disciples. That they still failed to grasp the nature of his Messiahship even as he went up to Jerusalem is suggested by the story of James and John asking for particular prominence in Jesus' kingdom (Mark 10:35–44). Jesus' response is to point to his own vocation: 'The Son of Man did not come to be served, but to serve, and to give his life as a ransom for many' (verse 45).

Jesus' death and the kingdom are explicitly linked in the words he used at the Last Supper, as recorded in Matthew 26:26–29 and Mark 14:22–25. Giving the disciples the cup he says: '... This is my blood of the (new) covenant, which is poured out for many for the forgiveness of sins. I tell you, I will not drink of this fruit of the vine from now on until that day when I drink it anew with you in my Father's kingdom.' Three aspects of this saying need to be stressed. First, there is the reference to his sacrificial death as establishing a new covenent between God and man. Second, that covenant is based on the forgiveness of sins, a healing of the rift between fallen man and holy God. Third, this sacrificial death and the new covenant are fundamental to the kingdom, to the reign of God. The celebration of the kingdom symbolized by the drinking of new wine comes after Christ has accomplished his work on the cross.

This then is the context in which we are to understand the teaching of Jesus concerning the kingdom. God, in his love and grace, has acted decisively in Jesus Christ to make a new covenant with man. The man who responds in faith to

God's initiative is summoned to involvement in the work of the kingdom. He becomes one of the people of God; his life should be conformed to the new standards of the kingdom. These standards are set out in Jesus' teaching about the kingdom.

(c) Jesus and the Law

Before we turn to the content of Jesus' teaching which is relevant to our theme, two preliminary points need to be considered. The first is the relationship between the teaching of Jesus and the Law of the Old Testament. The key passage here is in the Sermon on the Mount, which many interpreters believe Matthew structured so as to parallel the giving of the Law to Moses at Sinai. In Matthew 5:17–48, where a conscious dependence on the Ten Commandments can be discerned, Jesus begins by claiming that his teaching 'fulfils' the Law rather than 'abolishes' it. His requirements go beyond the Law, by demanding a righteousness which is far more rigorous. For example, the commandment to abstain from adultery is sharpened by Jesus' insistence that a lustful look is equivalent to committing adultery 'in the heart'. He sums up this teaching with the call to 'be perfect, as your heavenly Father is perfect' (verse 48). This can only be interpreted as a demand that our life should be modelled on Jesus himself.

The second point is that Jesus' teaching is authoritative. Thus six times in Matthew 5:17–48 he refers to various scribal interpretations of the Law, and six times he responds with, 'But I tell you . . .'. He is not offering just another interpretation. He speaks with a moral imperative that commands our assent, because what he speaks is entirely consonant with his own righteous life. It was an authority which was readily noted by the common people: 'When Jesus had finished saying these things the crowds were amazed at his teaching, because he taught as one who had authority, and not as their teachers of the law' (Matthew 7:28–29).

To sum up, we expect to see in Jesus' teaching definite continuity with the Law, but we also expect *new* authoritative emphases, not just interpretations.

(d) Jesus' teaching on wealth and possessions

The Gospel of Luke contains more of Jesus' teaching about wealth and possessions than the other gospels, and for the most part we shall concentrate on that gospel.[24] Two complementary themes stand out. The first concerns the *spiritual dangers* of riches. Jesus makes the point in various ways. Sometimes he is blunt and straightforward. 'No servant can serve two masters. Either he will hate the one and love the other, or he will be devoted to the one and despise the other. You cannot serve both God and Money' (16:13). 'But woe to you who are rich, for you have already received your comfort. Woe to you who are well fed now, for you will go hungry' (6:24–25). (These verses are to be read in contra-distinction to verses 20 and 21: 'Blessed are you who are poor, for yours is the kingdom of God. Blessed are you who hunger now, for you will be satisfied.') The rich man, who builds up his wealth to provide for a future of security and ease, is condemned by Jesus as a fool (12:16–21). At other times Jesus speaks with a twinkle in his eye. 'How hard it is for the rich to enter the kingdom of God! Indeed, it is easier for a camel to go through the eye of a needle than for a rich man to enter the kingdom of God' (18:24–25).

The second theme is perhaps more startling. Jesus tells his disciples to *find freedom in giving*. The upright, God-fearing young ruler of the synagogue is told: 'You still lack one thing. Sell everything you have and give to the poor, and you will have treasure in heaven. Then come, follow me' (Luke 18:22). His followers are told: 'Give to everyone who asks you, and if anyone takes what belongs to you, do not demand it back' (6:30); 'Sell your possessions and give to the poor . . .' (12:33); and 'Love your enemies, do good to them, and lend to them without expecting to get anything back . . .' (6:35).

In the parable of the rich man and Lazarus it is the failure of the rich man to care for the beggar at his door which is singled out as the cause of judgment upon him (16:19–31). When Zacchaeus decides to follow Jesus, the immediate consequences of his repentance are a generous restitution to those he had cheated, and a distribution of half of his wealth to the poor (19:8). In the parable of the sheep and the goats in Matthew 25:31–46, Jesus makes a willingness to help the hungry, the stranger, the poor and the oppressed a criterion for separating men at the final judgment. His argument is that feeding the hungry and thirsty, welcoming the stranger, clothing the naked, visiting the sick and the imprisoned are equivalent to doing him the same service: 'I tell you the truth, whatever you did for one of the least of these brothers of mine, you did for me' (Matthew 25:40).

This teaching presupposes the background of the Law. Indeed there are many echoes of Old Testament themes. The theme of God's providence in creation is powerfully restated:

> 'Therefore I tell you, do not worry about your life, what you will eat; or about your body, what you will wear. Life is more than food, and the body more than clothes. Consider the ravens: They do not sow or reap, they have no storeroom or barn; yet God feeds them. And how much more valuable you are than birds! . . .
>
> 'Consider how the lilies grow. They do not labour or spin. Yet I tell you, not even Solomon in all his splendour was dressed like one of these. If that is how God clothes the grass of the field, which is here today, and tomorrow is thrown into the fire, how much more will he clothe you, O you of little faith!' (Luke 12:22–28).

The same doctrine of providence in creation appears when Jesus is telling his disciples to love their enemies. This is no more than the Father does, for 'he causes his sun to rise on the evil and the good, and sends rain on the righteous and the unrighteous' (Matthew 5:44–45).

The theme of stewardship[25] in respect of wealth and possessions, most notable in respect of the allotment of land to families in the Law, reappears in the parable of the minas (talents, RSV) (Luke 19:11–27). This is placed in Luke's gospel immediately *after* the story of Zacchaeus, so it is natural to conclude that the parable has material as well as spiritual implications for the disciples. Second, the parable is told because '. . . the people thought that the kingdom of God was going to appear at once' (verse 11). The disciples are being reminded that life has still to be lived out in obedience to God. They cannot just sit back and wait for the kingdom to appear. The king is going away to a far country, and will be absent for some time (verse 12). So each servant is given talents to work with. At the return of the king, they are judged on the basis of what use they have made of those talents. But the talents belong to the king, not to the servants. And the reward for good servants is increased responsibility (verses 17–19).

The theme of the obligation on the rich to help the poor is the element of the Law which is given the greatest emphasis by Jesus, perhaps because it was the element which the people were least willing to obey. Thus if the rich man in the parable of the rich man and Lazarus had taken note of Leviticus 25:35, he would have accepted the obligation to take Lazarus into his house to provide for him and maintain him.

These examples indicate that Jesus was presupposing the Law in his teaching. He went much further in identifying the pursuit of wealth as idolatry. The word 'mammon' (RSV) has overtones of a personified wealth. Mammon is attacked because it can blind men to their need of God, and can divert them from the work of the kingdom. Jesus challenges his hearers: 'But seek his [God's] kingdom, and these things [food and clothing] will be given to you as well' (Luke 12:31), and, 'For where your treasure is, there your heart will be also' (12:34). It is a question of priorities. Are we putting Jesus first, trusting him and seeking his security for our lives ('Give us each day our daily bread' (11:3))? Or are we compromising to provide for our own security? If the latter, then our wealth has become an idol, a rival to God himself.

This is why the poor are blessed. They do not have the stumbling block of mammon in making a response to the kingdom. Jesus himself had renounced possessions and security: 'The Son of Man has nowhere to lay his head' (Luke 9:58). When he sends out the twelve, and later the seventy, on preaching missions, they are instructed to take no more than minimal possessions (9:3; 10:4). But at the same time Jesus does not teach a rigorous asceticism, such as that practised by the Qumran community. He was invited to banquets by the rich (Luke 7:36; 11:37; 14:1), and thereby incurred the mockery of the religious leaders, who described him as '... a glutton and a drunkard, a friend of tax collectors and "sinners"' (7:34). The explanation is that Jesus was not opposed to wealth in itself, but only insofar as it becomes an obstacle to response to God. An indication that it has become such an obstacle is an unwillingness to share the proceeds of wealth with those who are needy.

(e) The kingdom and the church

We now turn from the ideal to its implementation in the life of the New Testament church. Our first task is to examine the link between the kingdom of God and the church.

The kingdom of God in the gospels is the reign of God, *not* the community of disciples. The disciples are the people *in* whom the rule of God is to be manifest. They enter or join in the kingdom. That Jesus intended his disciples to form a community can be inferred from three elements in the gospels. The first is the parable of the vineyard in Matthew 21:33–43. Jesus first highlights the rejection of God's authority by the Jewish people. He then speaks of the owner of the vineyard throwing out the old tenants and finding new ones. He explains the import of the parable: 'Therefore I tell you that the kingdom of God will be taken away from you and given to a people who will produce its fruits' (verse 43). By 'you', his hearers understood him to be speaking of the Jewish religious leaders as the representatives of the people. By 'people', Jesus means a new community of the people of God.

The second element is the calling of twelve disciples to form the core of the new community. After Peter's confession at Caesarea Philippi, much more of Jesus' teaching is directed to his immediate circle, and his ministry to the multitude is restricted. The word 'church' appears only twice in the synoptic gospels, in Matthew 16:18 and 18:17. However the Greek word *ecclesia* is probably best understood not in the sense of a formal institution, but as a gathering of a community of disciples around Jesus. Finally, it is the eleven remaining disciples who receive the great commission, after the resurrection, to continue his work:

> 'All authority in heaven and on earth has been given to me. Therefore go and make disciples of all nations, baptising them in the name of the Father and of the Son and of the Holy Spirit, and teaching them to obey everything I have commanded you. And surely I am with you always, to the very end of the age' (Matthew 28:18–20).

The continuity between the disciples and the emerging church is confirmed by the events of the early chapters of Acts. It is to the disciples and close followers of Jesus that the gift of the Spirit is given at Pentecost, and they form the new community of the Spirit. The church is not synonymous with the kingdom of God, which is the whole of God's sovereignty in human affairs. But the church is a most important manifestation of that kingdom. We need therefore to look carefully at the characteristics of the emerging community.

(f) Economic relationships in the New Testament church

One characteristic of the New Testament church[26] is the stress on community.

> All the believers were together and had everything in common. Selling their possessions and goods, they gave to anyone as he had need. Every day they continued to meet together in the temple courts. They broke bread in their homes, and ate together with glad and sincere hearts, praising God and enjoying the favour of all the people (Acts 2:44–47).

This community ideal included a radical sharing of property:

> All the believers were one in heart and mind.
> No-one claimed that any of his possessions was his
> own, but they shared everything they had ...
> There were no needy persons among them. For
> from time to time those who owned lands or
> houses sold them, brought the money from the
> sales and put it at the apostles' feet and it was
> distributed to anyone as he had need (Acts
> 4:32–35).

It is probable that this spontaneous sharing of goods can be
related back to the teaching of Jesus on not being anxious
about food and clothing, and his exhortations to give to the
poor. However the application of the teaching was not
without its problems. Quite apart from the dissembling of
Ananias and Sapphira about the extent of their giving,[27]
difficulties quickly arose about the daily distribution to the
needy. These were solved by the appointment of deacons to
see that each needy person was properly looked after (Acts
6:1–6). The wisdom of the whole enterprise of sharing has
been questioned by some commentators, who point to the
later collections made by Paul for the poor church in Judaea
and Jerusalem. But its poverty may be attributed as much to
famine and persecution as to the initial community life of
the Jerusalem church.[28]

As the church spread outside Judaea, there is little evidence, in the epistles at least, that the experiment in radical
community living was repeated in the new churches. But
the ideal of the church as a new people of God, a new
community rooted in Christ, is very strongly emphasized.
The main images employed are those of the church as the
body (see especially 1 Corinthians 12:12–27; Ephesians
4:15–16; Colossians 1:18, 24), the church as a building (see
1 Corinthians 3:9–17; Ephesians 2:19–22; 1 Peter 2:4–8),
and the church as the people of God (see generally the
epistles to the Romans and the Hebrews). In each case, the
teaching about community is linked to ethical teaching, in
particular concerning the responsibilities of members of
these communities to one another. Ephesians 4:17 – 6:9 is a
good example of this kind of material. We restrict our

consideration in what follows to teaching specifically related to the theme of this book.

It can be summarized under the headings of work, and the obligation on the rich to help the poor. On the first, we may note that Paul maintained himself, when necessary, by his own labours, notably at Corinth (Acts 18:3), apparently at Ephesus (Acts 20:34), and at Thessalonica (1 Thessalonians 2:9). In part, he was glad to show that his preaching of the gospel was not for gain. But in other passages, it is apparent that Paul regards work as an integral part of the Christian life. He writes to the Thessalonians: '. . . we urge you . . . to work with your hands, just as we told you' (1 Thessalonians 4:10–11), and '. . . we gave you this rule: "If a man will not work, he shall not eat"' (2 Thessalonians 3:10).

The same instruction is given to the Ephesian church: 'He who has been stealing must steal no longer, but must work doing something useful with his own hands, that he may have something to share with those in need' (Ephesians 4:28). The motivation for the Christian to work comes out most clearly in the instruction given to slaves, of whom there must have been many in the early churches. They are to 'serve wholeheartedly, as if you were serving the Lord, not men' (Ephesians 6:7), and 'Whatever you do, work at it with all your heart, as working for the Lord, not for men' (Colossians 3:23).

The obligation on the rich to help the poor is a prominent theme of the epistles. One aspect was the collection which Paul organized among the Gentile churches for the poor among the church in Jerusalem (Romans 15:25–29; 1 Corinthians 16:1–4; 2 Corinthians 8, 9). In 2 Corinthians, Paul is clearly disappointed with the less than enthusiastic response to his previous appeal. So he goes to some lengths to urge them to think again. In part he tries to shame them by holding before them the example of the church in Macedonia. But more positively he points to the example of Christ: 'For you know the grace of our Lord Jesus Christ, that though he was rich, yet for your sakes he became poor, so that you through his poverty might become rich' (2 Corinthians 8:9). He explains that this giving should be commensurate with their means: 'Our desire is not that others might be relieved while you are hard pressed, but that there might be equality. At the present time your plenty will supply what they need ... Then there will be equality' (8:13–14). The motive for giving should be love (8:8), so there can be no compulsion: 'Each man should give what he has decided in his heart to give, not reluctantly or under compulsion, for God loves a cheerful giver' (9:7). The reward for giving is God's blessing: 'Remember this: Whoever sows sparingly will also reap sparingly, and whoever sows generously will also reap generously' (9:6). In 1 Corinthians 16:2 Paul also commends a pattern of regular giving, week by week, rather than on impulse to a particular appeal.

The teaching addressed to individuals in the Pastoral Epistles follows the same theme.

> If anyone has material possessions and sees his brother in need but has no pity on him, how can the love of God be in him? Dear children, let us not love with words or tongue but with actions and in truth (1 John 3:17–18).

This is linked with possible spiritual damage from riches in a way that suggests that the teaching is derivative from the teaching of Jesus. Thus Timothy is urged to include warnings to rich church members in his care:

> Command those who are rich in this present world not to be arrogant nor to put their hope in wealth, which is so uncertain, but to put their hope in God, who richly provides us with everything for our enjoyment. Command them to do good, to be rich in good deeds, willing to share ... (1 Timothy 6:17–19).

In a previous passage he is instructed to teach that 'godliness with contentment is great gain. For we brought nothing into the world, and we can take nothing out of it. But if we have food and clothing, we will be content with that' (1 Timothy 6:6–8). Then follows a stern warning against the pursuit of riches, including the famous dictum that 'the love of money is a root of all kinds of evil' (6:10).

The Epistle of James makes the same points, condemning the rich for their pursuit of wealth, luxury and status, and for their oppression of the poor, in language which is both dramatic and powerful (James 2:1–7; 4:13–5:6). It is apparent that the high ideals of the kingdom of God were not universally practised in the early church, any more than the actual social and economic life of the people of Israel incorporated the ideals of the Law.

The analysis of this section has set the New Testament teaching on economic themes in the context of Jesus' teaching about the kingdom of God, and the particular manifestation of that teaching in the life of the early church. In one sense there is little that is new in the discussion. The exercise of responsible stewardship through work, and the obligation on the rich to help the poor, are ideals carried over from the Old Testament. However these ideals are stated more radically, and with a new authority, in the teaching of Jesus. There is, for example, an emphasis on inner obedience as well as continued observance. Hence the teaching on the spiritual dangers of riches, and the stress on being willing to give generously and freely to the poor. The attempt to incorporate these radical ideals in the life of the early church is also instructive. But this begs the question as to how far this teaching is specific to the new covenant community of the church, and how far it can be 'applied' to secular communities. It is to this question that we turn in the next chapter.

CHAPTER TWO

Christianity and economics: theological ethics

1. Ethical method: from theology to ethics

We have now completed our review of the biblical material which is ostensibly relevant to the questions addressed in this book. We have yet to deal with the problem of how this material may fruitfully be used in Christian social ethics. Our hope is to be able to speak to problems of the social and economic order in general. We are looking for ethical principles that can be applied outside the people of God, as well as to the Christian community.

(a) Deriving principles of biblical social ethics

Our review has mapped out four biblical themes with ethical significance: creation with its themes of God's providence and man's stewardship; the fall and judgment with the associated covenant with Noah; Israel as the covenant people of God, and the detailed prescription for their common life in the Law; and the new covenant people of God in the church, with the radical ethic of the kingdom.

A preliminary view of the theological basis for each of these might lead to the conclusion that only the Noachic covenant is relevant for application outside the people of God. The creation material refers to an ideal state which is no longer with us because of the fall. The covenant with Israel and the new covenant are clearly for the people of God, and presuppose God's grace and man's response. This would indeed be a very disappointing conclusion, for although the Noachic covenant points to *mechanisms* by which evil is to be restrained in fallen human society, notably conscience, law and the authorities, it has little to say about the standards to which society should be directed by means of these mechanisms.

One conclusion of this view is that the Christian sees himself as a citizen of both the kingdom of God and of his secular nation or society. He submits to God in things concerning his spiritual life and personal conduct, and to the secular rulers as 'established by God' (Romans 13:1) to restrain evil conduct in society. This is, roughly speaking, the Lutheran position, characterized by Richard Niebuhr as 'Christ and culture in paradox'.[1] The 'paradox' arises from the tension that this position generates for the Christian: he acknowledges two authorities in his life to which he *must* submit, but with no guarantee that they will be in agreement.

An alternative conclusion is that the Christian identifies the secular authorities as being entirely under the control of the kingdom of darkness. He therefore withdraws from society as far as possible into the fellowship of the people of God, and shows no interest in what happens in society. Such radical separation may perhaps be justified from the first epistle of John. This is the stance entitled 'Christ against culture' by Niebuhr. It led in the second century to the radical separation advocated by Tertullian. He argued that sinfulness was enhanced by cultural contacts. So he urged Christians to withdraw from political and military life, from worldly occupations and from secular learning. Similar exclusive attitudes are prevalent in the teaching of some contemporary sects and house churches.

However there are a number of reasons for not accepting this interpretation. First, it is scarcely consistent with the doctrine of a gracious God that he should, in the Noachic covenant, make provision for the continuance of human existence after the fall, without giving any guidance as to the quality of that life. A more consistent view would be that although man has fallen, the image of God in him is marred but not destroyed. Man is therefore capable of living a useful life, including acts of goodness. This does not affect his spiritual status, but it does mean that human existence is not intolerable. An ethic based on creation can continue to tell us something about how fallen man should live.

Second, we have already noted that the people of God in the Old Testament are described as a light to the nations, and that Jesus calls his disciples to be a light to the world. No doubt an element in this is that they should be a witness to God's scheme of salvation. But that does not exclude a further purpose of instruction for all men as to the moral standards which God requires. Paul's conception of the Law as a 'custodian until Christ came' (Galatians 3:24 RSV) would seem to be not inconsistent with this view. Indeed it makes it clear that the proclamation of God's standards for all mankind is part of God's scheme of salvation. Without that knowledge man will not be aware of his need of salvation, and therefore will not have the motivation for repentance.

A third reason follows from this. The Old Testament prophets on many occasions direct their pronouncements of God's judgment not to Israel, but to the surrounding nations. For example, Amos speaks of punishment for transgression on Damascus, Tyre, Edom, Ammon and Moab (Amos 1–2:3) and Ezekiel pronounced God's judgment on Tyre (Ezekiel 27, 28). Such a judgment would be intolerable if God's standards only apply to his people, and have no relevance for other peoples.

Any interpretation which restricts the scope of God's moral rule and order to the people of God is in danger of implying a restriction on the sovereignty of God. But in Colossians 2:15 Paul speaks of God, in Christ and through the cross, disarming the 'powers and authorities' and triumphing over them. Although the precise origin of this phrase has been the subject of considerable scholarly debate, at the very least it must mean that all human affairs are now subject to the rule of Christ. Whether they acknowledge it or not, all nations and their rulers are subject to his moral rule and government. Our thesis therefore is that all the four areas we have detailed— creation, the Noachic covenant, the Law and the teaching about the kingdom— can contribute to the development of biblical ethics.

We distinguish three elements in any ethical theory.[2]

These are the perception of reality, the statement of ethical objectives, and the motivation to act in an ethical manner. All three elements were present in our review of the four areas. The Christian perception of reality is informed by an understanding of the fact of man's fallen nature, leading not only to separation from God, but also to various social disorders. The motivations to act ethically are various. For those outside the covenant of the people of God, one motivation is fear of temporal punishment and final judgment, related respectively to what Paul says about the authorities in Romans 13, and about conscience in Romans 2:12–16. Another motivation arises from the fact that man is made in the image of God; there is a striving after good which is not completely destroyed by the fall. For those within the covenants there is the further motivation of responding in love and gratitude for what God has done for them. The statement of ethical objectives is the substantive content of ethics. In our discussion this is a description of what God requires of men as they live their lives. Our analysis of creation, Law and the kingdom has already shown that there is considerable content in the biblical material relating to economic issues.

A further question is how these three elements relate to each other. The teaching of Jesus concerning divorce, in Matthew 19:3–9, can provide an example. The Pharisees ask Jesus a question: 'Is it lawful for a man to divorce his wife for any and every reason?' He directs them to the creation norm, with quotations from Genesis 1:27 and 2:24. The ethical objective is that marriage should involve the man and woman in becoming one flesh in the sight of God. Therefore divorce is a breaking of that creation principle.

The Pharisees are quick to point out that Moses (*i.e.* the Law) does permit divorce. To which Jesus replies: 'Moses permitted you to divorce your wives because your hearts were hard. But it was not this way from the beginning' (verse 8). The perception of reality is that sinful human nature will not always be able to aspire to the principle of lifelong union in marriage. Hence divorce is permitted, since if marriages are to break up, it is better that the process should be regulated, and the women, in particular, be protected. Divorce must, for example, be for good reasons, not just based on a whim or a groundless complaint.

Motivations for maintaining the principle of marriage will naturally vary. For the people of Israel there was the example of God's love for them, so movingly described by Hosea, using his own marriage as a parable. For Christians there is the example of Christ and the church (Ephesians 5:21-33); Christ's sacrificial love for the church is an ideal for the marriage relationship. For non-Christians, the capacity of man to aspire to the Christian ideal may be much affected by the degree to which Christian values have succeeded in permeating a particular society. We should not ignore the educative element in proclaiming Christian ethical principles in a non-Christian society, even if it would be extremely complex and even unwise to incorporate these standards in a formal legal framework. But it is important that non-Christians be reminded frequently of the standards that God requires. It is an essential part of any preaching of the gospel.

To sum up, our task involves three elements. The first is the identification from Scripture of those standards which God requires of man. In doing this we shall draw on all the strands of biblical teaching examined in Chapter One. Our examination has suggested a consistent approach in the area of economic life. In the next section we shall summarize this approach in terms of a number of social ethical principles.

The second element is the need for an accurate perception of reality in the areas in which we hope to apply these principles. A key theological element will be the fact of the fall, and its consequences for human life. But there will also be important contributions from the work of economists and social scientists.

The third element is a consideration of motivation. We shall naturally expect the people of God, in their economic relationships, to achieve standards which are much closer to the pattern God requires, than we would expect from non-Christians. For Christians not only have a better perception of what God requires, they also have the motivation of love for God, and the gift of the indwelling Holy Spirit, to enable them to live in obedience to what God requires. There is little point in advocating for a secular society economic structures which presuppose the existence of a closely-knit community of love, as in the early church in Jerusalem. That would be foolish utopianism. Instead we have to look for a second best, which approximates to what God requires, and which is credible, given the motivation and incentives which are present in a particular situation. The search for second-best solutions should not, however, be allowed to erode our perception that they are only second best and not fully consistent with what God requires. In pursuing the possible, we must not forget the ideal, and there should be an element of sadness and repentance that our solutions must fall so far short of the ideal.

The elements of this process will involve the making of provisional judgments. It must therefore be open to criticism and debate. Thus the derivation of social ethical principles from Scripture must be susceptible of correction from Scripture itself. It is all too easy for a single interpreter to allow his selection of material to be biased, or to allow prejudices or presumptions to affect his exegesis. So too our perception of reality is at best partial and incomplete; the fallenness of man has affected our capacity to discern truth in all its aspects. The difficulties that this can create are discussed in Chapter 3. Not surprisingly, therefore, our conclusions are at best provisional and incomplete.

All this may come as a disappointment to any who hoped that we would be able to give definitive 'Christian answers' to economic problems. But Jesus never promised us that Christian discipleship in a fallen world would be easy: the Christian who wishes to comment on economic issues has no short cuts available, no answers that he can read off directly. Submission to the scriptures, intellectual humility, a willingness to listen to other Christians, and openness to the guidance of the Holy Spirit are the qualities required.

Before we turn to the delineation of the biblical social principles which we will use in the rest of the book, it should be noted that others have advocated rather different procedures for Christian ethical thinking. Their advocacy involves, implicitly or explicitly, objections to the method we have outlined.

(b) First objection: social principles cannot be derived from Scripture

The first group says that the problems of interpreting Scripture are so overwhelming in the light of critical analysis of the texts, that the enterprise of deriving Christian social principles should not be attempted. One such is R. H. Preston.[3] He takes as his target a report of an ecumenical study conference, held in Oxford in 1949, which drew up four guidelines for the use of biblical material in social ethics. Since these share elements with the approach we wish to adopt, it is important to look carefully at Preston's criticisms.

The first guideline is that it is necessary to presuppose that there is a unity in the biblical material which permits us to derive consistent teaching. The second is that the meaning of particular passages can be adequately discerned by historico-critical methods, each passage being interpreted by reference to its context in the biblical story. The third is that the biblical material must be studied first on its own, not with reference to a particular ethical question we wish to solve. Fourth, in application, we should be aware of the distance in time and culture between the biblical situation and the modern world. Preston's criticism is that this set of guidelines tends to dodge the fundamental hermeneutical problems.

He dismisses the use of the Old Testament material on the grounds that the Law can only be understood in the context of the salvation events of the Exodus, and that in Israel there was no distinction between church and nation. Furthermore there is the problem of cultural distance: rules drawn up for a primitive society can have no relevance for modern ethical problems. He then argues that the use of material from the gospels and Acts is vitiated by its eschatological dimension. Jesus and the early church expected the kingdom to come to a full realization in the immediate future. So the ethics are those of a community expecting the parousia. This explains their radical nature:

the commitment to agape, the unworldly teaching on possessions, the ethic of giving.

Preston asserts a break with the Law in Jesus' dismissal of scribal teaching. As the eschatological hope faded in the early church, so new ethical teaching for the ongoing life of the church emerges in the epistles. But this is an amalgam of moral precepts from Jewish and Greek sources, and bears little relation to the agape ethic of the gospels. It should not therefore be treated in an authoritative fashion: it is conditioned by the cultural situation of the church, and therefore relative.

A detailed response to the critical views that lie behind Preston's stance is beyond the scope of this book. However we hope that our previous analysis has shown that there is much greater consistency in the material than Preston's view would allow. Moreover, while the point about cultural relativity is well taken, our own approach is to search for universal principles that govern the particular applications described in the biblical material. This is rooted in a belief that God's order and justice in relation to human nature and affairs have a timeless quality. Nor are we persuaded by the argument that New Testament ethics are the product of an eschatological hope, which was not fulfilled. There are too many references to the kingdom of God as a *present* reality as well as a future hope to make that interpretation satisfactory. Furthermore, we have shown that Jesus' teaching is to be understood as a development of the Law, not as a total break from it.

The consequence of Preston's position is that some other basis has to be found for Christian social ethics. He himself advocates a particular method for *doing* social ethics.[4] This involves bringing together Christian theologians and experts with detailed knowledge of some particular problem area. There can be no direct appeal to the Bible or even to Christian doctrine. The key to the process is *discernment*, which '. . . is achieved by putting one's understanding of human life, drawn ultimately from the biblical witness to Jesus Christ, alongside a diagnosis of what is going on'.[5] The end products of the process are described as 'middle axioms':

> ... it means roughly a statement indicating agree-
> ment, by those from different experiences work-
> ing together on an issue, about the general
> direction in which Christian opinion should try to
> influence change, without going into details of
> policy on the best way to bring it about.[6]

Preston believes it is difficult, if not impossible, to give any
prior description of what the Christian ethical input is going
to be. He acknowledges that it will come from Christian
theology in its understanding of God and man.[7] But the
content is not made clear. This precludes any rigorous
development of thinking about Christian social ethics. One
suspects that in the applications any distinctive Christian
contribution will be blunted by the strength of secular
viewpoints expounded in the group.

(c) Second objection: Scripture should be applied directly

At the other extreme to the standpoint of Preston are those
who argue for a direct application of biblical ethical teaching. Such a tendency was apparent in the exponents of the
social gospel beginning with F. D. Maurice. They made no
great distinction between the Christian church and non-
Christian society. For Maurice, Christ is Lord of mankind
and the King, whether men acknowledge him or not. Thus
in his most famous work, *The Kingdom of Christ*,[8] Maurice is
prepared to apply Johannine teaching to the whole of a
society, including, for example, Jesus' prayer in John 17.
He takes Jesus' petition, '... that all of them may be one,
Father, just as you are in me and I am in you. May they also
be in us' (John 17:21), and argues that society should enable
men to realize a unity based on love. This led him to
advocate a Christian socialism, which involves the church in
revealing to men a basic unity which they already possess in
Christ. He viewed men as inherently social and interdepen-
dent: his vision was to bring all human associations under
the kingship of Christ, so that the key to social life would
become cooperation and dependence, rather than competition and self-centredness.

The problem with this approach is that it fails to do

justice to the traditional Christian doctrines of sin, salvation and judgment. For example, many of the parables of the kingdom in Jesus' teaching speak of a separation of those who respond to the kingdom and those who do not. It is simply not the case that everyone is *in* the kingdom regardless of their response.

From a completely different theological standpoint, Clements and Schluter[9] have argued for a direct application of the Old Testament Law to the problems of modern societies. They first attempt to rebut a number of anticipated criticisms of any use of the Old Testament in this manner. The first is the criticism that cultural distance renders the Law irrelevant. They point out that there was also a large cultural gap between the society in which the Law was given, and that in which Jesus taught. But Jesus apparently did not find this a difficulty: 'Anyone who breaks one of the least of these commandments and teaches others to do the same will be called least in the kingdom of heaven, but whoever practises and teaches these commands will be called great in the kingdom of heaven' (Matthew 5:19).

A second objection is that the New Testament nowhere encourages the application of the Old Testament Law to the problems of contemporary societies. But it is equally plausible to argue that the New Testament simply presupposes the application, and concentrates on those areas where Christ has fulfilled the Law— in particular, salvation.

A third objection is that Old Testament ethics are imperfect relative to those of the New Testament. Clements and Schluter argue that this is because the Law applies to those who are unregenerate, whereas the ethics of the kingdom apply to the regenerate, whose lives are controlled by the Holy Spirit. Thus Jesus, in his teaching on divorce, says that the Law allowed divorce 'because your hearts were hard' (Matthew 19:8). It thus takes into account fallen human nature and proposes a second-best solution, rather than the higher calling of the follower of Christ. This view of the Law is also supported by the claim that Israel is to be a model for the nations.

But these arguments still leave open the question of *how*

the Law is to be applied in a modern context. Clements and Schluter argue against the method of social principles, and for a direct application of the Law. They present four criticisms of the method of deriving social principles. The first is that different interpreters can derive different principles from the same law, but there are no criteria by which we can determine which is correct. Second, there are no obvious rules for going up the 'ladder of abstraction', *i.e.* moving from the particularities of the Law to the principles. Third, there are no means for resolving conflicts of principles: this is part of the more general problem of discerning the common framework of which the principles are constituent parts. Fourth, the derivation of principles is a subjective enterprise, all too easily subject to bias by the interpreter's own prejudices or preoccupations.

The fourth criticism can be entirely accepted, without thereby denying the method of social principles. It is a warning to anyone who attempts to interpret the Bible on any issue. The interpreter should be prepared to submit his results to critical scrutiny within the Christian community.

The first three criticisms are more puzzling, since if they are taken seriously, they would threaten not just the derivation of Christian social principles, but also the whole attempt to derive a systematic biblical theology. Furthermore, they seem to imply a curious understanding of the nature of God. Presumably Clements and Schluter would not wish to suggest that God is anything less than entirely consistent in what he requires of men, and in his dealings with men. In which case it must be conceded that in the mind of God at least there is a set of principles for the social and economic life of his creatures. Furthermore the whole point of revelation is to give us an insight into his purposes for men. It would be extremely strange if he did this in such a way that we were totally unable to discern those purposes, however imperfectly. There can therefore be no objection, *in principle*, to the method of social principles which is being criticized.

This argument disposes of the first and third criticisms made by Clements and Schluter. Different, or opposing, principles *cannot* by definition be fully consistent with the

CHRISTIANITY AND ECONOMICS: THEOLOGICAL ETHICS   69

same biblical material. One or the other must be in error, and further consideration of the texts should be sufficient to resolve which has the best 'fit' with the biblical data. Further, the *conflict* of principles, and the question of the priority of one over another, is ruled out by a consistency in the mind of God, which is the common framework to which all the principles must relate.

Finally, there is the second criticism, which is that we have no criteria for abstraction. In response, we note that abstraction in this case is *not* a construct of the human mind, as Clements and Schluter seem to suggest, but rather an uncovering of what is already there in the mind of God. The process of abstraction is greatly helped by the existence of a range of biblical materials in which we can discern common features. Any principle must fit the whole range, without awkwardness or special pleading in interpretation. We shall be particularly suspicious of any 'principle' which is based on a single passage of Scripture. Further, we shall expect individual principles to fit together with others to form a consistent whole.

(d) Third objection: the use of the New Testament is inappropriate

A third objection stipulates the rejection of the New Testament as a source for social ethics, except in respect of relationships within the church. This is usually coupled with the assertion that the Old Testament Law *is* an appropriate source.

One argument is that Israel was a nation, a people living in a land with defined boundaries, a political and economic system and a place in secular history, whereas the church is a supra-national institution with none of these things. Apparently then Israel's Law is more readily applied. Second, membership of Israel was by birth, whereas membership of the church is by the spiritual process of new birth. Thus there is no direct parallel between the two communities. The only parallel is between the faithful remnant of Israel, which is a spiritual entity (Romans 9:6–8), and the church. Third, the Law presupposes a low level of behaviour in the community: it deals with questions of rape, murder, theft, bestiality and divorce. These are scarcely applicable to the community of the redeemed, but they are directly relevant to the real problems of societies made up of unregenerate people. Fourth, the ethic of the kingdom in the New Testament is impossible except for those who have experienced new birth, and by the power of the indwelling Holy Spirit are able to get to grips with the old, fallen human nature and put on Christ.

Without denying the force of these points, they do not conclusively render the New Testament irrelevant for our purposes. We have already stressed the fact that *both* the Law *and* the ethical teaching about the kingdom are addressed to covenant communities. It is simply not possible to take the Law outside the context of covenant. The difficulty that this creates in deriving general ethical principles is no less for the Law than for the New Testament.

There is also an implied disjunction between Old Testament and New Testament ethics that our previous analysis suggests is given too much weight. Jesus specifically sees his teaching as a fulfilment of the Old Testament. It is far from evident that what God requires of men has changed between Old and New Testaments; rather the New Testament sharpens the thrust of the Old Testament. What has changed is the quality of obedience that is expected from the covenant people.

In terms of our approach in deriving social principles, we would expect to find statements of ethical objectives in both Old and New Testaments. But the Old Testament may well be more useful than the New Testament in providing examples of second-best applications to a people who are less well motivated to obey.

2. Biblical principles for economic life

In this section, following the methodology described in the previous section, we expound those principles for the governance of economic life that may be derived from the biblical materials. In line with our theological understanding, we accept that these are ideals, for man as he was before the fall or for man as a member of the covenant people of God. The question of practicality in applying these to a fallen world does not arise at this point. That will be our main concern in the second part of the book when we come to application to particular areas of economic life.

The justification for each principle will be only briefly stated here, since the basis is the material earlier in the chapter which described the pattern of life that God requires of his covenant people. The derivation of these principles is provisional: they are open to a process of criticism and refinement in the light of the biblical material. We reiterate that their scope is quite limited. Few economic issues can be settled by direct appeal to Scripture. Bringing a Christian mind to bear will require disciplined thought, spiritual sensitivity and intellectual humility.[10]

The idea of stewardship is the organizing concept for the biblical principles we are about to derive. It reminds us that our personal talents and abilities, and the natural resources with which we work, are God's provision for us. They are not our personal possessions but are entrusted to us. We will, therefore, have to give account to God as to the use that we have made of them. We exercise our stewardship particularly in work, which involves an exercise of the will to direct our energies and talents. The fruits of our work are goods and services, the purpose of which is to enable man to live in a way which respects his human dignity as a person created in the image of God, placed in a good creation. But work does not imply the right to consume all the fruits of our labours, since we are stewards working on God's behalf with the talents he has provided. There is therefore an obligation on those who have much to provide for those who have little. There is also an implicit warning that the desire to hold on to what one has produced is a denial of God's ultimate ownership. Materialism is closely related to idolatry in biblical thought.

It is convenient to spell out the implications of the

concept of stewardship under three broad headings: creation and man's dominion, man and his work, and distribution of goods.

(a) Creation and man's dominion

In Genesis 1:26–30 and 2:15, man is given dominion over nature to care for it, and to use it to sustain his existence. The created order is God's provision for man. In the aftermath of the flood, God promises to maintain the natural cycle of day and night, seedtime and harvest (Genesis 8:22), and Noah is enjoined to replenish and subdue the earth. Exactly the same doctrine reappears in Jesus' teaching in the Sermon on the Mount (Matthew 6:25–32). Man's dominion over nature is regulated by a number of principles:

Principle 1: Man must use the resources of creation to provide for his existence, but he must not waste or destroy the created order.

This principle arises from the discussion of the doctrine of creation in section 2 of Chapter One. The idea of dominion, with its apparently harsh overtones, is offset by the injunctions to keep and work the garden, and by Adam's action in naming the animals. Even when animals become a source of food, in the context of the Noachic covenant (section 4 of Chapter One), their blood is to be respected, as a symbol of their life.

Principle 2: Every person has a calling to exercise stewardship of resources and talents.

Specific resources and talents are given by God to particular people or communities. An example was the provision of the promised land for the children of Israel. We saw in section 5 of Chapter One how the land was divided up in such a way that every family had an inheritance that was roughly equal. That inheritance was, in principle, to be protected in perpetuity by such devices as the laws for the redemption of debts, and by the institution of Jubilee. The parable of the talents in Luke 19:11–27 makes it clear that resources are delivered to individuals.

Principle 3: Stewardship implies responsibility to determine the disposition of resources. Each person is accountable to God for his stewardship.

The fact that we are stewards for God is implicit in the insistence of the Law that the land ultimately belonged to God (Leviticus 25), that it should be respected by keeping the seventh year as 'a sabbath of rest, a sabbath to the LORD', and that land should not be sold to foreigners, or even ceded to the king (1 Kings 21:3). It is also implied in the creation account, where God provides an environment for man to live, and grants him dominion.

The idea of accountability comes through clearly in the parable of the talents (Luke 19:11–27). Each steward is required to give an account of his dealings. Those stewards who have fulfilled their stewardship faithfully are rewarded by being given greater responsibilities. The condemnation of theft in the eighth commandment, and in more specific injunctions such as that against removing a neighbour's landmark, may also be interpreted as a defence of stewardship.

(b) Man and his work[11]

Principle 4: Man has a right and an obligation to work.

This is a creation provision, not a result of the fall. God himself, in whose image man is created, is described as a worker (Genesis 2:3). *Before* the fall man is required to 'fill the earth and subdue it. Rule over . . .' (Genesis 1:28), and he is placed in the garden to work it and take care of it (Genesis 2:15). The Psalmist regards work as being as natural as the rising of the sun or lions going out to hunt: 'Then man goes out to his work, to his labour until evening' (Psalm 104:23).

In the economic provisions of the Law, work on the family farm is regarded as the norm. Those who have lost their land for any reason are to be supported by being given work by another member of the family, if their land cannot be retrieved. Those without land are allotted the gleanings of the fields and vineyards for them to gather.

In the New Testament honest work is expected of

members of the Christian community who are fit and able to work. Paul's exhortation to the church at Thessalonica (2 Thessalonians 3:6–13) to get on with their work and not be idle, perhaps echoes the condemnation of Proverbs 6:6: 'Go to the ant, you sluggard; consider its ways and be wise.'

Principle 5: Work is the means of exercising stewardship. In his work man should have access to resources and control over them.

This principle is derived from the creation story. Man is given resources with which to work, *and* he is given the dominion over those resources.

The law concerning the land is a particular example. Each family was provided with a piece of land, which was to be held in perpetuity. The normal pattern of work was to be labour on the family land. Wage labour was a social safeguard (Deuteronomy 24: 15) for those who had lost possession of their land until the Jubilee. Decisions about the use of the land were made within the family: so those who did the work also controlled the land. Returns were earnings representing the labour and initiative of the family. They shared directly in the prosperity (or lack of prosperity) of the enterprise. The prohibition on usury within the community meant that savings would be applied within the family enterprise, rather than lent for interest. There were no returns on resources without a direct exercise of stewardship responsibilities in deciding the use to which they were to be put.

This close link between stewardship of resources, work and returns gives purpose and direction to work. Even the least interesting task can be seen as contributing to the outcome. It is true that as a consequence of the fall work becomes toil and is subject to a curse (Genesis 3:17–19). But that is the result of sin, and not God's intention for man. Work remains essential to human dignity, and integral to man's nature.

Principle 6: Work is a social activity in which men cooperate as stewards of their individual talents, and as joint stewards of resources.

It is fundamental to the biblical understanding of man

that although his individuality is very important, he is also meant to live in community with his fellow men. The smallest community for which provision is made in the creation story is the family. The social aspect of human nature is underlined by the fact that God calls a *people* of God, in both the old and the new covenants, and that the quality of their common life is given great significance.

This emphasis is particularly clear in the New Testament teaching concerning the church. The ideal for man is a community to which each member contributes according to his particular gifts. Extending the analogy to man's stewardship of resources, all employment by one man of another should take the form of an invitation to cooperate in a common enterprise. A man's labour should not be separated from his person. He is a whole person, not just a labour unit to be utilized.

(c) Distribution of goods

The combining of work and resources in the exercise of stewardship produces goods and services. We have already noted, in Principle 1, that these are to provide for man's existence. We now turn to the question of how they are to be distributed.

Principle 7: Every person has a right to share in God's provision for mankind for their basic needs of food, clothing and shelter. These needs are to be met primarily by productive work.

The creation ordinance was for man in general. Every person needs a minimum standard in food, clothing and shelter to maintain human existence and dignity. Thus in the Genesis story we see God providing food (2:16) and clothing (3:21) for Adam and Eve. In the wilderness, there was provision of manna and water sufficient for each man's need. In the Law, provision was made for the poor to share in the harvest (Leviticus 19:9–10; Deuteronomy 24:19–22). Jesus, in the Sermon on the Mount, specifically refers to food and clothing as God's provison for man (Matthew 6:25–32). Paul enjoins Timothy to be content with food and clothing (1 Timothy 6:8). Everything necessary for individual existence is also necessary *a fortiori* for families. We should ensure that families have sufficient goods and security for bringing up children.

The primary means of providing this minimum is the application of principles 2, 4 and 5 outlined above. The Law illustrates the point. A family's first defence against poverty was the fact that they had land on which they could work. Those who had no land were expected to work at gleaning in the fields. Those who lost their land were to be provided with work until their land was returned to them.

Principle 8: Personal stewardship of resources does not imply the right to consume the entire product of those resources. The rich have an obligation to help the poor who cannot provide for themselves by work.

If men are stewards of the resources and talents that God has entrusted to them, then it follows that they have no *right* to consume any more of the product than is essential to provide for their own basic needs. Within the covenant communities at least, God requires those who are rich to help those who are in need. This is a fundamental tenet of the Law, as evidenced by the obligation to provide for the disadvantaged (the widow, the orphan and the stranger), and to lend to a poor brother without charging interest and in expectation that the debt will be cancelled at the sabbatical year. We have also instanced numerous examples of a similar obligation laid on the rich in the teaching of Jesus, and in the practice of the early church. The condemnation of the rich fool (Luke 12:13–21) and of the rich man in the parable of the rich man and Lazarus (Luke 16:19–31) is consistent with this obligation. So too is the teaching about covetousness, forbidden in the tenth commandment, and placed by Jesus in the same list with such evils as murder and adultery (Mark 7:22). However there is an element additional to the implied condemnation of selfishness: riches themselves can become a spiritual snare which divert man's attention from God, substituting material security for the true security that only God can supply.

Our contention is that these *Principles* incorporate the essential features of biblical teaching concerning economic life. We have tried, deliberately, to abstract from the context in which particular teaching is found. They form a bridge in moving from the biblical material to the questions to be addressed in the second half of this book.

Having stated the *Principles* it is worth returning to two criticisms of our method advanced above. The first is that derivative social principles are likely to give rise to difficulties where they appear to conflict. The test of this objection is to see whether that is the case for our set of eight *Principles*. We do not believe that any fundamental conflicts arise, confirming our initial expectation that the biblical materials would give a consistent set. It might, of course, be possible for a casuist to invent hypothetical situations where two or more of the principles might be perceived, *prima facie*, to be in conflict. But moral judgment is seldom a matter of applying moral principles directly, but more frequently of discerning which principles are more applicable.

Nor does the consistency of the eight *Principles* preclude the possibility of conflicts arising when we come to practical application. Given man's sinful nature, an attempt to implement a particular principle may give rise to conflicts with another. For example, a stress on the obligation of the rich to help the poor may prove a disincentive to the exercise of responsible stewardship. But that is quite different from saying that the principles are fundamentally conflicting.

A second criticism is that there is no obvious control on the *Principles* that are derived from the biblical material. It has already been acknowledged that the task of producing universal principles from a diversity of biblical materials is fraught with difficulties, and can never be more than provisional. The test of whether it has been done successfully is to return to the text, to ask whether there are significant aspects which have been overlooked, and whether the principles are themselves fairly closely related to the text without too many intervening steps in the derivation. It is for the reader to decide whether our eight *Principles* pass this test.

Finally we need to explain why we have *not* adopted

principles which other writers have sought to derive from the same biblical material. One example is the attempt by Brian Griffiths[12] to argue that the biblical material requires private property rights, and that such rights in turn require a market economy. This could be argued in three ways, and in fact he presents an amalgam of the three approaches. The first is to argue that only such a system is consistent with the biblical material.

> The justification of private property rights ... is rooted in creation. Man was created as a responsible being. But freedom presupposes the ability to make choices concerning those things over which persons have control. In the material area of life this can be guaranteed only by the existence of private property rights.[13]

> To the extent that private property rights ... are the appropriate Christian starting point, then a market economy ... is the logical outcome.[14]

This is scarcely a convincing argument. It may be true that a market economy is consistent with biblical principles. That will be discussed in Chapter Four. But the word 'only' in the first quotation is quite unsubstantiated. Many people are highly responsible stewards of resources in which they have no private property rights: the examples of Christian ministers, hospital doctors, and university professors come to mind.

The second argument he advances is the various prohibitions against theft, which he takes as evidence of respect for private property rights. But as he himself is at pains to stress, these rights are not those of Roman law, which imply 'unconditional and exclusive use of the property by the individual'. They are rights which impose duties and obligations, in the sense of stewardship, as we have seen. The use of the term 'private property rights' in this context is therefore likely to confuse readers, who will assume that the Roman law view is implied.

The third argument is the least satisfactory. It is that the use by Jesus in his teaching of examples which are based on a market economy with private property is evidence that, at the very least, he did not disapprove of the market economy. But the argument imports too much significance in Jesus' choice of example. Are we, for example, to deduce from the parable of the wise and foolish house-builders that Jesus looked upon the building industry with particular favour? Our conclusion is that Griffiths claims too much in putting forward the market economy as a biblical ideal. It may be compatible with some or all aspects of biblical ideals, but it is not an ideal in itself.

3. Justice, and the authorities

The previous section established the principles that would govern an ideal economy. We now have to consider what allowance to make for the sinfulness of men. The key to resolving this question is the biblical concept of justice. Justice refers not so much to a state of affairs (in this world, at least), but to an activity— the activity of putting right a disordered or disproportioned state of affairs.

A full implementation of the *Principles* is out of the question. There can be no hope of a fully Christian economy, or of a kingdom of heaven on earth. Rather, a Christian's concern for justice in the economic sphere will be a persistent identification of areas of disorder or disproportion in the economy, whether capitalist, socialist or 'mixed', and then the attempt to get things put right in so far as the hardness of men's hearts will allow.

This leaves the question of *who* is to take action to ensure economic justice. The biblical view is that rulers, authorities and magistrates are responsible for justice (righting wrongs) in society.

(a) God's justice and human justice

The definition of justice requires us to make a distinction between God's justice and human justice.[15] The biblical material has much more to say about the former than about the latter.

We distinguish four aspects of God's justice. The first is the definition of good and evil, which derives from the moral character of God himself. He defines, for his creatures, how they ought to live. He calls them to live righteously. The content of righteousness for individuals and for the community in respect of economic life has been spelt out in the *Principles* of the previous section. In particular, God stresses his concern for the poor, the disadvantaged and the stranger (Deuteronomy 10:18; Amos 5:4–24), especially that they should not be oppressed by the perversion of justice by bribery and partiality.

The second element in God's judgment is retribution. Persistence in unrighteousness results in judgment and punishment. God will not tolerate evil for ever. This theme would be unbearable were it not for the third element in God's justice, which involves forgiveness and redemption. This theme is clearly present in the Old Testament promises of forgiveness and salvation which follow repentance (see, for example, Isaiah 1). It finds its climax, and perfect expression, in the cross. The themes of judgment for sin, and forgiveness and redemption by Jesus' death on the cross, are fully articulated in the epistle to the Romans (see particularly Romans 3:21–26).

The final element in God's justice is the promise of a new heaven and a new earth where righteousness will be established, and evil will be destroyed for ever (2 Peter 3:13). This comes about through the sovereign will of God.

Human justice, by contrast, operates mainly in respect of the first two elements, and even in those respects is at best a pale shadow of God's justice. God's justice provides a standard and a motivation for human justice. The first element, the stating of the content of justice, conforms very much to the pattern we have already described. God's principles for human life represent a first best towards which fallen man can at least strive. A second best, conscientiously developed with regard both to what God requires and to what sinful man can achieve, will be the content of human justice.

The second element, that of a judgment and punishment for wrongdoing, is also present in the practice of human justice. But it needs to be much more restricted in scope than God's judgment. Not only will the standards to be applied be less rigorous, we should also seek to minimize the degree of punishment to that which is compatible with the restraint of evils. Human judgment is too partial and too prone to error (for only God looks on the heart) to permit a process of justice that rigorously applies God's perfect Law. What was right practice for the covenant people of the Old Testament, we should hesitate to apply in a secular society.

The third and fourth elements in God's justice should be entirely absent from human justice. There is simply no basis on which human justice can offer redemption and forgiveness. These can come only from the redemptive grace of God. That is not to say that our justice should not be tempered with mercy. But that belongs to the first two elements of justice as we have defined them: the standards should not be too exacting, and the punishments should err on the side of mercy. Furthermore, there is no hope, in human justice, of bringing about 'a new heaven and a new earth'. Our achievements will be piecemeal, and subject to rapid erosion by evil. For that reason human justice is at best an activity which involves the identifying of wrongs according to the standards God has set for man, and then setting about putting them right.

(b) The role of the political authorities

Who then is responsible for securing a degree of justice in society? This role is ascribed, in the biblical material, to the rulers and leaders in society. Different kinds are recognized, from the judges in Israel and the various kings of the Old Testament, to the Roman magistrates of the New Testament. We shall use the term 'the political authorities' to describe them all.

The Christian doctrine of the authorities is by no means a settled theological issue.[16] All we may do here is to present what we believe to be a majority view on the interpretation of the biblical material, noting different emphases. The issue is discussed most explicitly in Romans 13:1–7, but our analysis must be extended to include other material, notably in the teaching and experience of Jesus. In the passage in

Romans, Paul is continuing the theme of God's sovereignty in human affairs which he has expounded in relation to sin and salvation in the first eleven chapters.[17] The question in Chapter 13 is how the Christian should relate to the authorities. The answer is to see the authorities as one aspect of God's providence— his moral rule and ordering of the world. (There is a parallel with the teaching about conscience in Romans 2.)

About the origin of the political authorities there is theological disagreement. One line of argument traces it back to the creation story in Genesis 2. God is the sovereign ruler of the world, but he delegates authority to human beings. The fall has disordered God's order, but not destroyed it. So it is still God's plan that man, even fallen man, should take responsibility for the rule of creation. Human rulers are God's representatives— men who by virtue of their position stand in God's place. This is made clear by a comparison of Romans 12:19–20, where wrath is specifically reserved to God, and 13:4, where the ruler is God's instrument to bring wrath on evildoers.

A second explanation of the origin of the political authorities is that of St Augustine,[18] interpreting the same basic biblical material. He argues that the dominion given to man in Genesis 2 is over creation and not over other men. In their original nature men were subject to God alone, and not to one another, since relationships (marriage, family) were based on love and not on power. It was the fall, with the disordering of relationships between men, which made political authority necessary to avoid the anarchy and destruction which proceeds from a free rein given to human selfishness. The authority of the rulers is an authority delegated from God. Their provision is an act of common grace on the part of God.

A third strand of interpretation links the authorities to the principalities and powers of Colossians 1:16 and 2:15 (RSV). Caird[19] traces the teaching about the powers to its Old Testament roots in the idea that the gods of heathen nations came to be regarded as subordinate forces acting under Yahweh (*e.g.* Psalms 29; 89; Deuteronomy 32:8–9). Since the power of each ruler was thought to be related to the power of the nation's god, it was natural to identify the rulers as subordinate ultimately to God. Assyria, for example, is so described in Isaiah 10:5–15. If this identification can be carried over into New Testament thought, then it is possible to interpret Colossians 1:16 as seeing the origin of the powers in the creative purposes of God. They are fallen, but can still be used for good in the providence of God. The authorities can still be described as 'ministers of God'.

The common theme in all three interpretations is that the authorities are seen as instruments of God's providence for preventing anarchy in human affairs. This conclusion is strengthened by consideration of the various attitudes of men and women of faith to heathen rulers in the biblical record.[20] In Jeremiah 29 the Jewish people are exhorted, and in the Book of Esther are shown, to be good citizens cooperating with the secular state. Nehemiah depends on the higher authority of the king in his dealings with Sanballat, the local governor. Daniel's loyalty to God leads him to civil disobedience, but despite the opposition of the rulers to God he is still prepared to continue in their service.

The life and teaching of Jesus suggest the same pattern. Quite apart from his famous dictum, 'Give to Caesar what is Caesar's . . .' (Matthew 22:21), and the acknowledgment that Pilate's power over him is 'given . . . from above' (John 19:11), it is clear that Jesus rejected the Zealot option, which advocated confrontation with the Roman authorities. He uses the title 'Son of Man' in his public utterances, rather than more definite assertions of his Messiahship. Finally, Paul himself maintains his teaching about the authorities apparently in the face of his experience. After illegal ill-treatment at Philippi (Acts 16:19–40), he merely reminds the rulers of their duty according to the law. He accepts their rightful authority. In Acts 25:11 he exercises his right of appeal to a secular authority.

The doctrine of the political authorities just outlined should serve to warn us against two alternative views. The first is that which identifies the authorities too closely with the work of God in the world. This tendency is apparent in Aquinas, who took the view that their authority is grounded in the natural order of things. In Thomist theology[21] the rulers have the duty and the right to enforce Christian morality on their citizens, following the analogy of a father requiring obedience from his children. The rulers may restrict the freedom of individuals in their own interests. However, all too easily a ruler may usurp God's privilege of legislating for thoughts and motives, becoming himself the arbiter of what is ultimately good for man. At this point the scepticism of Augustine is a healthy corrective, with its awareness of the sinfulness and corruptibility of the authorities. However we must also avoid a second alternative, which sees the authorities and the exercise of political power as intrinsically evil or demonic. This leads to exaggerated fears of state control and loss of individual freedom.

We need to be more precise as to the tasks which are entrusted to the authorities. The purely negative aspect of preventing anarchy and lawlessness has already been stressed above. God prefers any government to anarchy. However the authorities also have the positive task of promoting justice among their citizens. The biblical concept of justice describes both an ideal and an activity. The ideal is a purpose for man in society which will never be fully realized, because the effect of sin is that human relationships are predicated on a degree of selfishness and the use of power to attain selfish ends. It is the task of the authorities to protect those who will suffer injustice thereby, and to redress wrongs. So justice becomes the activity of putting right this disorder.

Now the authorities can fail to fulfil their responsibilities either by failing to act to reduce injustices, or by promoting the interests of one group in society, or by promoting their own self-interest. These accusations are levelled at the rulers of Israel and Judah on many occasions in their history (see for examples Amos 2; 4; Isaiah 1:10–26). It is for this reason that the Roman political authorities which are commended in Romans 13 can attract the fearsome denunciation of Revelation 13.

(c) Freedom
The view of the authorities just outlined involves an element

of coercion. In doing justice, the authorities will have to resort to sanctions against those whose behaviour is unacceptable. But this conclusion needs to be balanced by a discussion of human freedom, so that we can define more clearly what are the limits to what the authorities may do.

At first sight, the biblical material is not positive about human fredom. The existence of slavery is accepted in the Old Testament, without adverse comment. But a permissive attitude to the institution of slavery is confounded by consideration of some of the detailed teaching on the subject. For example, Deuteronomy 23:15–16 requires that a runaway slave should not be returned to his master, but should be free to live in a town of his choosing. In no way is he to be oppressed. Provision was made for slaves to be paid a fair wage as workers, and conditions for manumission were laid down. The effect of these provisions, if they had been applied, would have been the abolition of slavery as an institution. The slave who was treated badly could simply leave and obtain his freedom.

In the New Testament, Paul exhorts slaves to be subject to their masters, and restricts his advice to the masters that they are to treat slaves with consideration, remembering that both masters and slaves are subject to the same heavenly Master, who shows no partiality (Ephesians 6:5–9). In the case of the runaway slave, Onesimus, Paul urges Philemon to take him back, without suggesting any change in his status. But he exhorts Philemon to treat Onesimus as a 'dear brother', which scarcely suggests the continuation of a master-slave relationship (Philemon 1:16).

Theologically, the concept of freedom has an important role. Thus the Bible emphasizes human free will in the choice between good and evil. The responsibility for human sin is laid on all who are in Adam. As Romans 1–3 argues, every man has both a knowledge of the truth, and the responsibility for rejecting it. He also has the responsibility and freedom either to accept or to reject the gift of God's grace offered in Christ. He is a responsible moral being, not merely a creature.

Another theological theme concerns freedom from sin. In Romans 6 Paul describes the sinner as a slave to sin, unable to keep the law, and unable to please God. In Christ and through his atoning death, the sinner is delivered from his slavery to sin, and is enabled to live a new life of freedom, free to do God's will perfectly. The Christian becomes a 'slave of God'. However, chapters 12–14 make it clear that the new freedom which a man has in Christ has its practical consequences in a life of service to others, both within the Christian community and without. Personal liberty is to be sacrificed in order not to be an offence to others (chapter 14).

It is not evident that freedom in the theological sense has much to do with the secular concept of freedom in society, except that it reminds us of the very high value that God puts on human beings. That God should treat us as responsible agents suggests very strongly that we should extend the same respect to our fellow human beings. But as far as freedom in society is concerned, the biblical material emphasizes duties and obligations to our fellow men.

The key to this is that the Bible sees man as a social being, not in isolation. Adam is created in fellowship with God (who is himself 'plural' in the Trinity). This fellowship is supplemented by the provision of Eve. As sinners we all share in the race of Adam, of fallen man. The grace of God is extended first to a family, which becomes a nation, the people of Israel. Membership of that people involves relationships of obligation which are emphasized in the Law. The grace of God is then extended to a new people of God, the church. That new people is described as the body of Christ, with each member in an organic relation to the others. As Christians we are part of a new race, in Christ.

The conclusion must be that *ideal* humanity finds its expression not in individualism, but in membership of one another. It is the fall that generates self-seeking behaviour and disrupts human relationships of love and trust. However this argument must not be pushed to the point of attributing all expressions of human freedom to sinfulness. The correct model is of responsible individuals entering into loving relationships, and accepting responsibilities within those relationships, *i.e.* loving one's neighbour as oneself. Sin has perverted this scheme by tilting the balance in the direction of individualism, and by emphasizing power and domination in relationships in place of love, trust, and mutual responsibility.

Three related themes are relevant to the consideration of freedom within a society. First, individual freedom to act is likely to lead, if unchecked, to some individuals having power over others, and to a failure to accept responsibilities towards other human beings. Second, the power exercised by some individuals inevitably restricts the freedom of others. Hence it may be no contradiction to argue simultaneously for more restrictions on the freedom of those who are powerful, and for less restrictions on the freedom of the weak. Freedom, then, is not an end in itself, though it will be highly valued by the Christian. It must be evaluated with its other attributes, particularly the lack of responsibility that it engenders in sinful people. Where freedom is restricted, we need to ask why it is restricted, and what the consequences of the lifting of restrictions would be. Third, we should not treat freedom as an abstract ideal. We need to distinguish different types of freedom. Thus, freedom to worship God, or to love another person, are not likely to be in dispute. But economic freedom is more open to debate.

(d) The political authorities and the regulation of economic life

We now consider the specific responsibilities of the authorities in respect of economic life. The ideal is described by the *Principles* of the previous section. The reality is bound to be somewhat different.

What then is the role of the authorities, under God, in bridging the gap, and how far is it legitimate for the authorities to interfere with the freedom of their citizens to do what seems best to them in respect of economic activity?

On biblical grounds it is possible to rule out two extreme views in answer to the question. The first is that the authorities should not interfere at all in economic relations. That view is ruled out by the repeated condemnation in the Old Testament of those kings who failed to ensure that justice was done to the poor, the widow and the stranger. Their rights to land, to the fulfilment of contracts, and to payment for work are to be enforced. A legal framework to define basic rights in land, property and contracts should be established, with the means of seeing that these are enforced without partiality.

The opposite extreme is a political authority which attempts to establish an abstract 'state of justice' by coercion of its citizens. The parallel with the condemnation of Babel, *the* city, is appropriate here. The danger is that the enterprise of social control becomes an exercise in human pride, an expression of man's autonomy from God. The authorities become those who control and direct the destiny of their society. Nor would it help if the desired abstract 'state of justice' were close to the *Principles* of section 2. The imposition of such an ideal pays too little regard to the fallenness of man, and would no doubt involve considerable restrictions on human freedom. However laudable the ends, the means could be quite intolerable.

Consideration of those two extreme views leads to the following conclusions about the proper role of the authorities. First, they should seek to encourage those economic institutions whose functioning is most likely to be conducive to the ideals set out in the *Principles*. 'Functioning' here refers to the behaviour of economic actors within those institutions. The ideal is that they should be responsible stewards. The institutions then should be such that they give plenty of scope for personal responsibility in the use of resources, but also involve safeguards to prevent waste or exploitation of others.

The method by which such institutions may be encouraged is primarily a framework of law. Such laws should define the rights and responsibilities of those involved in a particular institution, and provide sanctions for clearly defined 'unacceptable' behaviour. These sanctions should, of course, be impartially applied.

Second, the authorities should be seen to be reacting to *perceived* injustices in specific situations. Suppose, for example, that a significant proportion of the society, through no fault of its own, has no work to do, and these people have no access to resources so that they may be responsible stewards. Then the authorities must seek means of rectifying the injustice. It is almost inevitable that in so doing they will harm the interests of others to some degree. If so, then care must be taken to keep that harm to a minimum, and its impact evenly distributed.

Third, the authorities should be ready to play an enabling role, by providing a focus and an institutional framework for responsible communal endeavour. Individuals probably recognize a responsibility to their fellow men, particularly where people have fallen on hard times through no fault of their own. In the case of near relations and friends that responsibility is motivated by love. But a sense of benevolence and goodwill is unlikely to be strong enough to lead to a wider responsibility through voluntary cooperation alone. Part of the problem is lack of organization. Part is the 'free rider' problem. The citizens may all agree, to a greater or lesser extent, that no one should be allowed to go without the basic necessities of life. But individuals are not willing to shoulder the responsibility unless they know that the burden of caring for the poor will be shared out among all those with sufficient substance to help. So an element of coercion may be entirely acceptable.

In providing an organizational focus for carrying out such a programme, a wise government will do all it can to strengthen the sense of individual responsibility that gave rise to it in the first place. For example, decentralized administration with maximum local participation will be preferable to a more efficient but centralized scheme.

CHAPTER THREE
Economic analysis: method and values

Methodology does not rank high in the preoccupations of the typical academic or applied economist. At the risk of some caricature, their methodological presumptions will contain the following elements.[1]

First, they will make a distinction between positive questions, which concern what is, and normative questions, which concern what ought to be. The former seek to elucidate the decisions of economic agents, and the economy as a system of interacting agents. The latter involve an evaluative framework for economic questions, and are much concerned with prescription, particularly but not exclusively in the area of government policy.

Second, dealing with the positive questions, economists will subscribe to a popular version of the scientific method. They will point to the development of economic theory, deriving predictions about the behaviour and outcomes that are to be expected from a few critical assumptions about the behaviour of economic agents. These predictions should then be 'tested' by comparison with data from an economy. This latter stage corresponds, somewhat imperfectly, to the experiments of the scientist. Only there are no controlled experiments, and the task of comparison is much more complicated. But nonetheless it is averred that there has been progress in replacing theories which do not 'fit the facts' very well with theories which correspond more closely to reality.

Third, in dealing with normative questions, there will be

an appeal to some weak form of utilitarian calculus. In evaluating an area of economic life, attention will be paid to the *consequences* for the individuals involved, in terms of costs and benefits. There are problems about aggregating gains and losses accruing to individuals to obtain a measure of social welfare; and economists differ about the weight to be attached to the distribution of welfare between individuals. But in principle utilitarian procedures are adopted.

A community of interest exists between the normative and positive sides of the subject. The positive side provides the predictions on which normative judgments can be made. The normative analysis provides a rationale for the emphasis on prediction in positive analysis.

This set of methodological presuppositions has been the subject of considerable criticism within the profession and without. In this chapter we seek to evaluate the presuppositions, and the criticisms made of them, from the standpoint of biblical theism. We will proceed by looking at the positive and normative aspects of economic analysis separately. We will then question whether the separation of the two aspects can in fact be maintained.

1. Positive economics

We will approach the analysis of positive economics indirectly, beginning with a brief review of the relevant developments in the philosophy of science.[2] One suspects that few economists have really grasped the implications of these developments, which have done much to undermine confidence in an 'accepted scientific method' to which economists might appeal. This leads on to a discussion of the apparent *practice* of economists, and the ways in which economists have sought to justify that practice. A specifically Christian perspective on these issues is then developed.

(a) Developments in the philosophy of science
Reading the history of the philosophy of science can be a frustrating experience, if we recall that in the past hundred

years science has been successful in providing knowledge, which when translated into technology has transformed the way in which human beings live. It comes, therefore, as a surprise that it has proved difficult to provide a coherent account of the methods of science. Every analysis appears to confront insuperable philosophical objections. The reaction to these philosophical objections has been to explain *how* scientists operate, without attempting any justification. Science is then justified by its results, without too much attention to its methods.

The nineteenth-century description of scientific method would have included the following elements. A scientist gives himself to careful observation of a set of natural phenomena. As he observes he organizes material in categories and classifications. In particular he notes that certain natural phenomena are associated with certain others. Reflection leads him to seek a characterization of the regularities that he observes. These characterizations are explanatory theories, which can then be revised and amended in the light of new facts as he collects new observations. The archetypal scientist of this kind was Charles Darwin, who took the opportunity of the famous voyage of the *Beagle* to make collections of biological material in different places around the world. He then worked on the same material for the rest of his life, seeking to provide a theoretical framework which would explain all the phenomena that he had in front of him.

The trouble with this plausible story of inductive reasoning is that almost every element of it is subject to challenge, if one imagines that it provides a logically rigorous method of arriving at the truth about anything. J. S. Mill[3] attempted to provide a rigorous justification of induction in his *System of Logic*. But philosophy of science has identified at least four objections to a formal logic of induction, three of which may be traced back to arguments presented by Mill's predecessor, David Hume.[4]

Hume's scepticism began with a denial that we can rely on our senses to give us information about the world. We have faith in our sense-perceptions and suppose that a natural world exists, and would continue to exist, without us.

Further, we suppose that the images of objects, conveyed to us by our senses, are those objects. But in fact, all we have are perceptions. We have no valid grounds for believing that it is an external, independent, real world which has caused these perceptions.

> It is a question of fact whether the perceptions of the senses be produced by external objects, resembling them: how shall this question be determined? By experience, surely, as all other questions of like nature. But here experience is, and must be, entirely silent. The mind has never anything present to it but the perceptions, and cannot possibly reach any experience of their connection with objects. The supposition of a connection is, therefore, without any foundation in reasoning.[5]

The difficulty with such unmitigated scepticism is that it scarcely rings true to common sense and experience. Mill, for example, assumed that we can obtain accurate information about the world from observation and experience. Yet if our senses are the *only* means of establishing truth about the world external to us, it is evident that Hume's difficulty is a real one.

A second objection to induction is due to Popper.[6] The number of facts that we might observe is infinite. No human mind could ever comprehend or contain them all. Hence the observer has to be selective. But there is no logical basis for making that selection. As soon as we impose criteria for selection, or even propose classifications of observations, we are implicitly bringing some prior theory to bear. All facts are 'theory laden'. For this reason Popper gives greater importance to our prior conjectures about the world in his account of the scientific method.[7]

A third objection to induction was also stated by Hume. But before we consider the objection, we will look at the strong case *for* induction made by J. S. Mill. He defines induction as follows:

> Induction, then, is that operation of the mind, by
> which we infer that what we know to be true in a
> particular case or cases, will be true in all cases
> which resemble the former in certain assignable
> respects. In other words, Induction is the process
> by which we conclude that what is true of certain
> individuals of a class is true of a whole class, or that
> what is true at certain times will be true in similar
> circumstances at all times.[8]

Mill argues that all our knowledge of the external world, with
the exception of intuitions and immediate observations,
comes from induction. The process can involve arguing
from the recurrence of one particular event to another
particular event of the same kind, *e.g.* the steam from the
kettle scalded my hand yesterday, and will do the same today
unless I keep my hand out of the way. Or it can involve moving
from a set of particular events to a general law, *e.g.* human
skin is unable to withstand being touched by very hot objects.

Hume's objection would be to deny the logical basis for this
reasoning. Thus men infer the general law that the sun rises
in the morning from their past experience that it always has.
But this cannot be *logically* conclusive, since we have no way
of knowing whether what we have experienced in the past
will continue.

Mill's response is again an appeal to experience. He *could*
conceive of a world where uniformity and regularity did not
exist, in which case inductive reasoning would be fruitless.
But we do experience a great deal of uniformity and regularity, and we can make use of that in acquiring knowledge.
The method of making inferences from a limited set of
observations has proved fruitful in the past, and will do so in
the future. Indeed the principle of the uniformity of nature
is the final step in the whole structure of inductive reasoning.
This principle is defined:

> The universe, so far as is known to us, is so con-
> stituted, that whatever is true in one case, is true in
> all cases of a certain description: the only difficulty
> is, to find what description.[9]

We arrive at this principle by discovering various physical laws, *e.g.* of motion, of light and of chemistry. These illustrate the principle of uniformity, and enable us to make the final step to that principle. However this response by Mill does not succeed in meeting Hume's criticism. All Mill has done is to provide a description of a way of reasoning without providing a philosophical justification. At the very least, an additional element to establish the principle of uniformity is required. Popper, for example, says that science has a 'metaphysical faith in the existence of regularities in our world (a faith which I share, and without which practical action is hardly conceivable)'.[10]

A fourth problem concerns the nature of the explanations which are provided to explain the observed regularities. Hume posed the question in the following way. The regularities which we observe are conjunctions of events. We then look for a causal mechanism to explain why one event always occurs with another. Unfortunately a causal mechanism cannot usually be directly observed. We can only infer its existence from the temporal sequence of events. This difficulty led Hume to deny the validity of any explanation of the conjunction of events in terms of real causes or reasons. He appealed instead to dispositions in the mind, which establish a customary connection between events, based on the repeated experience of temporal conjunction.[11] The event which comes first is the 'cause' of the second event, the 'effect'.

Mill's response to this was to claim the Law of Causation as another fruit of the 'inductive' process of thought.[12] This law is 'the truth [based on human experience] that every fact which has a beginning has a cause'. Rather than justify the law, he then proceeded to demonstrate how it should be applied to distinguish causation from correlation. The mere fact that two events are regularly observed to occur together does not imply causation. Day follows night, but night evidently does not *cause* the following day. So the task is to find that group of physical causes which can explain the event we are observing. Thus the cause of daybreak is the sun appearing above the horizon due to the natural rotation of the earth.

The ultimate intellectual enterprise, for Mill, was to link *all* phenomena in a single framework of cause and effect.

> An individual fact is said to be explained by pointing out its cause, that is, by stating the law or laws of causation, of which its production is an instance ... and in a similar manner, a law or uniformity in nature is said to be explained, when another law or laws are pointed out, of which that law itself is but a case, and from which it could be deduced.

The search is for the fewest general propositions from which all the uniformities in nature can be deduced.[13]

However we should not allow Mill's enthusiasm for this intellectual enterprise to blind us to the force of Hume's scepticism. If we rely on human experience, and nothing else, for knowledge of the external world, then we cannot prove that any particular event has occurred, or that X will follow Y on the basis that it always has in the past, or that X and Y are linked by some causal mechanism. These negative conclusions only apply to induction as a demonstrative logical argument. Nothing prevents us from using inductive inference to develop our understanding. It cannot give us *certainty*, but it is far from useless.

An alternative to the 'inductive' method described above emerged in the late nineteenth and early twentieth centuries, but was only given formal shape in 1948 by Hempel and Oppenheim as the 'hypothetico-deductive model'.[14] Explanation begins with a universal law to which are added relevant initial or boundary conditions. From these, by deductive logic, one arrives at a statement about an event for which an explanation is sought. The paradigm example is physics. A phenomenon in optics, for example, will be explained by appeal to fundamental laws concerning the behaviour of light. Typically the application will involve mathematical manipulation, which is an application of deductive logic.

In this account of scientific knowledge there is symmetry between explanation and prediction. Explanation involves identifying a particular phenomenon, and then finding universal laws and appropriate initial conditions that logically imply the phenomenon. Prediction involves the application of a universal law within a set of initial conditions to arrive by deductive logic at statements about unknown events. The underlying logic of the two procedures is precisely the same. But this symmetry thesis is not entirely satisfactory. For example, successful prediction need not imply a valid explanation: Newton's theory of gravity does not explain gravity, but in many instances it will predict quite well.

While this might not greatly concern someone who adopts the Humean notion that 'cause' is merely a description of temporal sequence (and hence a means to prediction), it will scarcely satisfy realists, who are seeking for explanations in terms of causal mechanisms to explain the sequence.[15] Similarly, some theories that are normally accepted as part of scientific discourse can explain but cannot predict: an example is Darwinian evolutionary theory which can only explain what has happened after the event. The source of the laws is not clearly specified. They are to be understood as inspired conjectures about the nature of the physical universe: they are certainly *not* the outcome of any strict logic of induction. But they may arise from inductive inference in the general sense described previously.

It is therefore of critical importance to consider how these hypotheses can be subjected to empirical scrutiny. Popper[16] makes the point that evidence can never *prove* a theory, it can only disprove it or falsify it. He illustrates this with an example borrowed from J. S. Mill: no amount of observation of white swans will ever prove that all swans are white, but *one* black swan is sufficient to disprove the generalization. Similarly, any number of empirical observations consistent with a theory are insufficient to establish the truth of the theory, but an observation inconsistent with the theory may be sufficient to falsify the theory. It is therefore important that scientific theories be open to being falsified.[17]

The concept of falsification is not however as straightforward as it seems. The Duhem-Quine[18] thesis is directed against any naïve reliance on empirical observation to decide the truth or falsity of any particular hypothesis.

There are two elements in the thesis. The first recalls a point made above in the discussion of induction. There are an infinite number of 'facts' in the world. In bringing an hypothesis to judgment, the facts are selected with respect to that hypothesis. So there may be an unknown and unknowable bias in selection: other relevant facts may be overlooked.

The second element is that hypothesis testing virtually always involves not only the theory itself but also a set of initial or boundary conditions. If therefore a set of empirical observations appears to disprove a theory, it is open to the scientist to discount the inconvenient observations as arising from the 'other' conditions. Popper makes this point succinctly:

> In point of fact, no conclusive disproof of a theory can ever be produced; for it is always possible to say that the experimental results are not reliable, or that discrepancies which are asserted to exist between the experimental result and the theory are only apparent and that they will disappear with the advance of our understanding.[19]

Popper calls this an 'immunizing stratagem': it enables a scientist to guard his theory against being falsified. Popper therefore devises a variety of methodological principles which will minimize the deployment of immunizing stratagems. These methodological principles define the content of 'sophisticated falsificationism'. They include the following: (a) all theories must be tested against the relevant evidence as soon as is feasible; (b) more credence should be given to theories that give scope for more severe testing; (c) preference should be given to theories that require fewer auxiliary hypotheses; (d) auxiliary hypotheses that increase the scope for testing are to be preferred to those that merely protect the theory from falsification. Popper suggests that the 'degree of corroboration' of a theory is to be assessed qualitatively by its track record in these respects. But however sensible these principles may be, they can do nothing to remove the second basic difficulty to which Duhem-Quine pointed.

Other analyses of the philosophy of science have abandoned the attempt to prescribe methods *a priori* for arriving at scientific truths. The emphasis has switched to insights from the sociology of knowledge, examining the role of the scientific community. The two leading proponents of this new view of science are Lakatos and Kuhn[20].

The work of Lakatos can be best understood as a development of Popper's views, in response to the Duhem-Quine thesis. The idea that hypotheses can be isolated and separately tested is replaced by the realization that scientists typically operate with a cluster of theories that comprise a scientific research programme (SRP). An SRP has a 'hard core' and a 'protective belt'. The hard core is the set of basic hypotheses which define the field of study. The protective belt consists of a combination of 'hard core' hypotheses with additional assumptions or conditions to generate theories which can be tested. Suppose that empirical observations are not consistent with a protective belt theory. Then an adjustment will be made in the protective belt theories in order to accommodate the observation. But the core will not be abandoned.

Lakatos makes a distinction between progressive and degenerate SRPs. A progressive SRP is one where the protective belt is proving fruitful in generating new theories, and those theories are being corroborated (or at least, not falsified) by evidence. A degenerate programme on the other hand suffers an increasing number of empirical failures, and can only accommodate these by making auxiliary assumptions which are increasingly ad hoc, and do not generate interesting new theories. Scientists vote with their feet, and desert degenerate SRPs for progressive ones, presumably because the progressive ones are producing results.

Kuhn[21] has no doubt that he is describing scientific methods rather than prescribing. He describes 'normal science' as being devoted to problem solving within a given theoretical framework or paradigm. 'Revolutionary science' occurs when one paradigm is replaced by another as a consequence of a series of empirical failures or anomalous results. The academic community has a critical role, both in defining the nature of normal science within the existing paradigm, and in achieving the transfer to a new one. According to Kuhn, this transfer is characterized by intense methodological and theoretical controversy. Scientists vote with their minds, and move to the new paradigm, but competing paradigms may persist for a long time. Kuhn did not view his analysis as a contribution to the formulation of a normative scientific method. In his view, science *is* whatever scientists currently happen to be doing.

The search for a unique rational scientific method within the hypothetico-deductive tradition seems to have failed. However we try to frame the rules for such a method, we end up by admitting an element of judgment on the part of the scientific community in making choices about which hypotheses to pursue.[22] This is not to adopt the extreme view that 'anything goes' in science.[23] Rather it acknowledges that rules, however useful, cannot be counted upon to be decisive.

(b) The methodology of economics

For the most part methods of investigation in economics have developed independently of philosophy of science, though doubtless sharing some of the same epistemological preoccupations. *Prima facie*, there are two reasons why a social science should be different from a physical science. First, the basic units of analysis are not physical entities such as atoms and molecules, but people. The analyst therefore has additional information besides detached observation. He can 'get inside' the behaviour of economic actors, and can use introspection as a source of information. Opinions differ as to how useful this information may be, as we shall see in our discussion of Friedman's methodology.[24] But most economists would agree that introspection ('How would *I* act in the circumstances under analysis?') is a useful source of hypotheses.

Second, human actions are to be understood in terms of reasons, preferences, and motives, rather than cause and effect. Thus if a person is asked about his economic actions, he is likely to respond with an explanation or justification of his behaviour. 'I bought this tin of beans because it was cheaper than the others on offer.' 'I decided to study for an M.B.A. because I reckoned it would improve my career prospects.' The emphasis is on an individual who weighs up alternatives, and then makes a decision. Attempts to provide explanations in economics without considering this aspect of human behaviour are, in our view, suspect.

Our discussion of economic methodology will focus on the antecedents of two major strands of contemporary analysis—economic theory and econometrics. We may trace the methodology of economic theory back to the work of J. S. Mill. Two important features of his approach are 'theoretical realism' and the deductive method.

Theoretical realism can be associated with his desire to provide cause-and-effect explanations for the temporal conjunction of events. Such explanations were to be sought in an understanding of how men take decisions and act. His advocacy of the deductive method may appear surprising in view of our earlier exposition of his arguments for inductive inference.[25] Towards the end of his *System of Logic*, he admits that induction cannot be applied in the social sciences: there are too many effects to be distinguished in a particular instance, and we cannot reduce the complexity by means of controlled experiments, as in the physical sciences.

Modern econometrics, on the other hand, has its intellectual roots in positivist empiricism. In its extreme Humean form, the sole criterion for a successful hypothesis is its power to predict. Economic theory is useful solely for providing testable hypotheses: the 'realism' of the theory, in Mill's sense, is not of particular interest.

In his *Essay on the Definition of Political Economy* in 1836,[26] Mill introduced the concept of 'economic man', which he took to be a partial description of man; but later economists argued that 'economic man' is the true nature of man, and not just an abstraction. Mill viewed economics as a science, which uses 'the method *a priori*', reasoning by deductive logic from basic assumptions about economic man. In the application to particular examples, the analyst also has to take account of 'disturbing causes', which correspond to those influences which modern economic analysis consigns to *ceteris paribus*. So predictions take the form of 'tendency laws', which may or may not hold depending on the significance of the 'disturbing causes'.

In practice, Mill accepted the Ricardian system with its various predictions: a rising price of corn, a rising rental share in national income, constant level of real wages, falling rate of profit. When all of these were 'falsified' in the 1830s and 1840s, Mill resorted to ever more ingenious special factors in the 'disturbing causes' to account for the apparent failure of the theory. For him the *validity* of the theories was never in doubt: only the correct application was open to argument.[27]

Mill's understanding of economic analysis was repeated with increasing refinement throughout the nineteenth century by writers such as Cairnes and J. M. Keynes.[28] The method is to start with a few indisputable assumptions about human nature, and to derive theories by abstract reasoning alone. This line of thought reached a classic expression in Robbins' *An Essay on the Nature and Significance of Economic Science*.[29] He defined economics as '. . . a science which studies human behaviour as a relationship between ends and scarce means which have alternative uses'. The two fundamental premises are diminishing marginal productivity, and that individuals have preferences. Neither of these is open to dispute, according to Robbins: '. . . we do not need controlled experiments to establish their validity: they are so much the stuff of our everyday experience that they only have to be stated to be recognized'. The correctness of a theory depends on the accuracy with which it is logically derived. Application of the theory is to be qualitative rather than quantitative, and depends on achieving a correspondence between the concepts that the theory is using and their real world counterparts. If a precise correspondence can be achieved, then the predictions of the model can be relied upon.

The degree of interaction with the real world in the development of theory may be very small. There are three rather different reasons for this. Some hold that economic theory is based on certain self-evident truths about human nature. These truths are the only 'facts' required. The modern proponents of this view are the neo-Austrians, who take their cue from von Mises and Hayek.[30] Methodological individualism, an emphasis on the rationality of purposeful individual action, is taken as a postulate, not open to argument. The consequences are radical: aggregation and macroeconomic analysis are rejected, and the whole modern apparatus of hypothesis testing, associated with econometrics, is a delusion.

Another viewpoint was taken by J. M. Keynes.[31] For him, the activity of theorizing should produce a *variety* of economic models. An empirical question then involves a judgment as to which model is the most apt for the economic problem under consideration. This judgment is more a matter of intuition, coupled with a willingness to immerse oneself in the facts of the situation. There is no rigorous logic of 'testing', because circumstances change so quickly that a model which is appropriate for today will not be appropriate for tomorrow.

A third viewpoint is that while it is in principle desirable to check our theories against empirical reality, it is in practice too complex. Theory is at best a 'parable' that enables us to get a handle on a complex reality. No theory will ever be complete: indeed, if it were, it would cease to be a theory.

It is this third viewpoint which dominates much of the theoretical work in economics done in the past twenty years.[32] This work usually starts by describing an economic problem in a way which is broadly recognizable as corresponding to some empirical reality. It proceeds by defining a model which is thought to capture some of the key features of that reality. The model is manipulated to provide conclusions. Some are consistent with reality, others are not, and a number of excuses ('extensions to the theory') are offered. The work usually ends by calling for studies to examine the correspondence with empirical reality more closely, but pointing out that this is not going to be simple (for any number of reasons, *e.g.* lack of data, theory too simplified, concepts not measurable). In practice what follows a seminal article is usually a stream of further theoretical papers proposing variants on the analysis using different assumptions or seeking more 'general' results. This reluctance to pursue empirical work suggests that testing of theories is not easy.

There is in fact an astonishing degree of agreement among theorists as to the model of man that forms the basic building block of economic theory. The individual is conceived of as 'rational economic man'. Rationality is given a formal content.[33] Man has preferences over the set of consequences of all his possible actions. These preferences have the following properties: (i) completeness: for any pair of actions he must be able to express a preference for the consequences of either one action or the other, or declare himself indifferent between them; (ii) transitivity: for any three actions with consequences C_1, C_2, C_3, if C_1 is preferred to C_2, and C_2 is preferred to C_3, then C_1 must be preferred to C_3.

These rules say nothing at all about the *content* of the preferences. In particular, they do not require economic man to be an egoist. If the set of consequences is restricted solely to the quantity of goods that the individual himself will consume, then there is some cause to call him selfish and egotistical. But the pure theory does not rule out the possibility that the consumption of *others* may enter his preference function, either positively (reflecting some concern for the welfare of others) or negatively (reflecting envy). This framework then leads to the economists' definition of rational choice: 'Given the set of available actions, the agent chooses rationally if there is no other action available to him the consequences of which he prefers to that of the chosen action.'[34]

The most common application of this framework of rational choice is in the theory of revealed preference. The set of consequences are 'goods', as defined by the principle of non-satiation: the consumer will prefer more of every good to less. Standard theorems in demand theory can then be derived.[35]

This particular model of man represents the final stage in the development of a concept with its roots in utilitarianism.[36] Nineteenth-century economists borrowed their concept of man from the utilitarian theory of Bentham. All experiences can be classified as generating either desirable or undesirable feelings. Individuals respond by increasing those experiences that generate desirable feelings, and by avoiding undesirable ones. An individual's goal in life is to promote his own interests, preserve his own life, increase his own pleasures and diminish his pains.

Bentham's contribution was to suggest that the pain–pleasure calculus could be captured in a single cardinal measure of utility. Seeking pleasure and avoiding pain is the same as maximizing utility, and all human efforts are directed towards that end. This idea was transferred more or less without amendment into economic analysis. So Edgeworth was able to assert that 'the first principle of Economics is that every agent is actuated only by self-interest'.[37]

The fact that utility cannot in fact be measured, linked to the desire to distance economic analysis from some of the cruder notions of utilitarianism, led Allen and Hicks,[38] in the 1930s, to redefine the model in terms of ordinal utility. Indifference curve analysis requires no more than the judgment that 'higher' curves are preferred to 'lower' ones, where in the usual textbook case these are defined with respect to quantities of goods. However the model of man is unchanged, since the objective remains to maximize 'satisfaction' given constraints. A higher indifference curve gives higher 'satisfactions'. Utility maximization still dominates the theory, but it is 'subjective' or 'introspective', and not susceptible to measurement by an outside observer.

In the logic of choice expounded above, there is no *need* to specify a utility function of either a cardinalist or ordinalist kind in order to derive theorems about consumer demand. However the utilitarian 'ghost' still lurks in the model of man used in most modern economic analysis. It is normal to postulate a utility function for consumers, and despite the fact that it does not *have* to be solely egotistical and self-regarding, it usually is.

This concept of man has attracted considerable criticism from within the economics profession. Sen states[39] that even Edgeworth felt uncomfortable with the concept, accepting other motivations for human conduct. But in the areas of contracts and human conflict he reckoned that the utilitarian egoist was an appropriate simplification.[40] Sen is not sure. He particularly attacks the equation of rationality with self-interest, *i.e.* the idea that action x is preferred to action y because one's personal interests are better served by the former's outcome. He notes that this requires assent to three fundamental principles. The first is consequentialism: only consequences count, not the action itself. The second is the evaluation of each action on its own, without any rules of conduct. The third is exclusion of everything except self-interest.

These are open to objection. For example, the principles fail to recognize that following rules may have value in itself. This is not just to make the distinction between act and rule utilitarianism, where rules are helpful to reduce the mental labour of employing the utility maximizing calculus at each and every moment. It may be that human beings actually like a life which is rule-guided to some degree. Secondly, if an individual is nothing more than a 'pleasure machine' (as a hedonistic utilitarian approach would require), then it is far from obvious why I should make any provision for my *own* future. To presume that I do requires some notion of continuing personal identity, which is difficult to reconcile with pure hedonism.

The third objection that Sen makes is that the model ignores commitment, which he believes to be an important human trait. Commitment is different from 'sympathy', which is the incorporation of externalities in the utility function. If your suffering directly and adversely affects my utility, or if your pleasure makes me feel better, then that is 'sympathy'. (It would, of course, be easy to incorporate an unpleasant, negative version as well!) Commitment is where there is no direct effect on my utility, but nonetheless I am inclined to act in a way which is not strictly consistent with personal interests.

A classic illustration is the Prisoner's Dilemma game.[41] The substance of the dilemma is that pursuit of self-interest, rather than cooperation, will lead to an inferior outcome for both players in the game. It is best to play a non-cooperative move when the other person plays a cooperative move. Hence neither has an incentive to cooperate, and the final outcome is inferior. (In fact this problem can be avoided if the game is being played sequentially into the future, or if the players collude to ensure the better outcome.) When the problem is put to people who understand the logic of the game, they frequently express discomfort at the application of rational self-interest. They want to include some commitment to the well-being of others.

Commitment may play an important role in public goods, welfare systems and workplace behaviour. Thus the 'free-rider' problem in the revelation of preferences for public goods is offset by a sense of commitment to the community in which I live: I am willing to pay my share (and perhaps more than my share), so that the community will have services which I regard as essential to its well-being even though my own benefit will be quite small. A similar commitment may govern my desire that the government should increase its overseas aid programme. *Esprit de corps* at work will lead me to put in more effort than rational self-interest would dictate, given the difficulty of measuring individual contributions to a joint effect. Finally, commitment may be a solution to the rational non-voter paradox: given the minimal scope for influencing the outcome of an election, the rational elector will stay at home and use his time more profitably (in the self-interested sense). But that is not what we observe when election time comes round.

A different attack on the rational economic man concept has come from Simon.[42] His claim is that the 'substantive rationality' which lies behind rational economic man is not consistent with psychological studies of how people actually make decisions. He proposes that a concept of 'procedural rationality' should be substituted. Given the computational complexity of any decision, especially where uncertainty is involved, economic man is looking for satisfactory solutions rather than optimizing solutions. Knowledge of the outcomes that will result from particular actions is likely to be sketchy: so the agent will gather information. This is unlikely to yield a complete description of outcomes, so he will gather information only up to the point where a particular action with satisfactory outcomes is identified. 'Satisfactory' will be defined in terms of target levels for different components or 'pay-offs'. These targets are 'aspiration levels'. If they prove easy to attain then the aspiration levels are relaxed. At the level of introspection, this description of human behaviour seems much more plausible than the maximizing behaviour of rational economic man.

However all these objections have been the subject of vigorous rebuttals in recent years. The roots of the argument can be found in the work of Friedman and Alchian.[43] Friedman regarded assumptions as of no great importance in the testing of economic theory. Thus evidence that firms did not see themselves as maximizing should not be allowed to detract from models which assumed *as if* profit maximization so long as they predicted reasonably well. The justification for 'as if' maximization was provided by Alchian: firms that failed to maximize would be eliminated from the market by competition. So the remaining firms would be *de facto* maximizers, even if they told a rather different story about their behaviour.

Similar arguments were subsequently put forward by Becker in respect of self-interested preferences, and by Muth in respect of beliefs. Becker[44] has borrowed from sociobiology the evolutionary mechanism of selection, which favours those genetic characteristics which give the organism a higher probability of surviving and reproducing itself. Natural selection will result in the elimination of those genetic characteristics which are not consistent with self-interest and survival. One difficulty is to reconcile a deterministic (or genetic) explanation of human preferences with the fact that persons are known to think about their preferences and advance reasons for them. A second objection is that for the mechanism of selection to work there must be at least some self-interested members in the population.

The selection argument has also been applied to beliefs about the future in Muth's theory of rational expectations.[45] The only consistent set of beliefs about the future is that arising from consideration of the relevant economic model. Those who think otherwise will always find that their expectations are not fulfilled, and therefore that their actions are not optimal. Furthermore, agents who act on rational expectations will have opportunities for profitable arbitrage. At the very least, other agents will observe their success and will copy them. So rational expectations emerge as the sole surviving determinant of rational agents' beliefs.

There are two objections to this theory.[46] The first is that it presumes that there exists a single 'true' structural model of the economy. But in constructing such a model the beliefs (and preferences) of economic agents will be important. Hence there is a diversity of models, given a diversity of beliefs, and there is no reason to think that convergence to a rational expectations model will necessarily occur.

The second objection concerns the cost of searching for information. Where there is uncertainty, the rational economic agent will proceed by acquiring information up to the point where the marginal cost of obtaining further information is equal to the marginal benefit. However to make this choice one needs information about the relevant marginal costs and benefits. This information is then the subject of a further search procedure equating marginal costs and benefits. But that search procedure also requires knowledge of *its* costs and benefits. There is therefore an infinite regress, with no *reason* to believe that it will be satisfactory to stop searching after a certain number of steps.

The final argument which concerns enforced maximization for firms has a long history in economic theory. It was originally linked to the theory of competitive product markets. Those firms which failed to minimize costs would be eliminated by the lower prices charged by more efficient firms. However this does not take account of the possibility of imperfect markets allowing inefficient firms to persist as suppliers.

The alternative mechanism is the market for corporate control. Any set of managers who failed to maximize returns would find their shareholders selling out to a more efficient managerial team. One doubt about this argument is that the concept of profit maximization is not well defined unless there exists a complete set of future and contingency markets (or their equivalent).[47] A second is that the takeover mechanism will fail if shareholders act rationally by attempting to 'free ride' on a takeover bid.[48] Since the effect of a successful takeover will be, by hypothesis, an increase in the efficiency and the value of the firm under new management, each shareholder would like others to sell, but would prefer to retain his own holding. Hence takeover bids will fail if shareholders act rationally.[49]

To conclude, the methodology of 'theoretical realism' introduced by Mill continues to exert a powerful influence in modern economic analysis. The rational behaviour of economic actors is presumed to explain economic phenomena. However the concept of economic man, which was for Mill a convenient simplification, has become *the* model of man for economists. The model has been bolstered against criticism by the selection arguments discussed above. The effect has been to protect the concept from qualms about its empirical relevance. The theory cannot be wrong, only inappropriately applied. So there is only limited interest in the positivist programme of testing hypotheses, to which we now turn.

The positivist methodology was first introduced to economics by Hutchison in 1938, in his book *The Significance and Basic Postulates of Economic Theory*,[50] which consciously drew on the work of Popper on method in science. His proposal was that economic inquiry should be confined to empirically testable propositions. The nature of the 'tests' is not made clear by Hutchison: for example, whether testing should be applied to the assumptions or to the predictions of a particular economic theory. However it seems likely that it was the assumptions or 'postulates' with which he was primarily concerned.

The positivist cause was given a major impetus by Samuelson's *Foundations of Economic Analysis* published in 1948.[51] He stated as his objective the derivation of 'operationally meaningful theorems': 'By a *meaningful* theorem I mean simply a hypothesis about empirical data which could conceivably be refuted if only under ideal conditions.' However the methodological significance of the book lay not so much with this affirmation, as with its demonstration of how *very* limited were the traditional methods of economic analysis as espoused by Robbins. For example, he shows that traditional comparative static analysis is useless, unless one can also specify the underlying dynamic system and show it to be stable. Further, he indicated that existing theorems often failed to provide even qualitative results concerning the direction of change of some key endogenous variable in a model, with respect to a change in some exogenous or control variable. The refutation of a theory that cannot even predict this much is not going to be easy.

However, the development of empirical methods in economics probably owed more to the practitioners of econometrics than to any writer on methodology. Schultz[52] was a pioneer in this field with his studies of demand, seeking to establish the numerical values for price elasticity, cross-price elasticity and income elasticity of demand for a number of different goods. The other impetus came from the Keynesian policies of the post-war period. Demand management called for fairly precise predictions both of the future path of the economy, and of the effect of different fiscal measures. The need to measure national income more precisely was linked to the development of relatively simple numerical models of the macroeconomy. To calibrate these models it was essential to have precise estimates of such magnitudes as the marginal propensity to consume and the marginal propensity to import. While the initial concern was to obtain parameter values to insert in the macro models, the econometric methods used to derive such values were also valuable in indicating how well some of the theories fitted the evidence. So refinement of the theory was stimulated.

The econometricians introduced to economics the concepts of hypothesis testing developed by mathematical statisticians, particularly the Neyman-Pearson theory. Suppose our hypothesis is that P 'causes' Y: for example, that the quantity of a commodity (Y) bought is, *ceteris paribus*, a negative function of the price (P). Because of the *ceteris paribus* clause, we know that an exact relation between P and Y will not exist. Other factors, such as income, taste differences, prices of substitutes and complements, will also affect the demand for Y. We may be able to include these in the analysis; or we may decide that these are likely to be small in magnitude and uncorrelated with the effects of prices, so that they can be subsumed in a normally-distributed random error. (An actual analysis is very unlikely to be so simple, but the example is for illustrative purposes only.)

We also have to face the possibility that there are errors in our observations of both prices and quantities sold: it is not easy to ensure that these have been accurately recorded, or that our statistical coverage is complete. So we know on both counts that the relationship between price and quantity, if it exists, is likely to show up imperfectly in our data. The question is: does the relationship exist? or rather what degree of imprecision will we accept without rejecting the hypothesis we started out with?

Typically, this kind of question is answered by means of regression analysis. Assume, for the moment, that we believe the underlying relationship to be linear or log-linear in the variables. Then we seek to test the hypothesis, H_1, *i.e.* that P 'causes' Y, against the null hypothesis, H_0, that there is no systematic relationship between them. The test, in this case, is for the coefficient on P, in a regression of Y on P. Our hypothesis, H_1, is that the coefficient is negative; the null hypothesis, H_0, is that the coefficient is not significantly different from zero.

The problem in constructing a statistical test is that there are two errors into which we may fall: Type I error is a decision to reject a hypothesis that is in fact true, Type II error is a decision to accept when the hypothesis is in fact false. On the whole, statistical methodology is conservative, in the sense that it presumes that the costs of Type II errors are likely to be higher (*e.g.* we may act on the erroneous conclusion that Y is determined by P) than Type I errors. (Ideally we should base our tests on the actual costs of the two types of error in the particular instance under consideration, but the information is probably not available.) Thus stringent rules are proposed: we are unlikely to give any credence to the hypothesis unless the chance of Type II error is less than one in twenty; and we will be more comfortable about accepting the hypothesis if the chance is less than one in a hundred. These correspond, of course, to the '5%' and '1%' levels of statistical significance. These are merely conventions. However they enable statistical results to be communicated and evaluated by other researchers.

In the example, the test can be applied directly to the coefficient of P in the regression equation. Other cases will require more complex applications of the same methodology. For example, we may wish to consider a number of 'explanatory' variables in the same equation; the hypotheses being tested may relate to the whole group of variables in conjunction, or to subsets of the group. Alternatively, the test may involve the consideration of several competing hypotheses, rather than just one hypothesis against the null. More narrowly, the test may be comparing different specifications of the same relationship, *e.g.* linear versus log-linear, to determine which accords more closely with the evidence.

This discussion of statistical technique and its applications does not however resolve fundamental methodological questions as to what is being achieved. This issue was opened up in a famous essay by Friedman.[53] His methodological position is that a hypothesis should be assessed by its predictive power:

> . . . the only relevant test of the validity of a hypothesis is comparison of its predictions with experience. The hypothesis is rejected if its predictions are contradicted ("frequently" or more often than predictions from an alternative hypothesis): it is accepted if its predictions are not contradicted: great confidence is attached to it if it has survived many opportunities for contradictions.[54]

This bold assertion is followed by an unequivocal rejection of any empirical test applied to the assumptions of a particular theory. The 'reality' of the assumptions is of no interest. The point of theory is to pare down reality: a good hypothesis is one which explains a great deal with minimal assumptions. It has to be descriptively inaccurate if it is to be useful.

Friedman is critical of those who require the assumed behaviour of economic actors to be feasible, in the sense of being consistent with the information available to them and with their powers of calculation. It is no criticism of the profit maximizing theory of the firm, according to Friedman, to protest that managers do not have the capacity or the information to act as the theory requires. He observes that the best managers will act *as if* they had these characteristics, and that inferior managers, who do not, will be weeded out, in Darwinian fashion, by the process of competition. This is the theory of *enforced* maximization which was considered above.

Critics of Friedman have pointed out certain pitfalls in his methodology. A good prediction is not necessarily coincident with explanation, since it gives no basis for distinguishing between correlation and causation. This is Hume's problem again. Friedman gives no particular *reason* for his objection to consideration of the empirical relevance of the assumptions of a theory. One might sympathize if tests of assumptions were claimed to be the *only* test. An open-minded approach might be to look at the whole model, assumptions, postulated mechanisms *and* predictions, in the light of the available evidence. A model would have to predict very well if it were to be maintained despite evidently counterfactual assumptions. The suspicion would remain that, for all its predictive power, it had failed to capture 'reality'. That leaves unanswered the question as to how 'unreal' the assumptions can be without becoming a reason for rejecting the theory.[55]

A more critical awareness of methodological issues has come into the practice of econometrics in recent years. This parallels frustration in the profession that econometrics has not been conspicuously successful in the task of discriminating between hypotheses. A notable example has been the debate between monetarists and neo-Keynesians over the significance of monetary policy in the determination of nominal national income.

The 'failure' of econometrics has been variously attributed. One view, due to Hendry,[56] is that econometricians have become careless in the methods they use. He makes a number of recommendations as to good practice. First, the econometrician should pay much greater attention to the detailed construction of data series. Data should conform closely to the actual concepts that underlie the relevant economic theory.

Second, particularly in the analysis of time series, the data should be allowed to dictate the dynamic lag structure, rather than the researcher imposing some arbitrary lag structure on them. The correct procedure is to specify initially a completely general lag pattern and then proceed by deletion. Furthermore, the model itself should have stable long run dynamic properties.

Third, if the test of a theory is its predictive power, then prediction outside the sample period is a very important part of any econometric evaluation. Failure to predict accurately suggests that the model is inadequate. Similarly, stability of the parameters over different sub-periods within the sample is confirmation that the econometric equation is capturing a stable behavioural relationship. Instability is an indicator that something is amiss.

Fourth, part of the 'failure' of econometrics has been the practice of each researcher presenting his own preferred equation and results, with no concern for quite different results obtained by someone else. For Hendry, an econometrician can only claim that his model represents an advance in knowledge if he is able to 'explain' the other results *within* his own framework. For example, it may be possible to show that other results have been biased by the omission of explanatory variables, or by the failure to prepare the data properly.

An alternative view of econometrics, which accords closely with Lakatos' description of an SRP, is that statistical testing on its own is inadequate to the task of discriminating between hypotheses. Cross has suggested,[57] for example, that the debate between monetarists and Keynesians over the demand for money function cannot be resolved by a simple appeal to the evidence. Each school of thought has its own 'hard core' of propositions which cannot be tested directly. Even large-scale tests of complete macroeconomic models are unlikely to be decisive, since each school could respond to unfavourable results by invoking the Duhem-Quine objection, or by making some adjustment to the 'protective belt' of the theory.

Quite apart from this, each school of thought will fashion definitions of variables according to its own theoretical presuppositions. Thus Keynesians and monetarists might find it difficult to agree on a definition of 'the money supply', relevant to a comparison of their two models. It looks as though the only 'test' of the adequacy of a particular SRP in economics is the long-term support of the profession. A degenerating SRP will lose support, a progressive one will gain, as economists perceive their relative advantages and disadvantages.

The distinction between economic theory and econometrics should not be pressed too far in respect of the practice of economists. Most economists would be prepared to concede a role for both theory and statistical analysis. But the role of econometrics often is the calibration of a particular economic model, rather than hypothesis testing in the Popperian sense. It is hard to identify any economic hypothesis which has actually been *falsified* by application of econometric techniques; though the poor predictive power of a model has sometimes generated substantial theoretical development. Few economists entertain seriously the possibility that the 'rational economic man' concept is itself inadequate.

(c) Christian reflections

The biblical affirmation is that the *locus* of truth is God. The creator knows all about his creation, so all truth about everything is his, and he knows it as a coherent whole. Truth therefore is absolute, unchanging and universal, since it reflects the nature and character of God himself.

One source for this affirmation is the doctrine of the *logos* or 'Word' in John's gospel. The term *logos* has a reference point external to the Bible, the closest link being the Hellenistic philosophy of Philo. The *logos* is an active, rational force that underlies the material universe, and gives order and unity to nature. An element of the *logos* is present in each man. In Philo the origin of the *logos* is God himself.

Logos also has a parallel in the personified 'wisdom' of the Old Testament Wisdom literature. This is the wisdom which governs the affairs of men, rewards the just and punishes the unjust. It existed from the beginning of creation (Proverbs 8:14–31).

In the prologue to his Gospel, John incorporated these meanings in identifying the *logos* as the Creator-God. The *logos* is the God who speaks in Genesis 1, and his decree effects what he declares. The *logos*, as revealed in the incarnation of Jesus, gives light and life to men. This personal concept of truth contrasts with the Platonic conception of impersonal universals which are eternal *and* autonomous, but cannot be discerned by man in either creation or history because man's perception varies and has no given reference point.

The personal nature of truth can be illustrated by the biblical words for truth, knowledge and wisdom. The word for truth normally carries the connotation of fidelity. The truth of a proposition is not abstract but is related to the truthfulness of the speaker. Thus the faithfulness of God is seen in his unchanging character, in his creation, in his mercy and in his justice (Psalm 89). The New Testament emphasizes the reliability of those who bear witness to Jesus, and have recorded his message faithfully (John 5:30–39; 16:13–15; 21:24). Jesus claims not only to bear witness to the truth, but to be the truth himself. In the incarnation, then, God discloses the truth, and Jesus becomes the key to seeing all things in their proper perspective.

The word for knowledge in the New Testament is not normally the Greek word from which the term 'epistemology' is derived. Instead, a word is used which implies personal involvement. Knowledge should affect personal standards and behaviour, and implies responsibility. Finally, wisdom is to be found in the knowledge of God and his ways. The wisdom of this world is condemned, precisely because it excludes God (1 Corinthians 1–2).

Holmes[58] summarizes his review of the biblical material as follows. Truth is absolute, unchanging and universally the same because it is derived from the eternal God, and grounded in his creation. Propositional truth depends ultimately on the fidelity of God, who can be trusted in all he declares, and all he does. Jesus Christ is himself *the* truth, and the focus to which all truth relates. The intelligibility of nature attests God's fidelity, and the cognitive powers of man reflect his creation in the image of God. But truth and knowledge should not be detached and purely theoretical. The pursuit of knowledge is an expression of trust in the faithfulness of God. Truth, in its fullness, demands a personal response.

Having discussed the concept of truth in its theological context, we need to consider how we are able to discover this objective truth for ourselves. First, we should note that there is 'no royal road'[59] through faith and the scriptures. Faith is a man's response to God's revelation, an opening of his life to God. But faith is not itself knowledge, nor is it a mysterious learning process. It is a response to what is already known.

Faith also alters our attitude to learning. It makes us more open to the truth and willing to learn. The scriptures are a source of information regarding the truth, *i.e.* they are propositional revelation. But that revelation is directed particularly to awakening sinful men to what God requires of them, and what he has done for them. Their purpose is redemptive. They need to be studied and interpreted, and then applied to our human experience. In the process of interpretation there is a problem of human fallibility. We must therefore acknowledge our dependence on God as we seek to interpret, keeping ourselves open to the leading of his Spirit. But, although the scriptures contain all that is necessary for us to know for faith and salvation, they are by no means *exhaustive* of all knowledge. They do however give us confidence in the rationality and order of God's creation, and in the cognitive capacity of men, to enable us to set about the task of understanding things on which the biblical revelation is silent.

But we should beware of placing too much reliance on the cognitive capacity of people to arrive at truth about these other matters. There is the problem of human error, arising in part from sin and unbelief, and in part from human finiteness. The Bible sometimes speaks of the inability of a person to comprehend the truth unless he or she is taught by the Spirit of God (1 Corinthians 1:18-2:14; John 7:15–18). But these passages refer to an understanding of God that lies apart from revelation, and do not deal with the limits of human knowledge in general.

Not all knowledge is closely tied to the central issue of Christian belief. For example, pure logic and mathematics are remote from these issues, while theology and ethics are (or should be) closely related. Hence it probably matters very little for his academic work whether or not a mathematician accepts the Christian revelation, while it is a serious matter for an ethicist. To explain error in mathematics, therefore, we cannot appeal to human fallenness. It is better to note that man was *created* a finite being, fallible and limited in his knowledge, not infallible and omniscient. This does not mean that we have to abandon all expectation of arriving at true knowledge. Rather we must accept that our knowledge is at best provisional, and must be open to criticism and correction, in those areas where there is no revealed biblical truth on which we may rely. This conclusion raises again the question of method.

We consider first the 'inductive method' described by J. S. Mill, which was discussed previously. This method corresponds with common sense descriptions of how we obtain knowledge about the world, but cannot be given a sound epistemological basis. However the philosophical problems are somewhat less acute if we approach the method from within in a Christian framework.

First, we no longer have any doubts about the metaphysical objectivity of the world we are observing. It is there, created by God, and that fact is revealed to us in Scripture. Hume's extreme scepticism is misplaced.

Second, we expect to observe regularities, and cause and effect sequences, since we know that God has created an orderly and unified universe. The principles that govern that ordering are there to be discerned (imperfectly, of course) by human reasoning and observation.

Third, the difficulty of having 'too many facts', and not knowing how to order them, can be somewhat reduced by noting two new elements. One is that revelation does in fact give us a starting point in our search for knowledge. We can use what we know as a bridgehead into areas where we know nothing. The other, more speculative, element is the idea that man in the image of God, although fallen, has a limited capacity to discern order in the creation. Our intuitions may be a better source of understanding than we usually credit. Certainly the biographies of great scientists suggest that a capacity for insight or intuition about the physical world was an important feature in their work. However it is essential that these insights, stated more formally as hypotheses, should be checked for consistency with the facts by careful observation.

This brings us to a fourth aspect in which the Christian framework is useful. We have already noted that when we observe reality, there is 'something there' to be observed. But that does not eliminate the possibility of observer error, so we are right to insist on methods of measurement that permit observations to be checked for their accuracy.

We suggest therefore that hypotheses are generated by a process of reflection on some aspect of the real world which gives rise to particular insights. These insights are then formulated in a more rigorous way to check for their consistency, both internally, and with provisional knowledge in related areas. This formulation is made the basis for tests of the hypothesis against the facts. If it performs well on the tests it will be accorded some limited status as provisional knowledge. This will then become a starting point for generating new hypotheses, directed at explaining areas where the provisional knowledge does not appear to be telling the whole story.

Obviously, this account is open to the objections of the Duhem-Quine thesis, and to the charge of relativism implicit in Lakatos' analysis. But our defence of the 'inductive method' (as opposed to the strict principle of induction) as a source of hypotheses rescues it to some extent. More importantly, our account emphasizes that the difficulties we experience in discovering knowledge do not arise from the lack of an objective truth to be discovered, but from our human finiteness and weakness.

It remains to see how far this account of knowledge, in a

Christian perspective, will help us with our economics. There are two major questions. First, can we expect the same order in human affairs as we have postulated for the natural order, on the basis of the doctrine of creation? The answer to this question will affect, for example, our capacity to use the 'inductive method' outlined. Second, does the biblical revelation give us any useful starting points for the development of hypotheses concerning economic behaviour?

For the physical and biological sciences the assumption of order in the natural world is based on the doctrines of creation and providence. It is not evident that the same assumption can be adopted in the social sciences. First, Christian theology has been at some pains to distinguish man *from* the natural order, while admitting that in his physical make-up he is a part of it. Second, the doctrine of original sin tells us that man has exercised his power of choice to cut himself off from God, and to make his own way in the world. Even if the fall has not destroyed the image of God in man, at the very least we expect human affairs to correspond only imperfectly to God's order. However that is different from saying that there is *no* order to be discerned. We expect men to act consistently, even if these actions are not motivated by obedience to God's laws, but by a desire to pursue their own ends. The image of God still prevails in this limited sense.

There is the further point that the Bible firmly asserts the view that God is still in control of human history.[60] Thus in Isaiah 41, God tells his people through the prophet that he is responsible for the rise of Cyrus, and in Isaiah 45 Cyrus is described as God's agent in history. The history of the people of Israel is set in the context of God's purposes not only for the nation but for all mankind. The New Testament sees human history as moving towards the climax of Christ's return, the final judgment and the destruction of evil. However we should not make too much of this biblical view of history as a basis for social science. It makes the point that history is not out of God's control, and that we are to trust him for the future. That does not give us any straightforward explanation of what we observe in finite human beings. But it can provide a presumption that a search for knowledge about human affairs is not likely to prove entirely fruitless.'[61]

The second question is whether the biblical revelation can give us starting points for the development of hypotheses concerning human behaviour. These starting points can be of two kinds. One is direct information about the nature of man, and about his motivations. The second is a set of criteria for deciding what aspects of economic behaviour are significant. These would help us to overcome the problem that there is an infinity of facts about economic life, and analysis has to have some criteria for deciding which facts should be selected for study.

The Bible devotes considerable attention to the nature of man. The aspects which are important here are man created in the image of God, and fallen man.

From creation we derive three elements. Man is personal, with the capacity for making real choices, and for entering into relationships. Man is a steward of the creation, to care for it, and to obtain from it those things which he needs for his existence. Man exercises his stewardship through work. From the doctrine of the fall we derive the notions that man's choices and actions are likely to be determined by selfish self-interest, that power and fear are present in human relationships, that dominion over nature can become exploitation, and that work can become toil.

The theological principle that the image of God in man was marred, but not destroyed, by the fall, suggests that our analysis of human behaviour needs to encompass *both* the aspect of creation *and* the aspect of fallen man. For example, an analysis based solely on the latter will emphasize self-interested behaviour, and will ignore or explain away genuinely altruistic behaviour. It will see work as toil, and fail to note that work is also good.

The concept of rational economic man in economic theory is not inconsistent with this biblical view of fallen man, which may explain why the concept has proved so enduring in the history of economic analysis. It also explains the discomfiture of those who see aspects of human behaviour that are not consistent with the concept.

Some of these, like the capacity for altruism, and the desire to work, come from the creation aspect. Others, like the presence of power and fear in human relationships, and man's destructive relationship to the natural order, come from the aspect of fallen man. Thus the standard economic analysis sees transactions as mediated impersonally through markets, and can therefore ignore the presence of power and altruism in transactions between those who also have a personal relationship. Similarly, the standard analysis takes work as a disutility and fails to register that many people like their work, and see it as a means of expressing themselves as persons.

The implications for economic analysis are not necessarily radical. There is no need to scrap all our theories and start again from scratch. But some reformulation of standard theory is essential. First, we need a richer set of hypotheses concerning the behaviour of economic actors. The model of rational economic man is an abstraction that captures only a part of reality. The most important step might be to escape completely from the utilitarian roots of the theory. This would permit a much wider range of preferences and motives to be considered. Choice theory needs to be reformulated, while retaining the concept of a person who can think about choices and make decisions. But choices should not be restricted to the consideration of the consequences of different actions (as in the utilitarian theory). They should allow for people to make choices of actions which have value in themselves, *e.g.* commitment to a particular way of life.

Secondly, theory should accept the importance of culture in explaining human behaviour. The rational economic man model holds out an enticing prospect of a unified cross-cultural theory of economic behaviour. But our analysis of the tensions in human nature between creation and fall suggests that some diversity is to be expected. For example, some cultures may give higher priority to creation values, and thereby affect the behaviour of their members. Other societies may be more rooted in hedonism, and the rational economic man model will be more appropriate.

The second sense in which the biblical material might

form a starting point for social science is by providing a set of criteria to determine what are the important issues. The biblical principles for economic life which we described at the end of Chapter One provide an agenda for economic analysis. They speak of what God requires of man in his economic life. It is appropriate that economic analysis be directed particularly to the issues that arise from those principles. They are the issues that God considers to be important.

The research programme should therefore include the following: (i) how far does the economic structure of the society allow man to exercise responsible stewardship? (ii) what is the relationship between economic activity and the use of resources? how far is the concept of *care* for the natural order a part of economic life? (iii) does the economy provide opportunities for satisfying work for its members? (iv) what are the causes of poverty? and does the economic system have mechanisms built into it to prevent some of its members becoming destitute? (v) how far has the pursuit of wealth, for its own sake, become the goal of society in detriment to other values? (vi) how effective are the authorities in promoting justice in the economic sphere?

All these elements are present in much economic analysis, which may reflect the key influence of Judaeo-Christian ethics in the Western economies. But the emphasis on 'efficiency, growth and progress', as defined within the neo-classical research programme, is missing from the list. (So too is the pursuit of macroeconomic stability, though this may be implied in (vi) in relation to promoting justice.) The reason for this omission is almost certainly due to the contrast between the biblical framework and the normative framework of economic analysis with its utilitarian roots. It is to this contrast that we turn in the next section of this chapter.

2. Normative economics

Our discussion of normative economics will follow the pattern established in the previous section. We will begin by

stating as concisely as possible the state of the art in normative economics. We will see that despite strenuous efforts on
the part of some theorists to purge the subject of its
utilitarian content, those efforts have not succeeded:
utilitarianism is alive and well in normative economics.
However the case for and against the utilitarian framework
is a subject of considerable debate within the economics
profession. So we shall take note of that discussion. Finally
we contrast the structure of normative economics with the
framework of biblical principles for economic life derived
in Chapter Two.

(a) The state of the art in normative economics

While some economists may reject it altogether, or would
wish to supplement it with other ethical judgments, welfare
economics is the standard normative analysis.[62] It seeks to
formulate criteria by which we can say that the social welfare in one economic situation is higher or lower than in
another. Such criteria are fundamental to the microeconomic aspects of government policy. The basic element
in the analysis of social welfare is 'individual welfare'. This is
the equivalent of individual well-being or happiness, where
'happiness' is broadly defined to include not only sensual
pleasure or pain, but also non-material or spiritual elements
in the individual's life. The presumption is that the individual is the best judge of his own welfare, and that he
maximizes it.

A social welfare function translates the vector of individual indicators of welfare into a single social welfare
indicator. Formally, if W^i are the welfare indicators for
individuals $i=1\ldots I$, then the social welfare function is of
the form:

$$W=f(W^1, W^2, \ldots W^I)$$

Social welfare then depends on individual welfares, and on
nothing else.

A particular example of a social welfare function is the
Benthamite formulation. This assumes that individual welfares can be measured in *utils*, which are comparable
between individuals. Social welfare is the sum of the utils of

the individuals. One objection to the Benthamite social welfare function is that it takes no account of the distribution of utilities between the members of society. If society has a preference for equality, then this can be incorporated in a function, f, which incorporates diminishing social returns to increased utility of individuals.[63]

For reasons which we will consider later, the concept of a cardinal measure of utility has been severely criticized. These criticisms led to the search for social welfare criteria which did not require cardinal utility. A particular criterion, which has captured the imagination of generations of economists, is the Pareto principle. Without defining the content of the welfare indicators, it states that social welfare increases if at least one individual is made better off without any individual being worse off. This requires of the indicators of individual welfare only the capacity to rank outcomes. An ordinal utility function may be a convenient way of summarizing this ranking.

The Pareto principle is astonishing in its capacity to generate conclusions about optimal social arrangements. The three 'marginal equivalences' for a Pareto 'efficient' economy can be derived without difficulty, and are part of the intellectual equipment that every student economist is expected to master. For example, if the marginal rate at which the economy can gain good X by giving up good Y is not equal to the rate at which consumers are willing to trade those two goods, then a rearrangement of production in a pure economy can yield higher welfare for at least one individual, all others remaining at the same level as before. The popularity of the concept of Pareto efficiency is almost certainly derived from the demonstration that a perfectly competitive economy satisfies the marginal equivalences. It is almost irresistible for economists to conclude that a competitive market economy has desirable 'efficiency' properties. However critics have been quick to point out some fundamental difficulties.

Consider, for example, the premise that each individual is the best judge of his own welfare in the sense that his ranking of different social states is reliable. This ignores the possibility that preferences may differ from his true welfare because he is ignorant, or his foresight is imperfect. His *ex post* welfare may be quite different from what he expected *ex ante*. Furthermore, his preferences may demonstrate irrationality or instability: the examples of someone suffering from mental illness, or a small child, should suffice to illustrate this possibility.

A further criticism is directed at the premise that only the welfare of individuals, and *nothing* else, should enter the evaluation of social welfare. For example, economic liberals would wish to give a high valuation to the extent to which economic institutions in society promoted individual freedom. Others might wish to preserve a traditional way of life, or be concerned about ecological issues. Furthermore, an economy might be Pareto efficient and yet affront some fundamental notion of justice. Consider, for example, a Pareto efficient oil-rich economy in which all the resources are owned by a feudal ruler. He enjoys a fabulous standard of living while his subjects live a life of abject misery. We might wish to say that Pareto efficiency is not enough to give satisfactory social arrangements in this case.

The Pareto criterion has also been much criticized for its practical conservatism. It is hard to find examples of economic changes that will satisfy the Pareto criterion. Almost any case gives rise to gains for some and losses for others.

Finally, the Paretian analysis does not in fact give us what we are looking for—a complete ranking of different social states. In principle, in an abstract economy, there may be an infinite number of social states which satisfy the Pareto criteria. The textbook analysis summarizes this by saying that fulfilment of the criteria will take society to the 'utility-possibility frontier', but cannot tell us which point on that frontier is preferred. The question can only be resolved by the introduction of a Bergson-Samuelson welfare function which explicitly ranks social states on the basis of the utility levels achieved by individuals. Unfortunately, such a function generally requires cardinal measures of utility which allow for interpersonal comparisons between the individuals. Hence the Paretian approach fails to dispense with the requirement of cardinal utility.[64]

In line with developments in economic theory generally,

welfare economics has tried to escape from its utilitarian origins by appealing to the concept of a rational economic man who can express preferences. It is often analytically convenient to express preferences in the form of an ordinal 'utility' function: but the 'utility' element is only for convenience, and does not place any restrictions on the preferences individuals are allowed to hold. Suppose that each individual has a preference ordering over a complete set of possible social states. Then the question arises whether it is possible to move from these preferences of individuals to a unique social ordering. Arrow's 'Impossibility Theorem'[65] shows that with five plausible conditions as to how the move is to be made, it is in fact impossible to obtain a social welfare function.

The five conditions are as follows. First, unrestricted domain requires that an individual may declare any preference ranking among the set of social states. The second condition is the weak Pareto principle: if everyone has more utility in state x than state y, then x is socially better than y. Third, the condition of non-dictatorship is that there should be no one person such that when he strictly prefers any x to any y, then invariably x is regarded as socially better than y. Fourth, the 'independence of irrelevant alternatives' condition requires that the social ranking of any pair of social states must be the same as long as the individual utility information about the pair of states remains the same. For example, suppose individuals have already declared a preference between states x and y, then the introduction of a completely new possibility, z, to the set of social states should have no effect on the preferences between x and y. A fifth condition is that the social welfare function should exhibit transitivity in choices between social states.

Convenient demonstrations of the Arrow Theorem can be found in Sen or Mueller.[66] Opinions differ as to whether the theorem is surprising or not. Discussion has proceeded along the lines of relaxing each condition in turn to see what it contributes to the outcome. The Pareto condition and the non-dictatorship condition are clearly central to the whole enterprise of moving from the individual preferences of *all* the citizens to a social welfare function. To relax them would destroy the analysis. 'Unrestricted domain' is akin to giving individuals freedom of choice. Given that a feature of different social states will be different income distributions, the preference rankings of individuals are likely to be widely divergent. But putting restrictions on the domain of choice is not possible without some prior presumption as to what the social welfare function 'ought' to look like.

The 'independence of irrelevant alternatives' condition apparently has two roles in the analysis. First, it rules out interpersonal comparisons of utilities for which information outside the two alternatives may be necessary. Second, it eliminates strategic misrepresentation in the statement of preferences: for example, if I don't like social state z very much, but I suspect that others do, I may be tempted to rank it very low in the whole set, if the *whole* ranking is relevant to the choice between z and some state y which I prefer. Finally, the assumption of transitivity rules out decision procedures which are commonly accepted. Arrow pointed out that transitivity required that the choice of social state had to be independent of any decision procedure. For example, a procedure which involves looking at sub-sets of social states first, with the 'winners' going on to subsequent decision rounds, is ruled out. Such a procedure is widely accepted as 'fair' in judging competitions. However the choice of a social welfare function is perhaps a more serious business than that!

Sen[67] argues that difficulties arise from the almost metaphysical attachment to 'welfarism', and from the very thin informational requirements of the theory. 'Welfarism' is the requirement that individual preferences, and *only* individual preferences, are to be taken into account in arriving at the social welfare function. So 'welfarism' excludes any general principles about desirable social states. For example, any presumption of bias in favour of the poor is ruled out. Indeed, since utility cannot be measured in the Arrow framework, one would not know who were rich and who were poor. Even if a majority of citizens were prepared to assent to some general principle of bias to the poor, it would not be allowed to influence the social welfare function.

The informational requirements of the theory can be summarized by noting that only preference *rankings* are considered. Suppose for example that I am more or less indifferent between social states x and y, but would rank x 'fractionally ahead' of y. You, on the other hand, detest x, but find y delightful. Common sense might lead one to suppose that y should be socially preferred. But under the Arrow conditions, the intensity of feelings about the two states is irrelevant.

If we relax the restriction that no interpersonal comparisons of utility are allowed we can make progress in the search for a social welfare function. In particular, with cardinal measures of welfare a range of social welfare functions becomes possible, incorporating various judgments about the weight to be given to equality as a social goal.

For a time it was hoped that explicit judgments could be avoided by the use of 'compensation tests'.[68] These tests were to be applied in those cases where an economic change resulted in both gainers and losers. Kaldor's criterion was that a change should be considered a social improvement if the gainers could fully compensate the losers and still be better off. Hick's criterion was that it was a social improvement if the losers could not profitably bribe the gainers to oppose the change. An important part of the methodology is that the payments are hypothetical. For example, if compensation was actually paid then the change would represent a Pareto improvement.

Unfortunately, as Scitovsky pointed out, the application of the criteria is not without difficulty. It is easy to construct examples where paradoxically the criteria would first recommend that a change take place, and then recommend that the change should be reversed. In the absence of actual compensation, the criteria can be interpreted as the application of a Benthamite utilitarian social welfare function which pays no regard to income distribution. This aspect is often concealed by the appeal to gains and losses measured in money values rather than utilities.

This has become a common practice in applied welfare

economics.[69] Under certain technical assumptions the 'utility' that a person obtains from consumption of a good may be expressed in monetary terms by willingness to pay, as measured by consumer surplus. (The derivation depends on a utility maximizing theory of demand underlying the demand function.) A similar method can be used to devise money measures of disutility or costs. Measures of costs and benefits are then aggregated across individuals to give a social evaluation. This is an illegitimate procedure to arrive at net social welfare, unless the utility derived from one dollar of expenditure is the same for all individuals involved. The fact that it patently is not may be shrugged off by the observation that we lack information as to who are the gainers and the losers and therefore it is impossible to make adjustments. Alternatively it is assumed that distribution of income is the concern of some other set of policy-makers. Hence any adverse effects from this policy will generate compensatory moves.

In theoretical analysis there has been an increasing willingness to specify interpersonally comparable utility functions for individuals as the arguments of social welfare functions. The social welfare functions specified are typically Benthamite, unless distributional consequences are of particular interest. Examples are to be found in the public finance literature on optimal taxes and public prices, and in the new industrial economics literature on the welfare economics of market structure, product differentiation, and research and development. The use of explicit welfare analysis is usually defended on the grounds that it may give some guidance to policy-makers.

The story has thus come full circle. The attempt to free normative economics from its utilitarian roots has failed to produce alternative criteria for social choice. Utility is now back in fashion—and old-fashioned cardinal utility at that.

(b) The debate about utilitarianism

Many students complete their studies of welfare economics without ever being made aware that utilitarian doctrines (that the moral value of an action lies in its consequences, and that a desirable feature of actions is that they should maximize 'utility', where utility represents preferences) have been strongly contested. Much of the criticism comes from philosophers rather than economists, though in recent years economists such as Sen have brought the discussion into economics more explicitly. It is impossible in a few pages to do justice to what is a complex debate, so our treatment is inevitably selective.

We begin with some general objections to utilitarianism which have been expressed persuasively by Williams.[70] We then carry the debate into economics itself, looking at the defence of utilitarian methods *in economics* by Mirrlees, and at some of the difficulties that have been identified by, among others, Sen, Hahn and Elster.[71] A brief section follows on alternatives to utilitarianism, which concentrates on the contractual theory of justice of John Rawls.

Williams[72] suggests that the test of a moral theory is whether we are prepared to live with that theory. His strategy in criticizing utilitarianism is therefore to indicate properties of the theory which leave us feeling uncomfortable about its application. His first criticism is that the stress on consequences rather than actions leads to an infinite regress in assigning values. Typically values are assigned to 'states of affairs' which are the outcomes of particular actions. But 'states of affairs' are not static objects: they include implications for future states of affairs which are consequent upon actions to be taken. The desire to exclude the valuation of actions, as opposed to the consequences of those actions, may make it difficult to create a pure 'state of affairs'.

A second criticism is that of negative responsibility. If consequences are *all* that count then we are equally culpable for our 'sins of omission' as for our 'sins of commission'. Williams uses the example of the botanist who wanders into a Latin American village, to find a group of soldiers preparing to shoot twenty Indians as a reprisal for Indian attacks. The soldiers' officer then offers the botanist a choice: either he can kill one Indian at random, letting the other nineteen go free, or the officer will order that they all be shot.

On utilitarian grounds it is hard to escape the unpalatable

conclusion that the botanist should act as requested. To fail to do so would result in much greater loss. Nor is an appeal to 'remote effects' going to hep very much. For example, on utilitarian grounds it is impossible for the botanist to argue that he should take into account his bad conscience if he kills the one Indian. Given the utilitarian framework he *has* acted rightly, so there is no reason for bad conscience. Nor can an appeal to 'thin end of the wedge' arguments get the botanist off the hook. If it is right to kill the Indian in these circumstances, then it will be right to kill Indians in all future like circumstances. So it is a good precedent which is being set, not a bad one!

A third criticism advanced by Williams is that utilitarianism requires us to take account of people's preferences in all cases. For example, if a racist white majority attaches a very large disutility to the presence of a black minority, then on utilitarian grounds it *could* be right to expel the black minority, in pursuit of the maximization of the sum of utilities. The usual response to this is to argue that such prejudices are irrational, uninformed and unacceptable. But we should note that to argue this we have to introduce some standards of rationality and acceptability that lie outside utilitarian debate.

Alternatively, we may follow Hare[73] in postulating two levels at which utilitarian methods should be applied. Level one is that of everyday decisions, where we may find it useful to follow rules and conventions. Level two is a more refined world of ethical debate where the rules and conventions are themselves criticized and developed in accordance with utilitarian principles. Level two interacts with level one, according to Hare, through education, broadly defined. Hare would like to see level two as the province of every man, exercising powers of cool and rational reflection. However not every man is capable of so doing: so the activity will be left to an élite to define acceptable elements to be taken into account in arriving at utility judgments. Such an élite could presumably rule out any preferences of a non-utilitarian nature as being not consistent with rational choice.

A fourth criticism is that utilitarianism has an exceptionally thin concept of man. In the cruder forms of utilitarianism, he is just a pleasure/pain centre. In which case it is hard to escape the conclusion that man's utility should be maximized by fixing him up with a drug to induce a permanent state of pleasure. In the more sophisticated versions, he becomes a bundle of preferences. However even then it is important to provide him with some sense of continuing identity: otherwise he would have no reason to make provision for the future, and just maximize his current satisfaction or preferences. The difficulty with these thin doctrines of man is that we know there is more to being a man. A man will have life projects and commitments which he will not easily abandon for the siren call of a higher utility. A perfectly proper sense of his own integrity will prevent the botanist from killing the Indian.

The fifth set of criticisms concerns the use of utilitarian methods for social decisions. It is not *obvious* that an individual should feel any obligation to abandon a life project to which he is committed simply because some utilitarian calculus informs him that the utility 'sum' (based on *other* agents' projects) requires him to give it up. Part of the difficulty is that utilitarian theory has no analysis of politics. Presumably the agency that presides over the calculations is a government of some sort, but there is no description of how it comes into being, of how it obtains legitimacy. For example, a utilitarian would find it hard to argue against a 'benevolent' dictator who is committed to pursuing the utilitarian calculus in all social decisions.

Sixth, it remains to be demonstrated why an individual, or a state, is required by rationality to abide by one overriding decision principle. Why not a multiplicity of goals? The utilitarian response is that pluralism can result in inconsistency and incompleteness of choices, which is irrational. But it is only irrational by the demanding standards of utilitarianism.

All these criticisms of utilitarianism have been contested in the philosophical debate. It is not our intention to convey the impression that the debate has been won by the anti-utilitarians. But the criticisms should warn economists against a too easy acceptance of utilitarian doctrines.

Utilitarian method in *economics* has been defended by

Mirrlees.[74] He argues that it is coherent to invite a person to consider 'alternative selves'—*all* that he will be in different states of the world at different stages of his life—and assign utilities. 'All' is emphasized since it is not just consumption goods that are under consideration, but mental states like memories, ambitions and accumulated experiences. In assigning utilities people may lack imagination, or may, on the basis of too little information, give the wrong values (*e.g.* a smoker who is ignorant of the health risks involved will not assign an accurate value to the consequences of smoking). So some 'guidance' in assigning utilities may be needed: it is real utility that counts, rather than inaccurate perceptions of it.

If that argument is accepted, then Mirrlees invites us to consider the case of an economy made up of identical individuals. They make identical decisions and have identical utility. Hence there can be no argument against the proposition that social utility is the sum of individual utilities in this case.

In the case where individuals are *not* identical, Mirrlees makes use of procedures from consumption theory. In essence, these involve making allowances for observable differences. The example he gives is one of differences in labour efficiency between individuals. He proposes the utility function, $u=u(x, z/n)$, where u=utility, x=disposable income, z=labour earnings and n=labour efficiency. He then argues that if two individuals have the same z/n, and the same x, then we can argue that both have the same experiences. Similar metrics can be established for other observable differences: for example, Mirrlees suggests that 'A child may be regarded as an adult for whom a unit consumption of ice-cream means twice as much, and a unit consumption of quiet conversation half as much as for a 'normal' adult; and so on for all aspects of consumption'. The objective is to scale different individuals in terms of a 'representative' utility maximizing individual, presumably with a given rational utility function. But individuals' preferences may differ sharply even *after* they have been scaled appropriately. Mirrlees admits there is no answer to this problem other than a 'quick compromise'!

Some of the objections raised by economists are borrowed directly from the philosophical critique of utilitarianism. However there are a number of criticisms specific to economic analysis. One is the question, raised by Sen,[75] of the allocation of resources to handicapped people. If they are poor at transforming resources into utility then they warrant few resources. In the case of handicapped people (especially mentally handicapped), it may be very difficult to perform the scaling relative to a 'representative' adult, described by Mirrlees. Hahn[76] invites us to compare two situations in which material circumstances are exactly the same with respect to work, leisure and consumption. In one case I am free to decide what to do, in the other I am the slave of a (benevolent) despot. Not unreasonably Hahn argues that if he is asked to decide between social states on the basis of utility, he is likely to ask for information about liberty. There *is* a difference, for example, between giving to the poor because I want to, and giving to the poor because I am rquired to do so through taxation, even though the consequences are exactly the same.

The question of preferences has also exercised some critics. The utilitarian method requires that individuals should have preferences which are independent of the final social states chosen. However there is little doubt that preferences depend on such things as culture, advertising, and the political process. Furthermore there is a process in society of criticism and development of preferences, which suggests that they are not by any means fixed and given. The response by Hare[77] would be that the latter represents level two application of utilitarian methods, refining and revising the level one preferences. Hence the bedrock is preferences over preferences. However there is no reason to stop there. Presumably there could in principle be an infinite regress with preferences at levels 3 . . . n.

Finally there is a question about the right treatment of uncertainty.[78] Outcomes (consequences) of different actions are never known with certainty, for two reasons. The first is uncertainty due to natural events outside the control of the agent (the weather, for example). The second is ignorance. If I take a particular action, its consequences may be quite unknown to me. Nor can I assume that the 'closer' effects are the only ones that matter. There is no reason to believe that the effects of actions die out, like ripples on a pond after a stone is dropped into the water.

The utilitarian calculus then requires that the rational agent maximizes expected utility, which is the utility of different states of the world multiplied by his subjective probability of each state, and then summed across all states. However this raises problems for social decision-taking: the agents' preferences now have to be reviewed not only for a 'reasonable' utility content, but also for 'reasonable' probability assignments. The alternative is to allow the agents to report their utilities in different states of the world, and then assign a 'social probability' to each state. But this may give a completely different ordering to the previous procedure, and it is not obvious that either is the only correct method. Nor is it always possible to attach probabilities: many people would, for example, believe that there is some chance of a nuclear war in the foreseeable future, but few could assign a probability to such an event.

These criticisms of utilitarianism are not necessarily conclusive. They raise difficulties which may or may not be satisfactorily resolved within the utilitarian framework. But the ultimate test is not whether such a resolution is possible, but whether the whole framework is adequate in its description of humanity. We will argue below that it is incompatible with the Christian doctrine of man. But that argument aside, there has been a revival of interest in recent years in alternative social ethical theories. One of these is the libertarian theory with its strong emphasis on rights, espoused by, among others, Hayek and Nozick.[79] Rights are postulated as the basic values in society. Man is autonomous, and his rights are what constitute his autonomy. The libertarian tradition has been developed particularly in the defence of market capitalism. It is therefore convenient to discuss it in Chapter Four, where the case for and against capitalism is treated. The other alternative, to which we now turn, is the contractarian theory, and in particular Rawls' Theory of Justice[80], which constitutes a major challenge to utilitarianism. The applications of the theory in economics have however been minimal.

The focus of the theory is on the process or context of decisions. The search is for just institutions for decision-taking. There is no presumption that these institutions or their decisions will maximize the social welfare.

The argument proceeds in two stages. The first is a social contract arising from an 'original position'. The second deals with the principles involved in that contract. The context for the social contract is that life is a game of chances in which Nature deals out attributes, and social positions, in a more or less random way. This natural distribution is neither just nor unjust. But it would be unjust for society simply to accept these chance distributions. So a set of just institutions is one which mitigates the effects of chance on the positions of individuals in the social structure. Rawls proposes that decisions on the social institutions are made behind a 'veil of ignorance'. Individuals make decisions unaware of their present or future position, and of the economic environment. Rational individuals will then reach agreement on the following two principles of justice: (i) each person is to have an equal right to the most extensive basic liberty compatible with a similar liberty for others; (ii) social and economic inequalities are to be arranged so that they are both (a) reasonably expected to be to everyone's advantage, and (b) attached to positions and offices open to all.

There is a lexicographical ordering attached to these principles. The first principle has priority over the second, once a reasonable level of material life is reached. Liberty is more important than material goods once basic needs have been met. The second principle (or Difference principle) also applies lexicographically. The rule is to maximize the welfare of the worst off: then if his welfare cannot be improved, the second worst off, and so on. Welfare is defined *not* in terms of utility, but in terms of 'primary goods'. These are the basic liberties, and freedom of movement and choice of occupation in respect of principle (i), and powers and prerogatives attached to offices, income and wealth, and social bases of self-respect, in respect of principle (ii). The Difference principle has affinities with the minimax strategy in decision theory: choose that option with the highest minimum pay-off, regardless of other pay-offs, or the probabilities of attaining them. The principle is justified by Rawls on the grounds that behind the veil of ignorance there is no basis for attaching probabilities to different pay-offs, since the economic environment is unknown.

This theory has attracted a number of criticisms. Hart has pointed out[81] that the original position does not contain enough information to decide priorities between basic liberties where they conflict. Another criticism is that the Difference principle may involve the rich in making quite large sacrifices in order to improve the position of the poorest person by a fraction. Quite apart from the fact that the rich may not be willing to comply, it is not obvious that such sacrifices can be justified. It is also somewhat extreme to rule out completely any information (even of a probabilistic nature) about the likely income distribution. If *something* is known about the income distribution, then it would be desirable to do more than just improve the position of the poorest person. Finally, some critics have doubted whether Rawls has convincingly shown that his two principles *have* to emerge from the discussions in the original position. To do that he would have to consider all other possible principles, and demonstrate their inadequacy. For example, Hare[82] utilizes the concepts of anonymity and universalizability, which are not dissimilar, in effect, to the 'veil of ignorance', and emerges with a modified utilitarianism. The hope that unprejudiced reflection will generate a consensus on moral principles seems somewhat forlorn.

Whatever one may think of the particular principles of justice proposed by Rawls, we may draw two conclusions from his work. First it is evident that there can be alternatives to utilitarian procedures in normative economics. These alternatives may have drawbacks and snags, but so does utilitarianism. Even within the *secular* discipline of economics one can hope for rather more debate about normative principles than we have witnessed during the ascendancy of welfare economics. Second, it challenges the requirement that there should be a single decision rule based on maximizing a single criterion such as utility. A plurality of objectives is possible, perhaps a lexicographically ordered set of rights, related to freedom and needs.

(c) A Christian critique of welfare economics

The utilitarian analysis, and the Christian analysis of man and his purposes in life, are so far apart that it is difficult to know how to use the latter to critique the former. They simply belong to different worlds. Here we will draw attention to some of the major points of contrast.

First, they differ sharply as to what is the good. For utilitarians (and in welfare economics), the good is to maximize personal satisfactions in the fulfilment of personal preferences. This can be expressed either in an hedonistic fashion, or in a manner which allows for 'higher' values. In *practice*, economic analysis has tended to the former, using the excuse that it is analysing the production of goods and services in the economy. However expressed, the focus of the good is the individual himself, and perhaps his immediate kin. The Christian conception of the good is that man should love God with all his heart and mind, and that he should love his neighbour as himself. Whatever *content* is given to these commands to love, one thing is clear: the good is defined in terms of persons *other* than the individual himself, though a proper self-love is not excluded.

Second, they differ in respect of the evaluation of states of the world. The strict utilitarian is a consequentialist, and will not admit values attached to actions. A Christian on the other hand believes that a situation should be judged in terms of its conformity to what God requires of man in his everyday life. That includes, as we saw in Chapter Two, righteous motives and actions, the maintenance of particular social institutions, and a sensitivity to unjust outcomes. Thus the concern of the economist for efficiency, growth and equality is replaced for the Christian by a concern with stewardship, useful work, protection for the disadvantaged and the preservation of institutions such as marriage and family life.

A third contrast is the emphasis given to community as

opposed to individual values. For the strict utilitarian, social values are to be derived from some summation or function of individual values. But a Christian sees community as more than the aggregate of individuals. First, human beings are made for relationships in community. These relationships are important in defining his personal identity and worth: he is made to be loved. Second, man is instructed to love his neighbour, and thus contribute *to* the community. So the Christian ethic is a community ethic, which defines the goals of the individual in terms of his responsibilities to others.

A further contrast concerns the role of the political authorities in society. The utilitarian analysis lacks a theory of the state. At best it is a device for aggregating individual utilities, and reporting the outcomes. Once a social optimum has been found, it makes an appropriate announcement to the populace, who see the wisdom of the calculus and adjust their plans accordingly. At worst, it could be some sort of 'benevolent' tyrant, who decides rationally what it is appropriate to permit in the evaluation of individual welfare, and once the social optimum has been uncovered will proceed to impose it 'for the good of the populace'. It would need to be imposed, because the tyrant's evaluation of individual welfare would differ from that of the ignorant, prejudiced, irrational individuals. The Christian view of the political authorities is quite different. They are ordained by God to promote God's justice between the citizens. They are to keep the peace, to ensure justice for the disadvantaged and to prevent evil from getting the upper hand. This view is realistic about the consequences of human sin—in particular, the human capacity for selfishness and violence. It also insists that the authorities, however they are appointed, are themselves under God and ultimately responsible to him.

The contrast could hardly be greater, and it is difficult to see any reconciliation. Does this mean that an economist who is a Christian must abandon welfare economics? In terms of using it as a tool for policy recommendations, I believe it does. However it is very important that Christians should understand the basis in utilitarianism of much advice from economic experts. An example illustrates the point. One of the benefits of road improvements is that they reduce fatal accidents. An exercise in applied welfare economics is a cost-benefit analysis of a road improvement. On the cost side will enter the cost of construction; on the benefit side the 'value' of lives saved. Various methods have been applied for estimating this value. As a Christian, and a non-utilitarian, I would object that lives cannot be valued in this way without in some fundamental sense treating a fellow human being as an object like an expensive car. We do not allow human beings to be bought and sold, and for very good reasons. The procedure is therefore ethically unacceptable.

A proponent of cost-benefit analysis will typically reply by asking how a critic would analyse this case. One response is to provide an analysis which details costs on one side, and potential benefits on the other; but the benefits are simply listed as reductions in fatalities, serious injuries, *etc*. This report will then be for the relevant authority to wrestle with and to reach a decision. Their responsibility for doing justice should not be taken away from them by an analysis that purports to give a definite 'right answer'. However, if a particular road improvement is undertaken, with an estimated reduction in fatalities, then the *cost* of saving a life can be deduced. It may be helpful to remind decision-takers of these implicit costs, to assist them in assessing different demands on the scarce resources for roads and other social investments.

In place of the emphasis on efficiency in welfare economics, with perhaps a nod in the direction of equality, a Christian normative economics would ask a range of questions about economic life and institutions. These were summarized in the Christian principles for economic life listed in Chapter Two. The Christian is committed to a multiplicity of criteria, not to a single objective.

3. Normative versus positive economics

In this section we look at the traditional distinction made between positive and normative economics. A number of

factors suggest that the distinction cannot be rigidly maintained, though it may retain value as an intellectual
organizing device.

The root of the problem goes back to our previous discussion on how we are to find out anything in the real
world, given that there are an infinity of facts which we
might consider. We need some framework to sift what is
significant from what is not. In practice, these 'characterizing value judgments' are based in presuppositions
about what has value. These may be simply asserted, as in
the libertarian analysis of rights, or in the utilitarian
emphasis on preferences. Or they may be deduced from
some more general metaphysical or theological world-view.
They affect not only the domain of study, but also the
concepts that are used. Hence it is generally true that a pure
positive economics, without reference to any value system,
is simply not available.

But *within* any framework of values it is possible to distinguish 'appraising value judgments' from 'characterizing
value judgments'.[83] Within the utilitarian framework, attention is directed to the efficiency of the economy. Hence it
will be worth looking at indicators of efficiency like productivity (output per man). Analysis will be directed to the
causes of differences in productivity, which is a 'positive'
question.

There are also normative questions to be addressed. The
economist may wish to compare the level of productivity
with that which could be attained under some optimal
arrangement of production. He may also explore policy
options with both positive and normative aspects: for
example, he might wish to consider the likely effects of
different tax reforms (positive question), and then assess
the costs and benefits of each one (normative question). The
categories used in the positive analysis will be determined
by the use to which the results are to be put in the normative
analysis.

If this discussion of the relation between positive and
normative economics is correct, then the implications of the
analysis of methodology in this chapter are quite radical.
Those who reject the utilitarian basis of welfare economics

will be wise to examine carefully the bases for any positive analysis to which they commit themselves. They may find that the concepts which are utilized in positive economics are fashioned specifically with respect to the utilitarian framework. If that framework is *untrue* in its claims about man in his social relationships and economic life, then the analysis will be seriously flawed. There is therefore a *prima facie* case for reconstituting economics within a Christian framework.

CHAPTER FOUR
The capitalist market economy

1. Introduction: an outline of the approach

In this chapter, and throughout the rest of the book, we seek to apply the principles described in the first three chapters to questions which have traditionally attracted the attention of economists. These include the relative merits of market and planned economies, and the problems of macroeconomic policy, limits to economic growth and the relations between rich and poor nations. Our approach will be to evaluate economic institutions and behaviour in the light of the biblical principles enunciated in Chapter Two.

This does however present a difficulty. The descriptive and analytic material which we will use to portray the issues is derived from standard economic analysis. As we saw in Chapter Three, such analysis has been developed from a normative viewpoint which differs markedly from that of our biblical principles. For example, the concern for economic efficiency, which is derived from utilitarian welfare economics, is *not* a major focus of those principles. We therefore have to be very cautious in our use of standard economic analysis, since the questions which are being asked are possibly very different from the questions we might want to ask. In the present state of our knowledge there is no alternative to such careful use.

A second general problem lies in achieving the appropriate balance in analysis between abstract descriptions and actual situations. For example, in the next section of this

chapter we will attempt to outline in abstract the characteristics of a market capitalist economy. We will have in mind the
kind of market economy which is to be found in the United
States, the United Kingdom or West Germany, but *without*
interventions by government in markets, or to modify market outcomes, which exist in those economies (*e.g.* competition policy, taxation, social security, and controls on
externalities such as pollution).

A critic may complain that the outline does not correspond
to any single economy. The danger is that we are setting up a
'straw' economy, and that our evaluation bears no relation to
the 'real world'. The alternative approach would be to consider a particular market economy in full empirical detail.
The disadvantages of so doing are that such material quickly
becomes dated, and that the task of translating the argument
to a different economy, or even to the same economy ten
years later, is likely to prove difficult. We have chosen the
abstract approach, in the hope that this will provide the
reader with the tools for looking at a particular economy or
economic problem. However, we emphasize our conviction
that economics needs both theoretical and empirical analysis: we have no wish to emulate contemporary economic
analysis in its undue emphasis on theory (as described in
Chapter Three).

In the next section, we give a general description of an
abstract capitalist market economy. Our focus is on microeconomic aspects: the use of markets as an organizing device
for economic activity. Macroeconomic aspects will be treated
fully in Chapter Six. In sections 3 and 4 we will examine
critically the arguments in favour of markets which are
advanced by utilitarians (welfare economics), and libertarians (the Austrian school of economics). This clears the
path for an assessment, based on our biblical principles, in
section 5.

This chapter leads naturally into the next chapter, where
socialism (or economic planning) is given the same treatment. The chapters are linked in two ways. First, socialism
developed as a response to the perceived deficiencies of the
capitalist system: a critique of capitalism is therefore an
appropriate starting point. Second, there is a symmetry in

the use of arguments in the two chapters. For example, an argument for 'economic freedom' will count for capitalism and against socialism. However it is not our intention to set them up as alternatives in this way, but to develop a critique of both from a distinctive Christian position. We also take this approach for a practical reason. The choice between socialist or capitalist systems is not one that, in practice, many people have to make. Political choices are more likely to take the form of more or less 'market forces', more or less intervention by the authorities in the economy. Our objective is to provide a framework within which such choices may be evaluated.

2. Description of a capitalist market economy

In abstract the two essential features of a market (capitalist) economy are the institution of private property, and the fact that exchange is mediated through markets, in which prices play a decisive role. Lying behind these there must exist a body of law or social norms, which protects property rights and which ensures that market contracts are enforceable.

The concept of private property can be defined in two complementary ways. Negatively, it requires the protection of law or social mores to prevent others taking property by force. Positively, it involves freedom of individual action in respect of the use and disposition of that property. Laissez-faire requires that the government or other authorities should not interfere in any way with my decisions. Their role is to protect my rights of self-determination. This doctrine of the unconditional and exclusive use of property by an individual is derived from the concept of natural rights in Roman law, which will be considered further in section 4.

The role of markets and prices in exchange is so familiar that it is difficult to convey its full significance. First, we note that it requires an acceptable medium of exchange in the form of money, which acts as a store of value. This delivers economic agents from the difficulties of a pure barter system, in which if I wish to obtain a good I have to find someone with that good who also wishes to obtain something which I have on offer. Such a system is likely to work extremely imperfectly. An advanced economy, with a range of goods and services being supplied, would be an impossibility. The market system does away with the need for reciprocal coincidence of wants and supplies. I sell what I have to sell to a wide range of purchasers, and with the proceeds I can then buy from a wide range of quite different sellers. Among the inventions of mankind that have produced great social benefits, that of money must rank very high.

Second, the market system has two important further features, in respect of the role of prices. Prices provide both incentives and information. The incentive function relates to the concept of private property rights. Given alternative uses for a piece of property, the owner can make up his mind on the basis of a comparison of money returns in different uses. Prices enable those comparisons to be made easily. The expectation is that as relative prices change, so property owners will divert their resources from activities with falling returns to activities with higher returns.

The implications for resource allocation will be discussed in the next section of this chapter. However this role of markets immediately indicates the information aspects of prices. Suppose I own a resource, the demand for which is increasing. Then, in the absence of a price system, I would require a very extensive information network to register the increased demands from a large number of potential customers. I would also need to know about other potential or actual suppliers, and how they are going to respond. In a competitive price system where prices are responsive to increased demands and supplies, all this information is unnecessary. I observe what is happening to prices, and adjust my supplies accordingly. In practice, markets may not be quite as simple in their functioning as that. But the information role of markets is nonetheless very important.

It is doubtful, however, if markets can function without the support of some wider framework of law or social custom.[1] Contracts freely entered into should be enforceable in some ways and suppliers should tell the truth about their products. Thus for Adam Smith, market capitalism rested on a moral base external to the system itself, since markets will fail without standards of truth, trust, acceptance and obligation, which the system cannot itself provide.[2] The point has been succinctly put by Arrow:

> ... the definition of property rights based on the price system depends precisely on the lack of universality of private property and the price system.[3]

If, to take an extreme example, the judiciary were regularly to sell their services to the highest bidder, a system of property rights and market contracts would soon fail. An incorruptible judiciary is necessary, but probably not sufficient. Market relations are so pervasive in a capitalist economy, that it would be impossible to regulate every transaction by a legal contract. An element of general social assent to standards of honesty and truth is also needed.

We now consider the substantive features of market capitalism as it is experienced in the Western economies today. These are the institutional flesh on the abstract system we have described above.

The two main groups of economic actors in the economy, ignoring any role for government, are private households and firms. Relationships between them are mediated through markets. In the markets for final goods and services, the firms are suppliers and the households are purchasers. In the markets for productive factors, such as labour, capital and land, the households are the suppliers, and the firms are purchasers. There is a circular flow of income and payments in the whole economy: households receive payment for factor services, which they can then use to purchase goods or services from firms, or which they can save by adding to their assets. In the long term a household is only able to spend the equivalent of its stream of income from supply of factor services, excluding any gifts or transfers from other households.

Firms are the economic institutions where most of production takes place (a certain amount of production occurs within the household sector). The role of the firm is to purchase the requisite inputs in factor markets, to provide the organizing structure for production, and to sell the output. These sales may be to other firms in a vertically related production chain, or to final consumers. In each case, the firm has to ensure that the value of sales in the long term covers all the costs of production. Otherwise it will eventually go out of business. A particularly important role is ascribed to entrepreneurs: their task is to perceive business opportunities, and to take the risks inherent in organizing firms to meet these opportunities.

A distinctive feature of the household sector in market capitalist economies is inequality in income and wealth.[4] Low incomes can be due to a number of causes. Some households fail to enter factor markets as suppliers. They may be prevented from working for a wage by ill health, old age or the need to look after young children. Or they may not be able to find an employer for their particular skills (or lack of skills) in the area in which they live. Alternatively they may be able to find work, but their incomes will still be small, because their particular talents do not command a high wage. They may, furthermore, have no financial or other assets to give a return. High incomes, on the other hand, can arise from the ownership of considerable assets, or from the possession of a skill which is highly valued in labour markets. Such a skill is likely to arise from a combination of natural abilities and specific training. Natural ability without training is unlikely to realize its potential value in markets. But training can only be a partial substitute for talent in many skilled occupations (consider, for example, a musician). Another element determining rewards in labour markets is experience on the job. A newly trained worker is unlikely to be as productive as one who has been doing the job for some time.

Inequality of wealth can arise in a number of ways. We define wealth as the value of assets, excluding the value of a person's own 'human capital' (their capacity to earn in the labour market, reflecting their training and experience). Assets are created by a process of saving and accumulation. Thus a certain amount of inequality in wealth reflects a life cycle. A person may borrow money early in their life cycle to buy a house. Later in their career they will probably pay that back, and begin to accumulate assets depending on their willingness to save. Assets will reach a peak just before they retire. They are likely to be run down in retirement, though the motive of handing on a bequest to one's children, as well as uncertainty as to when one is likely to die, usually prevent assets being completely dissipated at death. Assets can also be created by entrepreneurship: the businessman who is fortunate to spot an opportunity, and skilful in exploiting it, may be able to build a personal fortune in the firm which he establishes.[5]

The significance of inequality in wealth is twofold. First, those with assets will have higher incomes than those without, the returns on assets being additional to labour incomes. Second, those with wealth will be better placed to cope with the vagaries of the market system with its shifting pattern of returns and rewards. A person with wealth who loses his job can run down his assets while he looks for another, or even undergoes retraining. A person without assets will have to find a new job more rapidly, and may not be able to afford a period of retraining. (We are ignoring here the fact that in virtually all Western economies some government system of income maintenance or welfare is available to the unemployed. In a 'pure' market capitalist economy this system would not exist, but might be replaced in part by private insurance markets.)

The significance of the distribution of income (and wealth) is the relation between the money income which a household receives, and its ability to purchase goods and services. Low income implies low consumption and nothing left over. High income can provide both for adequate consumption, and for adding to assets via saving.

The firm sector of modern capitalist economies has a number of characteristics which are of particular significance. The first is the legal framework of limited liability within which most firms operate. In formal terms, the firm becomes a legal entity, which is distinct from its owners and all others who participate in the firm. The consequence is that the firm is liable for its debts, and not the owners. If the firm goes bankrupt, the liability of the shareholders is limited to their initial stake in the firm.

The implications are far-reaching. The first is that the personal risk to the shareholders is greatly reduced. Such firms are able to grow by issuing share capital to people with no involvement whatsoever in the operations of the firm. Such shareholders can reduce their own risks by holding, either directly or indirectly via unit trusts or investment trusts, a portfolio of assets. The second implication is that responsibility for the direction and running of the firm is delegated to managers,[6] since the shareholdings are too widely dispersed for shareholders to be effective in control of the firm, always presuming that they wanted to be. Characteristically, the legal constitution of the firm recognizes only the participation of the shareholders. The rights and responsibilities of workers and management are not included, though they will normally be provided for in contracts of employment.

A second major characteristic of modern capitalist economies is the size distribution of the firms.[7] Whatever size measure is employed— assets, sales, workers employed— typically the largest 100 firms (or 200 in the US) account for more than half of the manufacturing sector. Concentration is less in other sectors, such as finance or distribution, but it is still very substantial. This characteristic often carries over into markets for particular goods and services. Typically, an industrial market will be dominated by a few suppliers.

Industrial economics has explored some of the consequences for competition.[8] Competition among the few, or oligopoly, means that firms are aware of their interdependence in the markets in which they operate. They avoid direct competition in price, since that will reduce the profitability for them all as price cuts are matched. Competition is long-term, and involves a race to produce new products ahead of their rivals, or to introduce new processes. A fringe of smaller firms may be able to thrive under the umbrella of the dominant firms, particularly if they specialize in supplying a particular niche in the market. However they, and any potential rival from outside, may be disciplined by predatory behaviour— price cutting or aggressive marketing. The aim of the dominant firm is to establish a reputation for responding aggressively, in the expectation that future challenges to its dominance will be deterred.

Turning to factor markets, we consider first the labour

market. The organization of the labour market varies considerably between the industrial economies.[9] However a common feature is the growth of labour market institutions such as trade unions and employers' federations, the latter often in response to the former.

The basis on which trade unions operate is that a joint approach by particular groups of workers is likely to be more successful in protecting the interests of their members at work, and at increasing wages, than if workers attempt to bargain in a fragmented way. They have been successful both in building membership, and in obtaining a degree of legal protection for their activities such as strikes. For example, they have sometimes won concessions from employers that only union members should be employed. They have also done much to improve working conditions. But with their increasing influence has come the ability to protect their workers from technological change by insisting on restrictive working practices. They have also been able to use the threat of a strike to pressure employers into the concession of wage increases which cannot be justified on the basis of higher output.

Finally, we consider capital markets and financial intermediaries such as banks.[10] The role of capital markets is to collect the savings of the economy, and to pass them on to those who wish to borrow for investment. Three aspects are of particular importance. The first is that there is no need to match savers and borrowers. Savings can be collected from a wide range of small savers, and lent on in larger units, without savers and borrowers ever knowing the destinations and origins of the funds. The second aspect is that of risk reduction. Investment in physical capital represents a commitment to future output, but before the demand for that output is at all certain. However well planned and thought out, there is inevitably an element of risk. As we saw in our discussion of shareholding, capital markets can reduce the risk for the saver by spreading the funds across a portfolio of assets. And, through the device of limited liability, the risk of borrowing and investing in physical assets is reduced. The third aspect is that the capital market, like every other market, provides both incentives and information. A high return or interest rate, which is the relevant price in a capital market, is a signal of expected future demand, and an incentive for capital resources to flow into a sector.

Market capitalism has been defended, within the mainstream of economic analysis, as an efficient system for allocating scarce resources. It has also been defended by libertarian analysts as the natural outcome of a concern to preserve and enlarge human freedom. In the next two sections we will examine these two arguments for the defence of market capitalism, and ask to what extent, if any, they may gain the assent of Christians. In a final section we will attempt a direct evaluation of market capitalism using the biblical principles developed in Chapter Two.

3. Market capitalism as an efficient system for allocating resources

When asked to assess the efficiency of the market capitalist system, an economist trained in the mainstream of Western economic analysis will look to welfare economics to provide a framework.[11] Our immediate objective is to assess the case for market capitalism within that utilitarian framework: it turns out that at best the argument has to be hedged about with many qualifications.

We recall that welfare analysis takes as its starting point a deceptively simple value judgment which is termed the Pareto principle. It states that an economic change constitutes an improvement if it makes at least one consumer better off, leaving all others in the community as satisfied as before. Clearly if *all* such improvements are carried through, a point will be reached at which no citizen can be better off except at the expense of others.

Now it can be shown that a pure capitalist or free enterprise system would lead to a pattern of production and distribution of goods that satisfied the Pareto principle.[12] That is, it would be impossible to make any economic change that constituted an improvement under the Pareto principle. The critical assumptions are that consumers can bid freely for goods in markets; that the prices of goods should reflect the cost of making them, competition between firms having eliminated any excess profit; and that competition between firms for scarce resources ensures that they go to the most efficient firms.

Now this analysis may be challenged as to the reality of its assumptions concerning the functioning of the market capitalist system. We may identify at least five matters in which the reality falls short of the ideal. These are not abstractions, but matters in which governments in Western economies have taken an active policy interest.

First, the actual behaviour of firms does not conform to the requirements of the competitive model of the economy, particularly where a market is served by a few firms (oligopoly). Prices no longer necessarily reflect the cost of making goods, and lack of competition may permit inefficient firms to survive. Instead of being responsive to consumers' demands, the firms may use advertising and other sales techniques to plan and control their markets.

Second, there is the problem of external costs that are not paid for. For example, a private firm will have no incentive to incur the cost of safe disposal of a poisonous effluent which will pollute the water supply to other citizens or firms. A private motorist will drive his car in a crowded city without paying for the costs of congestion that his car is inflicting on other users of the city. An aeroplane flying overhead may cause acute discomfort because of noise, but the airline pays no price for it. These matters used to be thought of as textbook curiosities, but in a crowded world troubled by the problems of pollution they constitute a serious defect of economic freedom.[13] The problem is that it is not easy to create markets for these 'bads' (as opposed to 'goods'), where firms could buy the 'right' to cause a nuisance from those affected by it, thus effecting some compensation for their discomfort.

Third, there are the cases of public goods. The best examples are government, the defence forces and the police. It is impossible to create a market for these because citizens who failed to pay for the services provided could not be excluded from the benefits.

Fourth, there are goods which create a natural monopoly.[14] The best examples are the telephone and electricity systems where the essence of the good is the interconnection of the network. It would clearly be a waste of resources to have a large number of electricity companies competing with each other, since that would involve multiplication of electricity mains all over the country. But a monopoly, operating within the free enterprise system, does not have the competitive incentive to be efficient or to price at cost.

Fifth, a free enterprise system has no mechanism for ensuring that sufficient investment is done, or for ensuring that the pattern of investment is the right one. There are two problems here. The first is that a great deal of investment will benefit not only the present generation but also future generations (consider for example the Channel tunnel). But the system has no way of taking the wishes of future generations into account. The current generation may take sufficient thought to provide for the future, but we cannot be sure. The second is that, because the future is uncertain, firms may refrain from investing as much as society would like, particularly in sectors where there is little information concerning future needs, and they may get the wrong pattern of investment altogether.

Now we must beware of asking too much. It is possible to set up a theoretical model to give a perfect allocation of resources to investment for the foreseeable future. However such a model has been aptly described by one economist as the 'economics of Nirvana'.[15] The conditions are so stringent that we could not conceive of their satisfaction under any economic system. But the fact remains that there are serious doubts about the ability of a capitalist system to provide a tolerably correct pattern of investment.

We must now return to the Pareto principle. The attraction of the principle lies in the apparently innocuous value judgment that it contains. However it is not without its defects. An immediate question that arises is how we are to deal with the problem of envy. If one citizen is better off in material terms, while all the others are as before, then they may well be envious of him and therefore not so happy. A moment's reflection will be sufficient to convince the reader that this matter cannot easily be dismissed. A second query concerns income distribution. The pattern of resource ownership is taken to be a given. The distribution of income is the resultant of the distribution of resources and labour skills, and the prices which these can earn in markets. The analysis stops at this point, and probes no further.

Market capitalism clearly has considerable deficiencies when evaluated by the standards of Paretian welfare economics. Nor are the problems entirely abstract in nature. They have been perceived to be sufficiently serious for intervention by the authorities. It is common to the advanced industrial economies that natural monopolies are regulated directly or indirectly, that the market behaviour of large firms is subjected to scrutiny by relevant competition authorities, and that provisions to deal with externalities such as pollution are enacted. In addition discomfort with market outcomes in the area of income distribution have generated tax and transfer mechanisms to transfer income from the rich to the poor.

However there is also a reluctance to abandon market capitalism, which is seen to have many virtues, of which the price system is perhaps the most remarkable. The 'invisible hand' of the price system as described by Adam Smith is able to co-ordinate the supply and demand of thousands of commodities and services arising from thousands of firms and millions of households in an economy. It does so with remarkable precision, and with the minimum of information passing between consumer and firms.

Equally important are the desirable incentive properties of market capitalism, with the linking of reward to effort, and the disciplining of slack and inefficient enterprises. It is these properties that are usually credited with the measured success of market capitalist economies, in terms of economic growth. Despite the difficulties of measuring the growth of national income in different economies, those countries which have favoured market capitalist systems have apparently experienced faster growth than those that have not. The difference is particularly dramatic in developing economies, where market-oriented economies such as South Korea, Singapore and Kenya in the 1970s outperformed countries such as Liberia, Sri Lanka and India, where planned development was more significant.[16]

These differences in performance have generated a lively debate as to their interpretation. A particular question is whether the more rapid growth in the market economies has led to greater inequality. It is alleged that in a fast-growing capitalist economy most of the additional wealth and income accrues to business élites, and there is little 'trickle-down' to other sections of the community. The evidence is not clear-cut. In some cases, like Taiwan, everyone seems to benefit. In others, like Brazil in the 1960s and '70s, trickle-down was limited.[17]

Whatever the outcome of this debate, the criteria employed to evaluate performance — the growth and distribution of national income — are derived from the framework of utilitarian welfare analysis. It is therefore appropriate to remind ourselves that this framework was subjected to critical Christian scrutiny in Chapter Three,[18] and was found to be lacking in many respects. In particular, we criticized the individualistic basis of welfare economics, in comparison with the Christian emphasis on man in community with responsibilities for others, and the emphasis on attaching values to consequences (growth, efficiency, equality) rather than to actions and institutions (useful work, protection for the disadvantaged, preservation of family life).

Before we leave the evaluation of market capitalism within a secular framework, we should return to the issue of the need for a moral basis, a need first identified by Adam Smith. The concern of a number of recent writers is that market capitalism is only sustainable if there is an external moral basis, which capitalism cannot provide, and which it tends to erode. This issue has been sensitively explored by Hirsch.[19] A market economy can only operate successfully if there is acceptance of standards of honesty, truth, trust and refraining from the exercise of physical violence. While a moral consensus probably needs to be reinforced by a body of law, *e.g.* a law of contract, or laws protecting consumers, the law is not sufficient in the absence of social consent. The entry of legal procedures into every contract would rapidly destroy the advantages of decentralization— perceived to be the particular genius of markets.

The malfunctioning of markets in the absence of honesty

and trust was described analytically by Akerlof,[20] with the example of markets for second-hand cars. Buyers are unable to determine precisely the quality of the cars on offer. Hence, a self-interested seller of a poor quality car has an incentive to pass off his car as better than it really is. Unable to distinguish quality, a purchaser will bid on the basis of his estimate of average quality of the cars on offer. Sellers of good quality cars then have an incentive to withdraw their cars from the market, and the average quality falls. A rather different example is the effect of possible legal action for damages on the doctor–patient relationship in the United States. Lack of trust has had bizarre consequences: patients are asked to pay for a range of tests which are probably quite unnecessary, and high-risk medical procedures are no longer practised by doctors.

The problem for market capitalism is how to generate the requisite moral standards. A commitment to moral standards in economic and social life might be forthcoming, *if* the outcomes of the market economy were seen to be just. But if the outcomes cannot be obviously validated on moral criteria, then why should the individual exercise restraint?

Hirsch's thesis[21] is that market capitalism originally succeeded because it had inherited a strong religious and moral basis, which acted to prevent the pursuit of self-interest in ways which would be damaging. However, with the erosion of the religious sanction markets operate less effectively, for the reasons outlined above, and market behaviour starts to spread to areas where it is very damaging— the corruption of civil servants and the judiciary.

The response, according to Hirsch, is an increase in *intervention* by the authorities in the market economy. Examples are the regulation of securities and insurance markets to prevent fraud, the development of consumer protection legislation, and the increased sophistication of competition authorities in regulating behaviour in markets where the participants no longer have any agreed basis for what is 'fair' competition.

The raising of taxation is another case in point: the complexity of taxation legislation is the result of the growth of an industry concerned with evasion. There is no ethic which sees the payment of taxes as a social responsibility: on the contrary every last detail of the law is scrutinized to see how they may be avoided. The irony is that intervention by the authorities in markets also tends to erode the market freedom on which the system is based.

4. The liberal defence of the market system

The liberal tradition places its emphasis on the market economy as the system which arises naturally from an insistence on two fundamental absolute rights – individual freedom and individual property rights. The link is both logical and evolutionary. It is logical in that only a free market economy is compatible with these rights. It is evolutionary in that a market system arises spontaneously where individuals have these rights. The corollary of this argument is that only a minimal state, arising out of agreements between individuals, is acceptable. We will now explore this argument, taking each element in turn and examining it for compatibility with a Christian analysis.

The liberal theory of property rights is based on a natural rights doctrine which has two important presuppositions. The first refers to justice in acquisition. Locke[22] imagines an original state of nature in which there are no property rights. But every man has rights over his own person. By his own labour he wrests from nature a patch of land for cultivation. Thereby he establishes a property right in that piece of nature. 'It hath by this labour something annexed to it that excludes the common right of other men.' 'God by commanding to subdue, gave authority to appropriate.'

The second presupposition is justice in transfers. After the initial phase of acquisition, individuals enter freely into exchanges, or make gifts, *e.g.* bequests to children. Over a period of time these actions, together with the action of chance factors, *e.g.* good and bad harvests, may well generate inequalities. But so long as justice in acquisition and justice in transfers have been observed, then the 'rights' which emerge as a result of the historical process of acquisition and exchange are vindicated.

This argument attracts a number of critical comments. First, the Lockean notion of the pioneer wresting his plot of land from virgin nature is more romantic than apposite. Very few new assets are created as the outcome of *one* person's labour. Second, there is every reason to believe the present distribution reflects previous injustices in transfers. Even if we could somehow ensure that all future transfers were just, since the starting point would be unjust so would be the outcomes of a continuing historical process.

Third, a Christian critique of the liberal theory would dissent from the emphasis on property rights, implying use for one's own ends, and would emphasize stewardship rights, implying use for the good of society in general. Fourth, the Jubilee provisions of the Law specifically abrogated the rights created by transfers on equal terms (Leviticus 25). The regulations concerning the Year of Jubilee emphasize that God gave the trusteeship of particular areas of land to particular families. Over a period of years, in a predominantly agricultural community, it was likely that some families would lose control over their land by incurring debts. However at the end of seven sabbath years, *i.e.* after forty-nine years, there was to be a Jubilee year in which all land was restored to its original owners. They were the trustees appointed by God for that land, and it was to be returned to them.

The second fundamental right identified by liberal thought[23] is freedom, especially economic freedom. The starting point is that 'freedom of the individual, or perhaps the family, is our ultimate goal in judging social arrangements'. Freedom is defined negatively as that condition in which the degree of coercion of some individuals by others is reduced to the minimum. Freedom is independence of the arbitrary will of another, lack of interference, and lack of coercion. This is Locke's 'state of nature' where individuals are in a 'state of perfect freedom to order their actions and dispose of their persons and possessions as they think fit, within the bounds of the law of nature, without asking leave or dependency upon the will of any other man'.

Liberal thought also argues that freedom is all of a piece, so that freedom is predicated on the existence of a free market economy. It accepts a hierarchy of freedoms in cases where these conflict. Moral and intellectual freedom are ranked highest, followed by political freedom. The economic freedoms of markets, competition, entry, choice of consumption and occupation, rank higher than 'freedoms' of contract and coalition. But it is argued, especially by Friedman,[24] that the different types of freedom are intimately connected. The attempted separation of economic freedom and individual freedom (*e.g.* in democratic socialism) is a delusion. Only in a market economy can the individual obtain resources to achieve his own ends and purposes without being dependent on others, apart from contracts freely entered into by both parties. The only prerequisites are the existence of 'law and order' to prevent coercion, and to enforce contracts. What an individual does is strictly a private affair.

The singling out of individual freedom as the overriding value in assessing social arrangements is incompatible with biblical criteria. That freedom is a positive good is not denied. But it needs to be taken in conjunction with an equal emphasis on man in society with both rights and obligations. The biblical doctrine of fallen man should make us suspicious of any promotion of individual self-seeking as an ultimate value. Friedman's association of freedom with market freedoms is also open to objection. The outcome may well be freedom for the strong, and a greatly restricted range of options for the weak.

Given the two fundamental rights, it is Hayek's contention that a market economy will evolve.[25] His thesis is that social arrangements are not designed for the purposes they serve, but evolve spontaneously into orderly structures. A market economy is the paradigm of spontaneous order. Hayek prefers not to use the word 'economy', since it implies a set of activities by which resources are allocated to specific ends. But in the market order there are no ends as such. So he uses the word 'catallaxy'. Individuals with property rights enter freely into barter or exchange within a framework of law governing contracts. They enter because they perceive personal benefit in exchange, and thus new wealth is created.

The market economy which evolves has all the advantageous properties with respect to incentives and information previously identified in section 2. It is an advantage that there is no common purpose towards which society is organized. Individuals' objectives may differ, but these are painlessly reconciled within the framework of the market. Each individual seeks his own ends within the opportunities that markets offer.

Obviously, the outcome of the market game need not correspond to any ideal of distributive justice. It will be the result of the resources individuals have to contribute, how these resources are valued in markets, and a mixture of luck and the skill with which the individual manages his affairs. Ideas of social justice are simply irrelevant. The only evaluative judgment permitted by Hayek is this: '. . . the economist is therefore entitled to insist that conduciveness to [the market] order be accepted as a standard by which all particular institutions are judged'.[26]

Griffiths[27] rightly objects to this analysis on biblical grounds. First, the idea that there is no overall purpose in human activities arises from acceptance of a theory of cultural evolution, which is incompatible with Christian conceptions of creation, providence in history and relevation of God's will for mankind. In his economic life, man is intended by God to be a steward of the created order, as set out in our biblical principles at the end of Chapter Two.

Second, the theory of guaranteed social harmony within the market order fits awkwardly with the doctrine of the fall, with its emphasis on the exercise of power and force in human relationships.

Third, the Christian concept of economic justice is concerned with more than just property rights and the enforcement of contracts, as an inspection of our biblical principles makes clear. There is, for example, the need to ensure that the basic needs of the poor are provided.

Fourth, the stress on *individual* rights derives from a view of man as a rational being, the proprietor of his own person and capabilities. Community only arises from contracts between freely consenting individuals. By contrast, the Christian doctrine of man is that his dignity and worth derive from God, and that community is part of the creation order — man is intended to be responsible for his fellow men. We conclude, with Griffiths, that the liberal justification for the market economy is incompatible with the Christian doctrine of man and society.

The final element in the libertarian position is that only a 'minimal' state can be justified within the market order. The liberal theory of the state was first developed by Locke and has been given a sophisticated modern treatment by Nozick.[28] Locke begins with individuals in a state of nature, 'a state of perfect freedom to order their actions and dispose of their persons and possessions as they think fit, within the bounds of the law of nature, without asking leave, or dependency upon the will of any other man'. No-one ought to harm another in his life, health, liberty or possessions. If he does, the injured party may punish or exact compensation. But, although the individual is free in the 'state of nature', he is also insecure against the invasion of his rights by others. He may have insufficient power to punish or exact compensation. Agreements freely entered into may prove difficult to enforce. Feuds may develop in the private settling of scores.

These difficulties drive men into commonwealths (Locke) or protective associations (Nozick) to secure their rights. The protective association, according to Nozick, arises naturally out of a state of nature, even though no-one intends it or tries to bring it about. It establishes a legal framework for relationships between the citizens, it acts as an impartial judge in disputes, and it has the power to carry out its judgments, including the exaction of compensation. In these tasks it is dependent on the consent of the members of the protective association, who have agreed to enter on the basis of the predefined constitution. In Locke's analysis this includes legislators, chosen by the members of society, who have powers to make laws within certain constitutional constraints. They have no arbitrary power over life, liberty, or possessions of individuals. They may act only on the basis of settled and agreed laws, which apply impartially to all citizens. They may not take from any man any part of his property without his consent. (What about taxes to pay for common purposes, *e.g.* the expenses of the protective association? Consent here is redefined as consent of the majority to the taxation.) Finally the legislators cannot transfer power to any other hands.

Nozick sees these features arising by an 'invisible hand' process, from local protective associations to a dominant protective association, which is the minimal state including all the citizens. He is mainly concerned with the rights of 'independents'— those who do not wish to join the association. First he argues that the protective association will have to prohibit the private enforcement of justice on the grounds that it is risky or unreliable in procedure. If there are too many independents, there is a non-negligible risk for everyone else that they will be unfairly punished by an independent, and they will therefore live in fear. Punishment has to be based on agreed procedures for determining guilt or damages. So the dominant association may find itself having to protect one of its members against an independent who has used an unreliable or unfair procedure, and who has punished one of the members against his will. It therefore prohibits independents from exercising self-enforcement of their rights (including the right to punish), and compensates them by extending its own protective services to them. Thus the dominant association becomes a *de facto* monopoly, since it is the only institution in society which has the *power* to prevent others from exercising their right to punish. It has no *de jure* power. Nozick rejects the free rider argument that independents should be compelled to join the protective association because they benefit from its existence.

Whatever the merits of Nozick's description of the 'invisible hand' process by which states are formed, it is clear that the minimal state so described is not consistent with the biblical view outlined in Chapter Two. The minimal state is a *de facto* state deriving its authority solely from the consent of its members. The biblical political authorities derive their authority from God. The minimal state is restricted to a narrow range of activities determined solely by the ceding of rights on the part of the citizens. It is mainly concerned with providing the framework for transactions between citizens, and with punishing infringements of absolute personal rights. The biblical political authorities have a more positive role in promoting *justice* in the society, not merely protecting rights.

Our conclusion on the libertarian case for the market system is that, whatever its merits as a secular analysis of the emergence of the market economy, its prescriptive claims have no basis in Christian ethics and are indeed incompatible with them in substantive respects.

5. A Christian evaluation of market capitalism

Our first task is to provide a critique, based on the biblical principles derived in Chapter Two. In the light of that critique, we will ask whether market capitalism is nonetheless an imperfect second best, given the sinfulness of man; and whether there are ways in which the gap between market capitalism and Christian ideals could be narrowed.

The first three *Principles* are about man's exercise of dominion over creation. *Principle 1* asks how far the concept of *care* for the natural order is a part of economic life. Man must use the resources of the created order to provide for his existence, but he must not waste or destroy that order. This issue is discussed in detail with respect to a market economy in Chapter Eight, but we may anticipate the conclusions here. A market economy has no concept of care for the natural order, and under a wide range of conditions is likely to be destructive of it. Interestingly though, part of the problem arises from the lack of property rights in particular resources, though that is not a problem that can be easily rectified.

Principles 2 and *3* deal with man's role as steward of the resources and talents that God has entrusted to him. Every person has a calling to exercise stewardship, which implies responsibility for deciding how resources and talents should be used. In the exercise of that responsibility, the individual should look beyond immediate self-interest to see how resources may be used for the good of others.

When judged by these principles, a market capitalist system has both good and bad features. The good features are the scope that private property and markets afford for the exercise of stewardship, and the responsibility that rests with each person or household to see that what they have to contribute by way of skills and natural resources is used effectively. However there are less desirable features. The Roman law concept of 'private property', on which market capitalism rests, is different from the Christian ideal of personal responsibility. 'Private property' implies the right of use to advance personal interests; the Christian concept sees responsibility as being exercised in service to others as well as to oneself.

A market economy can provide an apt setting for the exercise of such stewardship. But there is nothing in the system as such which is conducive to it. Economic freedom within a market system gives equal scope for behaviour which is narrowly self-interested and indeed prejudicial to the wider community. For example, aspects of predatory behaviour in markets by large companies can prevent the emergence of alternative sources of supply for consumers. It is naïve to presume that market behaviour is always innocently competitive in the textbook sense.

Furthermore certain characteristic features of a modern capitalist economy encourage a lack of responsibility for personal resources. The first is the institution of limited liability stockholder companies[29]. The owners of a company can duck out of responsibility for the consequences of poor judgment, mismanagement or even misfortune. In bankruptcy, debts which are incurred in their name can be left unpaid.

The second feature is indirect shareholding. The growth of financial intermediaries such as pension funds, unit trusts and insurance companies means that the ultimate owners of the assets may have no clear idea of what assets they own, let alone exercise any stewardship responsibilities for how those assets are used. Thus a pacifist may unwittingly be holding shares in a weapons company, and a champion of the poor in the Third World in some multinational with a bad record in respect of its Third World employees.

The next three *Principles* concern man and his work. Work is the means by which man exercises his stewardship. So *Principle 4* is that man has a right and an obligation to work.

But market capitalist economies appear to have an endemic problem about the provision of work opportunities for their citizens. The reasons for unemployment are complex, and are explored further in Chapter Six. While at least some unemployment is due to institutional obstacles to the functioning of labour markets (*e.g.* trade union power), that is by no means the whole story. 'Making markets work' is only a partial solution.

The other two *Principles* are concerned with the nature and organization of work. *Principle 6* states that work is a social activity in which men cooperate as stewards of their individual talents, and as joint stewards of resources. The position with respect to employment in a market capitalist firm is quite distinct from this *Principle*. The formal structure of the firm is that it is owned by the shareholders, who may take no interest in the running of the enterprise. This is delegated to management, which is appointed by the directors on behalf of the shareholders, and with the brief of running the firm in the interests of the shareholders. Their task is to hire labour to perform production and other necessary tasks, with a contract which specifies the work, the conditions under which it is to be done and the remuneration. In formal terms, the worker is not given any voice in how the firm is run or what its objectives should be. He has no stake in it.

It takes no great imagination to envisage what a fruitful source of conflict between capital (the shareholders) and labour this arrangement could be. The owners' interest is to keep wages down and to seek higher productivity, so that profits may be higher. The workers' interest is to maximize their returns consistent with retaining their jobs, avoiding any behaviour which might put the long-term viability of the firm in jeopardy.

In practice any wise management will know that conflict is not a viable strategy and will try to encourage responsible involvement by workers and union representatives in the organization of the firm. But that only softens the impact of a formal arrangement which, from a Christian point of view, is unjust. It is wrong to treat a worker as labour input: he should be given a formal status which recognizes that he too has responsibilities for the way in which resources are used and the firm conducts itself. How this might be achieved is discussed briefly at the end of this section.

Principles 7 and *8* are concerned with the distribution of income. *Principle 7* is that every person has a right to share in God's provision for mankind for their basic needs of food, clothing and shelter. These basic needs are to be met, in the first instance, by productive work. But we have already noted that market capitalism is not particularly effective in ensuring that everyone has work to do. Nor is it evident, among those who do work, that their talents are properly utilized.

Principle 8 reminds us that personal stewardship of resources does not imply the right to consume the entire product of those resources, and that the rich have an obligation to help the poor, who cannot provide adequately for themselves by work. Neither of these aspects is evident in the concept of private property which underlies market capitalism. Those who have highly valued resources or talents will have high incomes *and* the right to dispose of that income to their own advantage. They may be disposed to act altruistically and give much of it away. But there is no sense of obligation to do so within a private property framework. Nor is this an incidental feature: the incentive of higher rewards for a greater contribution is fundamental to the operation of the system, justified on the basis of efficient use of resources.

This would not matter if market capitalism did not, in practice, generate a problem of poverty. But the existence of the problem is undeniable. There will always be those without work or who cannot work, or whose talents and resources are of little value and so generate an income too small for the basic necessities. However it is not only the poor who are harmed: it is also the rich. The biblical material is quite explicit that the pursuit of wealth for its own sake can become an idol, which hinders men from considering their status before God ('You cannot serve both God and money').

It is evident that, on biblical criteria, we are right to feel uneasy about many aspects of market capitalism. But we have to consider whether the system is nonetheless an imperfect second-best, given the fallen nature of man: and whether the force of the critique could be softened by the introduction of additional elements, within a framework of law, more conducive to the kind of society envisaged by the biblical principles, but remaining recognizably a market capitalist system.

This approach has been persuasively argued by Brian Griffiths in recent writings.[30] The essence of his approach is that a market system itself is morally neutral, and should be judged on the basis of its effectiveness as a decentralized information and incentive system. What matters is the set of cultural norms and values, some of them enshrined in law, which are motivating the economic actors within the system.[31] Thus he makes the distinction between a set of values based on faith in God, and a set based on Mammon (Money). He believes that the former values, which were those of the Reformation generally and of the Calvinist Puritans in particular, were those which generated the development of market capitalism in England, a thesis first advanced by Weber in his classic *The Protestant Ethic and the Spirit of Capitalism*.[32] These values include work as a 'calling' before God, avoidance of personal extravagance and waste, responsibility to provide for one's family and close relatives, and a concern to provide for the poor. The values of Mammon, on the other hand, are those which see work as a means of getting money and consumption as a route to happiness, and do not accept any obligation to care for others.

This distinction between different sets of values within the market system is illustrated by Griffiths in a number of ways.[33] He makes the distinction between the pursuit of self-interest (out of a proper self-love, responsibility before God for oneself and one's dependents) and selfishness (which is the desire of fallen man to pursue his own ends without regard to others). Adam Smith showed how self-interest could be harnessed for the public good within the structure of a market economy, and it is to this goal that Griffiths believes we should direct our attention.

For Griffiths, 'competition is simply a way of resolving conflicts in society', a human phenomenon which results from the facts of scarcity. He is thus able to distinguish a benign form of market capitalism, which looks like a textbook version of perfect competition, from the rivalries and destructive competition of oligopolistic markets. Inequality must be accepted, Griffiths believes, as an outcome of acknowledging the fact of human differences as bestowed by God, and of safeguarding the right to private property. But he adds a Christian responsibility to help others, as a steward of God's resources. He accepts that unemployment is a serious evil, but prefers to see this as largely due to technical failures of the market system, arising from intervention by governments or trade unions. Finally, he argues that a market system is the only means of preserving human freedom and dignity. If there is no market, then there are no economic incentives, and the authorities will have to resort to coercion to get things done.

What Griffiths succeeds in showing is that a market capitalism founded on the values of faith would look very different from one founded on the values of Mammon. It is the latter, and not the market system *per se*, which attracts criticism of the kind with which we began this section. Given that he would not disagree that the market capitalism we observe is largely motivated by the spirit of Mammon, it is relevant to ask how he expects the older Reformation values to be re-established.

The question is precisely that raised by Hirsch in respect of the depleting moral legacy of market capitalism. Hirsch[34] points to the decline of traditional Christian morality, but he does not discuss the possibility of religious revival as a solution to the problem which that decline poses for the survival of market capitalism. He argues that a new social ethic is urgently needed, and asserts: 'The functional need for change in social ethic can be expected, over time, to promote it'.[35] But he is far from optimistic about the efficacy of the processes by which that ethic might evolve. Griffiths, as one would expect from a Christian writer, is prepared to stress a need for evangelism and a revival of Christian social values.

Both writers also see a role for institutional reforms which might help to alleviate the problems. Hirsch sees the distributional struggle as the fundamental problem of market capitalism: the outcomes of the market system are not perceived to be just, and therefore the moral basis for the whole system is called into question. He therefore advocates institutional reforms which will result in distributional issues being explicitly addressed, resulting, for example, in an agreed narrowing of pay differentials over time.

Griffiths is more precise concerning the kinds of reforms he would like to see. He would like to see trade union powers reduced, and is unhappy about their involvement in collective bargaining.[36] He believes that competition policy should be vigorously promoted to prevent the abuse of market power by dominant firms.[37] He acknowledges that the limited liability company, which gives sole control to the shareholders, is inconsistent with Christian notions of responsible stewardship. But he believes that there is sufficient legislation to protect the interests of workers, consumers and the public at large.[38] (Indeed, in the UK case he hints that this legislation may have become too protective.) So while he is prepared to encourage different structures of ownership and control of firms, he does not recommend that legislation should be amended to require this. Useful though these reforms might be, it is evident that Griffiths places great reliance on the re-emergence of Christian moral values to restore moral validity to the market economy. Institutional reforms cannot alone bridge the gap between market capitalism based on Mammon and market capitalism based on faith in God.

Our discussion of Griffiths' contribution would be incomplete without a consideration of the role of the political authorities in his analysis. He believes that the state in the United Kingdom has grown too large, in respect of the level of public expenditure, particularly the welfare state.[39] His argument is that the consequence has been a reduction in personal freedom of choice, and in individual responsibility. He is strongly opposed to public deficits, a point to which we will return in Chapter Six. But at no point does he try to state in a systematic fashion what he believes should be the responsibilities of the authorities in the context of a market economy. Piecing together material from various parts of his writings, it appears that he sees their primary task as the provision of a framework of laws, hopefully consistent with Christian principles, within which the market economy can function. He is apparently reluctant to concede to the state an enabling role as a focus for responsible communal endeavour. Such a role might include an element of coercion to overcome the free-rider problem, where citizens are generally agreed on some desirable social end, but individual action will not work, *e.g.* the provision of public goods, or the provision of income support for the poor.

Griffiths' defence of market capitalism is *too* dependent on a revival of Christian social values. Such a revival is, in human terms, extremely unlikely, even if there were to be a major Christian renewal. Our experience is that the values of the secular market economy have taken deep roots in the Christian church, perhaps particularly the evangelical churches. The fundamentalist churches of North America have, for example, espoused the secular market doctrines of libertarian thought,[40] which we dissected critically in section 4 of this chapter. Sadly, there is too little tradition of biblical thought to counter this secular infiltration, though Griffiths is to be applauded for his biblical critique of libertarian ideology. But one wonders whether the church is prepared to listen.

Without a revival of Christian social values, the market economy is likely to continue to be based on the values of Mammon, with all the unjust features described. What then might a conscientious Christian citizen prescribe? First, we suggest that institutional reform could go much further than Griffiths is prepared to contemplate. For example, the legal and fiscal constitution of companies could be changed so that ownership and responsibility is shifted, in part if not completely, to the people who work in it. One suggestion is that shareholders should no longer have ownership rights: their status would be that of bondholders, though their dividend returns might continue to be dependent on the success of the firm. Alternatively they might be permitted to retain ownership rights, but only if they would forgo limited liability. Such an arrangement would give them an incentive to act responsibly in their ownership.

The other part of any such reform would be to give ownership rights in the firm to those who actually work in it. These rights would confer not only a share in the profits, but also the potential to influence the activity of the firm. A simple means to achieve this would be equity participation by long-standing workers. An alternative would be a recognition in the legal constitution of the firm that its objectives include the long-term provision of employment for the labour force. This could be given substantive content by provision for worker participation in major decisions. Worker participation schemes are given further consideration in Chapter Five.

Second, we believe that government should be encouraged to tackle particular injustices like unemployment directly, even if it means 'interfering' in the market mechanisms. A job guarantee system,[41] for example, would be a proper objective, and certainly much more consistent with Christian principles than an extensive welfare support system for the unemployed. Further consideration will be given in Chapter Six to measures to tackle unemployment in a market economy.

Third, a Christian would wish the political authorities to act to restrain the exercise of economic power in capital and labour markets, and in markets for goods and services. Our preference is for a framework of law regulating the activities of trade unions, financial institutions and firms, but we would not entirely rule out discretionary intervention where a perceived injustice cannot be adequately put right within the legal framework. Detailed recommendations, for example in respect of competition policy, cannot be pursued here. However, a Christian will approach the issue somewhat differently from secular analysts. Traditional economic analysis of competition policy has stressed the issue of economic efficiency to the virtual exclusion of everything else. It is, however, doubtful whether this approach does justice to the considerations that have motivated the historical development of competition policy in the United States and the UK. These have included a commitment to defend small businesses from the power of large firms to destroy their business, and to protect the poor consumer from being exploited by high prices charged by monopolistic firms and cartels. The latter is motivated more by considerations of income distribution and 'fair play' in market competition

than by a desire for economic efficiency. These considerations would also be appropriate concerns for a Christian.

Fourth, the government should not hesitate to use the
traditional tax and transfer mechanisms to ensure that those
without the means to acquire the basic necessities of life are
provided for.[42] Given that the objective is to build on any
latent sense of responsibility that the citizens may feel for
their less economically privileged members, there are
obvious advantages if the system of transfers can be administered in a decentralized manner.

In all this, a Christian would also wish to insist that the role
of the authorities be kept under constant scrutiny to ensure
that their involvement is limited to creating a legal framework for responsible individual decisions, to intervening in
cases of perceived social injustice, and to meeting genuine
economic need. The danger is always that they will exceed
their God-given responsibilities, and use their powers for
their own ends. The political question of how to make
governments responsive and self-restrained is beyond the
scope of this book, though some form of direct accountability
to the citizens (as in a democracy) is obviously desirable. But
given that governments are corruptible, just as much as
businessmen, we are right to be sceptical about too great a
reliance on government to right wrongs in a capitalist
economy.

CHAPTER FIVE
Socialism and the planned economy

1. Introduction

Three types of socialism are distinguished in this chapter, though the differences between them are not in practice so clearly defined. The first is communism, characterized by a powerful state which directs the economy by means of planning. The second is a neo-Marxist socialism, which has updated the Marxist analysis of capitalism, and seeks to introduce socialism by a quiet revolution in which the state takes over giant companies and coordinates their activities by a limited planning mechanism, and by strict control of the financial sector of the economy. The third is the social democratic tradition, which rejects much of Marx's analysis of capitalism, and proposes detailed regulation of a capitalist economy without the abandonment of independent firms as the basic productive units. These three types of socialism, and their programmes, are described in sections 2 and 3 of this chapter.

It may surprise some readers that so much of the analysis will concern economics. They might ask whether the proper emphasis ought not to be a broader vision of the nature of man in society. Thus the comparison between capitalism and socialism might be made in terms of individualist versus collectivist philosophies. However the fundamental point which all types of socialism have inherited from Marx is that the organization of production is the key to understanding all relationships in society, not least the question of the locus of power, and how that power is exercised. Hence the focus of socialist programmes *is* economics, and unless we understand the economics we will not understand the socialist system and ideals. However, the economic analysis cannot be divorced from ethical issues, as if it were merely a technical matter. On the contrary, all sorts of ethical issues arise concerning the state, property, planning, freedom, work, equality. So we have chosen to tackle these one at a time in sections 4 to 9, providing the biblical ethical tools for the evaluation of each variety of socialism. The degree to which these issues arise will vary between one variety and another.

2. Socialist analysis and socialist ideals

Each variety of socialism starts at the same point, a fundamental dislike of capitalism and its effects. This is the source of its moral purpose, and it is towards the solution of the problems of capitalism that socialist programmes are directed. So it is necessary to outline briefly the socialist critique of capitalism before directing our attention to the socialist society or programme.

(a) The Marxist critique of capitalism

The Marxist analysis of capitalist development is conveniently outlined in *The Communist Manifesto*,[1] though the full subtlety of Marx's system did not emerge until the publication of *Capital*.[2] According to Marx, the industrial revolution destroyed the simple hierarchies of feudal societies, and replaced them with a two-class system. The bourgeoisie are the owners of capital, the proletariat are the workers employed by them. The emergence of the bourgeoisie is based on the technological revolution in manufacturing industry and the development of free trade. Competition ensures that only the efficient survive in the market-place. Large scale and mechanization (with consequent division of labour) are the means to achieve efficiency. So success is related to the accumulation and concentration of capital.

However, the system has two fundamental flaws. The first

is that competition between capitalists tends to drive down the rate of profit, thus removing the capitalist incentive to accumulation. The trend decline in the profit rate is accentuated in crises of overproduction, when the intensity of competition between capitalists leads to the closing down of productive plant and to losses for some of the bourgeoisie. But, despite this, because they retain control of the means of production the bourgeoisie are able to maintain their grip on society.

The second flaw in the system is its ultimate dependence on the proletariat. The capitalist system can only develop insofar as it develops a working class. The workers survive by selling their labour as a commodity to the capitalists. In production they become appendages to the machine. Because of the nature of the productive process, they become alienated from their work. Competition between the workers for employment keeps the wage at a subsistence level, and hence the surplus from their labour accrues to the bourgeoisie. The workforce is 'disciplined' by periodic crises in the capitalist system which leave many of them unemployed for a while. This only serves to increase their dependence on the bourgeoisie.

Eventually, the process of capitalist production, in bringing the proletariat together for production and giving them a common lot, provides the means for combinations of workers to form trade unions. Initially they will operate locally, seeking to raise wages, combat closures of factories, and improve working conditions. Later they will seek to strengthen themselves by forming alliances with trade unions in other areas. Despite this, they will not be able to improve conditions materially because of the long-run decline in the profitability of manufacturing which will lead the bourgeoisie to resist vigorously the attempts of the trade unions to raise wages. The proletariat will realize that improvement can only come by the destruction of the system. The capitalists must be dispossessed of the means of production, since their interests block any reform. So the organization of the proletariat turns itself into a revolutionary movement:

> The Communists disdain to conceal their views and aims. They openly declare that their ends can only be attained by the forcible overthrow of all existing social conditions. Let the ruling classes tremble at a Communistic revolution. The proletarians have nothing to lose but their chains. They have a world to win.

The Marxist analysis is a mixture of descriptive and moral elements. Whatever the merits of the historical analysis and its historicism, the moral fervour still commands attention.

Four moral criticisms can be distinguished. First, the conditions of the working classes in nineteenth-century Britain, as described in *Capital*, chapters 10 and 15, were simply appalling. Second, the alienation of man from his labour, so that he becomes a wage-slave and his work merely another commodity, is evidently wrong. Third, the fact that the system, while keeping the workers in poverty, also generates a surplus for the capitalists to maintain their lifestyle, is open to objection on the grounds of inequity.[3] Fourth, the control by the bourgeoisie of the means of production enables them to maintain a grip on society and to make decisions in their own interests without reference to the interests of the vast mass of the people, the proletariat. In a capitalist crisis the bourgeoisie arrange for the costs to fall on the working class, in terms of lower real wages and unemployment. So the lot of the working class is made worse by uncertainty about their future, which is entirely in the hands of the bourgeoisie.

(b) The neo-Marxist critique of capitalism

The Marxist analysis still attracts a substantial following among socialists, though the context of the analysis has been updated[4]. The centrepiece is the development of giant manufacturing firms, particularly those with a multinational flavour. These are the logical outcome of the capitalist process of accumulation. Confronted with the threat to profit posed by competition, the large firm has sought a monopoly to control its market. If the market is worldwide, then only a multinational can achieve this. By this means the capitalist sector has held off the long-run decline in profits foreseen by Marx, and has also made itself less vulnerable to 'local' capitalist crises. However the crises of world capitalism are still a difficulty for the system.

The relationship of capitalism to the bourgeoisie has also changed subtly. No longer is there a direct link between the ownership and the control of capital. The diffusion of shareholding has enabled a new managerial class to assume control. The managerial élite are distinguished by their identification with the companies which they control. The company rewards them with power, prestige, salary, and all manner of non-pecuniary benefits. Their interests are served by the continuing existence and growth of their company. They have made an alliance with the remaining bourgeois class of property-owners and shareholders, and they have aspired to adopt the lifestyle of that class. They have been successful in obtaining a policy of aid to the capitalist sector in terms of grants and subsidies from general taxation. These have helped to keep the profit rate up, and have enabled the system to weather the occasional capitalist crisis.

The material position of the workers has improved very greatly, for two reasons. First, the extension of monopoly and the obtaining of subsidies from the state, has enabled firms to concede trade union demands for rising wages, since there has not been so much pressure on profits. Second, the development of a welfare state paid for from general taxation, and not from capitalist surpluses, has reduced the militancy of the proletariat.

But the other essential features outlined by Marx have not changed. The worker is still alienated from his work: indeed the pace of technological advance has made this more critical. A new breed of worker has emerged who accepts passively an utterly dehumanizing job for the sake of a large wage to spend in his leisure time. Though there may have been some reduction in income inequality, the managerial/ bourgeois class maintains a high standard of living on the basis of the surplus created by the workers. Class interests and identification are as strong as ever. The power of big business has largely replaced the power of the bourgeoisie, and the worker is at the mercy of the decisions taken by the managers. Elected socialist governments have been able to do little to weaken their power over the workers. For example, a multinational corporation can use its threat to transfer its operations to another country to fend off an intervention by the government on behalf of workers.

(c) The social democratic analysis of capitalism

Even less of the Marxist analysis survives in the social democratic writings of the late 1940s and early 1950s.[5] Their analysis was particularly directed to the situation in Britain.

Crosland argued that Britain could no longer be classed as a capitalist country. First, government intervention in the economy had become more pervasive during the Second World War. Governments were more prepared to control the economy generally, using Keynesian demand management to maintain full employment. Second, the owner-manager class was disappearing, and being replaced by professional management. Shareholder control was weak.

Third, as a consequence of the previous point, the ownership of the means of production was becoming irrelevant to its control. The alienation of workers derived more from the technological basis of modern methods of production. Fourth, the simple Marxist analysis of class conflict between the bourgeoisie (capitalists) and the proletariat (workers) no longer applied. The new conflict was between workers and management, and it was a conflict where significant transfer of power to workers had occurred. Keynesian full employment policies had blunted the capitalist weapon of unemployment as a means of disciplining the workers. The nature of modern production methods made strikes extremely costly for the management, so that industrial action had become a powerful instrument in the hands of the trade unions. Fifth, the unequal distribution of wealth and income was no longer a strictly class matter: wealth was not concentrated in the hands of an identifiable capitalist 'class'.

The conclusion is that the social democratic analysis rejected much of the Marxist analysis. But the moral motivation for social reform remains. Crossman[6] writes that social progress is measured by

> the degree of equality and respect for individual personality expressed in the distribution of power and in the institutions of law and property within the state. This standard is what we mean by the socialist ideal.

Jenkins[7] spells this out:

> Where there is no egalitarianism, there is no socialism.

For him, a classless society is the goal:

> one in which men will be separated from each other less sharply by variations in wealth and origin, than by differences in character.

With this general ideal, particular areas for action are identified. In any market economy there are likely to be significant minorities who are materially disadvantaged. The relief of poverty is therefore an important goal.

Even when material poverty is absent, capitalism will generate significant disparities in income and wealth. Crosland[8] argues that this will lead to social discontent based on envy. He regards envy as a basic human response, which must enter any realistic social analysis. It manifests itself in collective discontent, which feeds on itself and generates social tensions. The analysis is reminiscent of Hirsch's analysis[9] of the failure of material progress to bring happiness. The lot of the workers has improved in absolute terms, but they are no nearer to obtaining the coveted 'positional goods'[10] which by definition are available only to the few.

The achievement of equality of opportunity is an important socialist ideal. But this is not enough, if the resultant distribution of income and wealth is markedly unequal. Equality of opportunity is hindered by the privileged access to education and to positions of economic power fostered by birth into the wealthy classes.

Democratic socialism is also motivated by the rejection of competition as a social organizing device, and by the espousing of an ideal of cooperation. Personal motives should involve the idea of working for the common good rather than for oneself, and relations at work should be guided by cooperation rather than antagonism between workers and managers.

Finally, there is an awareness of the dangers of the concentration of power into the hands of the few, as the result of technological and organizational progress. Crossman[11] quotes approvingly the view of Reinhold Niebuhr[12] that human institutions have an unceasing proclivity to act immorally. So a constant watch must be kept on their performance with a view to preventing the worst excesses. Large companies in the private sector must be scrutinized in their activities and made responsible to social objectives. Large institutions, whether in the public or the private sector, must not become the preserves of small managerial or civil service élites. Managerial positions should be filled on the basis of merit, and the managers themselves should be subject to some wider democratic control. In particular, decisions affecting employment should not be taken solely with regard to the interests of the institution.

3. Socialist programmes

Corresponding to the social analysis described above, there is a variety of socialist programmes. The purpose of this section is to describe these in broad outline. At the end we will identify those issues that require scrutiny from a Christian ethical viewpoint.

(a) The communist programme

Marx gave little detailed attention in his writings to the kind of society which would follow the proletarian revolution. The main sources are *The Communist Manifesto*[13] and the *Critique of the Gotha Programme*.[14] His lack of precision is related to his theory of history. The new society would *arise* out of the capitalist society by means of the revolution. So its form would be historically conditioned. He had no socialist utopian ideal, and tended to criticize those who had.

In the *Critique of the Gotha Programme* he saw two stages in the development of the society after the revolution. In the first stage the proletariat achieves power, and extends to all the workers the principles of the bourgeois society. The producers become the state and take control of the instruments of production. This stage was given the title of 'socialism' by Lenin.

Marx outlined in *The Communist Manifesto* ten regulations which would be characteristic of this first stage: they included abolition of property in land, a graduated income tax, abolition of inheritance, central control of financial institutions and the means of transport and communication, extension of State ownership of the means of production, and free education for children. A number of features of this list are noted by Avineri.[15] Nationalization of industry is not included as an immediate measure: the private sector will wither away in the socialist state without direct expropriation. The abolition of private property is not advocated. Marx himself criticized the advocacy of 'crude communism' by idealist socialists. In Marx's scheme the proletariat uses the power of the state for its own ends. The programme itself is not particularly revolutionary.

But for Marx this was merely a first step. He distinguished a 'higher phase of communist society' which would succeed it, and which was entitled 'communism' by Lenin. This phase is even less defined in his writings. However it is to be marked by a new consciousness in man, a new attitude to work, a new basis for production, and a new form of state. Man's relation to things will be creative rather than hedonistic. Work is not the evil which it appears in capitalism: it is part of being human. The creation of needs will simultaneously create the means to ensure their satisfaction. Work constantly unfolds the potentialities of the individual. Each person contributes in accordance with his abilities.

The precise form that productive activities will take in this phase is not spelt out. Marx relies on illustrations from agrarian societies, where rigid differentiation or social division of labour is less apparent. Nor is the role of planning clear, except insofar as cooperation between workers is necessary to achieve social objectives in the absence of a market mechanism. The State itself is to 'wither away', but not in the sense (due to Engels) of its total disappearance. Rather it is to cease to operate as a social institution divorced from the totality of economic life: universal suffrage will ensure that it remains responsive to the needs of the people and not separated from them. Finally, the 'communist' phase can only be reached when there is abundance in terms of material production. We might note that Lenin predicted that the Soviet Union would move into this second phase in about 1980!

Whatever Marx might have thought would follow the revolution, the reality in Eastern Europe has been somewhat different. The basic pattern was developed by Lenin and propagated by Russia in its East European satellites. There are variants, particularly outside the Soviet bloc. There are four basic elements involved:[16]

First, power in economic matters is concentrated in the Communist Party which seeks to promote the interests of the working classes. The party provides for continuity in economic policy, and makes the basic value judgments about the long-term objectives of society. Second, the means of production are socially owned, especially natural resources and capital equipment. This applies to agriculture, industry, banking, finance, distribution and foreign trade. Small private or individual sectors may survive, but their activities are severely curtailed. Third, market processes are replaced by, or supplemented by, economic planning. The macro-economic objectives are determined by the Communist Party. The economic planners operate to those objectives. Fourth, the system seeks a socially equitable distribution of the national income. There is no money income from property: earned incomes are based on the quantity and quality of work done. Private consumption is supplemented by a well-developed system of collective goods, provided by the State.

In principle, this system is designed to meet the objections to capitalism identified by Marx. The absence of a capitalist class, and the control of the State by the proletariat, remove the major source of class conflict. Since all capital is owned by the State on behalf of the proletariat the alienation of workers is partly removed. There is no longer a surplus that is appropriated by the bourgeoisie: the surplus is used by the State to further the interests of the workers. Such alienation as remains relates to the technology used in production, and possible antagonisms between a managerial class and the workers. Planning is intended to remove the uncertainties of the market economy, particularly avoiding the crisis of overproduction. Thus long-run security in income and employment is supposedly assured. Finally, the control of the distribution of income, together with abolition of property income and the plentiful provision of public goods, removes the threat of extreme poverty, and could prevent persistent disparities in income levels. Whether the system can actually deliver these social objectives, and at what cost in other areas, is something which we must discuss further below.

An alternative to the Soviet model, though still claiming to be 'socialist', is the Yugoslav system of worker-managed enterprises. Any group of workers may set up an enterprise, subject to no more legal restriction than applies to a public company in a capitalist economy. The enterprise is owned by the workers. Most firms of any size operate by means of a workers' council which has the responsibility of recruiting managers and other key personnel, and which approves an annual plan of operation for the enterprise. This plan approves in advance the rules for remuneration of the workers in the enterprise, the principle being that each worker is remunerated according to his work. The level of remuneration actually paid then depends on the success or otherwise of the enterprise. The plan also specifies the distribution of the firms' income to other objects— notably reserves, acquisition of new capital assets, and social or welfare expenditure, *e.g.* housing or sports facilities. Within the guidelines laid down by the workers' council, management has in practice considerable freedom of action.

The role of the State and the central Communist Party is much truncated under this system. 'Planning' is reduced to

determination of the over-all allocations to capital investment, social and personal consumption. The supply of
finance to enterprises is controlled by State banks, which in
principle can be used to guide investment decisions. The
provision of social goods, especially education, health, and
social insurance, is paid for by taxation on both enterprise
and personal incomes. Taken together with the collective
goods provided by the enterprises, the ratio of social consumption to personal consumption is much higher than in a
capitalist economy.

(b) The neo-Marxist socialist programme

Neo-Marxist analysis has also generated a socialist programme.[17] The power base for the execution of such a
programme is a democratically elected socialist party with
its origins in the trade union movement. Even Marx suggested that attainment of universal suffrage in Britain could
obviate the need for a revolution[18]. So the absence of a
revolution in Britain is not necessarily an embarrassment to
orthodox Marxists who wish to support the more gradual
transformation of capitalism envisaged in the neo-Marxist
programme.

The objectives of the programme are the nationalization
of a number of the largest companies in the manufacturing
sector, the extension of a limited version of planning to all
the largest firms and measures to reduce the inequalities of
wealth, particularly those accumulations arising from
inheritance. The logic behind the programme is straightforward. The largest firms, especially multinationals, have
not acted in the interests of society as a whole. They have
failed to invest in the face of uncertainty about the future;
they have closed down plant without regard to the effects
on workers; and they have taken state subsidies to maintain
payments to shareholders. They need therefore to be made
more accountable to their workforces and to society as a
whole.

The key is planning agreements between firms, the trade
unions, and the government. All large firms would be
involved in the exercise. They would prepare long-term
strategic plans for one to five years ahead. These plans

would specify investment and production plans with their employment consequences, especially those involving redundancies and/or regional effects. The plan would then be subject to negotiation with the government and trade unions involved to reach agreement.

Nationalization is essential to this strategy. First, it would be necessary for the state to control the banking and insurance sectors to give the state a financial lever to use against recalcitrant companies. Second, nationalization would be an ultimate sanction against a firm, especially a multinational, which failed to comply with the planning agreement procedure. Third, twenty to twenty-five firms would be taken into public ownership. This would give the state direct control of a substantial part of the manufacturing sector. These enterprises could exercise leadership within their sectors, and hence 'pull up' the investment of the remaining private firms. Fourth, a National Enterprise Board could operate to create new public enterprises in sectors where the private firms were failing to take profitable opportunities.

Lying behind the planning and nationalization strategy is a 'virtuous circle' theory of growth in the economy. The defect of capitalist enterprise is seen to be lack of investment, due to the capitalist phenomenon of falling profit rates identified by Marx. The difficulty is that each enterprise takes the current situation as given, and so is not prepared to respond. Suppose, however, that all firms *together* expand investment and production. The investment would improve productivity, enabling firms both to reduce prices (especially in export markets) and to increase wages. These in turn would generate the growth in demand to justify the initial expansion in capacity and output. So a cumulative process of growth could be generated. The 'Planning Agreements' could serve to initiate this process.

The system does not involve abandonment of the market in the allocation of resources. However it does seek to overcome a deficiency of information in the market system. Where the economy is dominated by a few large firms, the profitability of investment for one firm is critically dependent on the investment and production plans of other large firms. The planning system enables firms to assess prospects more accurately.

How would this system deal with the problems of worker alienation, which are a critical part of the neo-Marxist analysis? The solution lies in worker participation in the economic planning process, and in measures to reduce inequalities in wealth.

Worker participation in economic decision-making is envisaged at all levels. Within the firm, worker control of management is preferred to the appointment of worker directors. Worker directors would tend to undermine the bargaining power of workers, would bring class conflict into the boardroom, and could enhance the sense of alienation. Worker control, with a workers' council appointing and controlling the management, would avoid these difficulties.

Within the planning agreement system trade unions would have the power to influence the activities of large firms, particularly with regard to employment and redundancies. The trade unions are more likely to accept needed redundancies if there is a publicly-owned sector which is actively engaged in the provision of new employment on a regional basis, where it is most needed. Finally, the planning system would bring the trade unions into the processes of government in a more formal and detailed way, as they would be involved in the formation of national economic policy and its translation into plans for the major enterprises, and on a regional basis.

Measures to reduce inequality would include more progressive income taxation, taxation of wealth and inheritance, and reduction in the level of income from property and shareholding. The last would be achieved by limiting payments to shareholders as part of the planning agreements with companies. More provision for social consumption goods is also part of the programme for greater equality. The hope is that greater equality in wealth would undermine the basis of class, and hence the class antagonism. It would also, together with trade union involvement in industrial decision-making, reduce the militancy of the workers in making inflationary wage demands.

(c) The democratic socialist programme

The less avowedly Marxist analysis of the democratic
socialists is matched by a less radical socialist programme.
The emphasis shifts from the replacement of capitalism by a
socialist system, to a modified system which Crossman[19]
terms 'welfare capitalism'. The aim is to intervene in the
working of the capitalist system in order to improve its social
performance. The political basis for action is a democratic
socialist party which can draw support from all voters of
goodwill, not exclusively the working classes. The middle
classes are to be persuaded of the moral rightness of the
programme, even if some aspects are not entirely in their
interests. The socialist party will draw considerable support
from the trade unions, but it should not be dependent on
them.

Nationalization is regarded as a policy tool which is to be
used with caution. The case for public utilities is accepted.
But in other sectors the prevailing market form is seen to be
oligopoly[20] rather than monopoly. If anti-monopoly policy is
ineffective in these sectors, then 'competitive public ownership' of a part of the sector is a solution to maintain the
competitiveness of the private firms. It may be helpful to
have a state bank in competition with the private banking
sector. The emphasis in the public sector is to be on efficiency
and profitability. Long term the public sector should contribute to public resources: it should not become dependent
on subsidies. Within the firm the ideal is seen to be cooperation between all the workers in a common enterprise. There
is no dogmatic prescription as to how this might be achieved,
though industrial democracy is cautiously welcomed. The
hope of the neo-Marxists that nationalization will reduce the
sense of alienation on the part of the workers is dismissed.
Workers can be just as alienated by state capital as by private
capital.

Planning is also given cautious treatment.[21] 'Planning' is
already an internal feature of the large firms that operate in
different sectors of the economy. The question is whether
this 'planning' needs supplementation to improve the performance of the private sector. First, there may be sectors
where private enterprise is not willing or able to accept the

risks involved. This may be because of technological uncertainty: private finance is not likely to be available for very risky research and development. Or it may be related to extreme market uncertainty: if the market is subject to great fluctuations then private firms may be unable to maintain the level of capacity necessary to avoid supply constraints in the upswing of the trade cycle. Steel is sometimes thought to be such a sector. Second, there may be sectors where there is a definite divergence between the private and social costs. Planning processes can take into account social cost-benefit in assessing the proper levels of capacity and output.

Third, planning may be related to the perceived information defects of the capitalist system. Durbin describes planning as 'the extension of the size of the unit of management, and the consequent enlargement of the field surveyed when any economic decision is taken'. Pooling of information and forecasts between the major firms in a sector, under the aegis of government, could lead to better investment decisions. The institutional form that this type of planning could take is exemplified by the operation of the economic development committees for a number of sectors set up under the umbrella of the National Economic Development Council in the late 1960s. Interestingly, Crosland[22] suggested in 1952 that in Britain the advantages of such planning were well recognized, but that the major difficulty was the lack of political will to make such planning work.

The above analysis concentrates on the supply side of the economy. However the democratic socialists are also committed to Keynesian macro-economic policy intervention on the demand side to ensure full employment. The forecasting of the economy, and the adjustment of fiscal and monetary instruments to keep aggregate demand in line with productive capacity, is as much part of the planning process as intervention on the supply side of the economy.

The social democratic analysis emphasizes the social disharmony caused by great disparities in income and wealth, rather than absolute poverty, as the main reason for redistributive taxation. The aspect of class conflict is played down, except insofar as it is based on inequality. Apart from extensive provision for the economically disadvantaged— the old, the sick, the chronically unemployed, large families, or single-parent families— the main emphasis is on taxation. Unearned income is to be taxed heavily: Crosland[23] envisages a situation where the return to shareholders will be reduced by taxation to a level commensurate with. a 'fair' return on capital.[24] This is linked to the proposition that the 'surplus' above this level should be used to generate new investment rather than to swell the consumption of the rich. Presumably he has in mind an arrangement whereby the tax proceeds are diverted into productive investments via a state bank. Taxes on capital gains, capital transfers and wealth are also advocated, to supplement the taxation on inheritance. The intention is to reduce the accumulations of wealth in individual hands, and to prevent new accumulations. On the other hand, saving for retirement, via private superannuation schemes, is to be encouraged.

As in most socialist programmes, extensive provision of public goods such as education, health, and other amenities is seen as a redistributive device. It is also the basis for providing better life chances for the poorer sections of the community, particularly in education, which is seen as a major contributor to social mobility. On the other hand, Crosland[25] is concerned that equal opportunity should not merely provide a means for able children from the working class to escape into the middle class meritocracy, thus leaving the working class bereft of able leadership. But equal opportunity is seen by Crossman[26] as a tool for preventing the control of the state and the economy falling into the hands of a self-perpetuating class, arising from private schools and élite universities. Preservation of strict meritocratic methods of appointment to top jobs is to be preferred.

Finally, Crosland[27] is unwilling to countenance government intervention in the labour market, except in the most extreme inflationary circumstances. He admits the dangers of wage inflation and labour immobility in a full employment economy. But he argues that intervention would have to come to terms with the political fact of trade union autonomy and independence. He is not prepared to interfere with that: or at least he is not prepared to face the political consequences of trying to do so.

(d) The questions for ethical discussion

In the preceding paragraphs we have set out the socialist analysis of capitalism, and a description of a variety of socialist programmes. Our next task is to outline the major questions for ethical enquiry[28].

We have chosen for discussion six areas in which socialism has characteristic features. These are not mutually exclusive, nor are they intended to be exhaustive: but they do serve to distinguish socialism from the capitalist market economy of Chapter Four.

We begin with the role of the state. In all varieties of socialist analysis it is envisaged that the state will take an active part in the regulation of socio-economic life. Second, regulation is facilitated by social ownership of all or part of the means of production, with obvious implications for private property. Third, economic planning replaces or supplements the market in the allocation of resources. The main issue here is the efficiency or otherwise of the planning mechanism.

Fourth, the existence of social ownership and planning is often said to be inimical to freedom. We examine the truth or otherwise of this accusation, and assess the weight which should be ascribed to freedom. Fifth, socialist programmes are motivated by ideals for the nature of work in relation to human values. Finally, a tenet of all socialist programmes is a belief in social and economic 'equality'. In the rest of the chapter these six areas will be subjected to critical scrutiny on the basis of the biblical principles of Chapter Two.

4. The socialist state

We have already seen that the Marxist utopian ideal of the 'withering away' of the state is to be interpreted as a diminution of the alienation of the citizen from the state, rather than its disappearance. So for all practical socialist analysis the state remains as an active organizer. It is involved in the direction of economic activity, in 'ownership' of the means of production, in the provision of public goods and in measures to redistribute income and wealth. How should we evaluate this involvement?

First we note that a state cannot be rejected solely because it is powerful. Our concern must be with the content of the socialist programme and the means that the socialist state uses to achieve its ends. However that does not prevent us from being sceptical about the ability of powerful states to remain uncorrupted.[29] We ought not to be sanguine about a state which has cut itself off from any real political constraints in terms of responsibility and accountability to its citizens.

The tendency of the state to misuse its power has been used by Niebuhr[30] to argue for a 'democratic' system. In such a system, ideally, power is widely dispersed in order to prevent its misuse by the state for its own ends. 'Man's capacity for justice makes democracy possible: but man's inclination to injustice makes democracy necessary.' This is a deduction from biblical premises, but it has no direct biblical support: on the contrary, in the Bible all kinds of régimes are taken for granted, and are accepted as the 'ministers of God', so long as they attend to their God-appointed task. They cannot be rejected *a priori*. However we are right to prefer a democratic socialist solution to the communist one in practice.

Second, we must condemn any state that sets itself up as the sole arbiter of what is good in society, and aspires to the total commitment and loyalty of the citizens. This is true of the state in Russia and Eastern Europe where it is linked to an atheistic stance. The question then arises as to whether this is a necessary outcome of socialist principles, or whether a socialist state would be perfectly feasible without it.

The issue arises with respect to the objectives of economic planning. In our discussion of the biblical understanding of the political authorities in Chapter Two, we concluded that they exist in order to ensure justice. This involves encouraging, within a framework of law, those institutions which are most conducive to the ideals set out in the *Principles*. Second, it requires the authorities to react to *perceived* injustices in specific situations. Third, they should be ready to play an enabling role, by providing a focus and an institutional framework for responsible communal endeavour. This may, in the case of 'free-rider' problems, require an element of coercion.

Our criticism of a socialist state would be that it goes well beyond these biblical limits, by specifying a goal for society in terms of a particular distributive outcome, and by using the institutions of planning to ensure that this goal is achieved. It is to be condemned precisely because by doing this the state is putting itself in the place of God. Human justice should be partial and provisional, reacting to wrongs and putting them right: it should not try to achieve some abstract ideal.[31]

The *planning* of justice, with its idea of ensuring a particular future for a society, can be objected to on three grounds. First, it is an act of *hubris*, which attempts to substitute a human control of the destiny of man for the providential workings of God in history. It is precisely this sin which beset the builders of Babel, and for which judgment was visited upon them. They set out to make a name for themselves, and to secure their future. This point was discussed in section 3 of Chapter One.

Second, it requires that the citizens act in accordance with the plan. Even if they consent, it is hard to reconcile this with the idea of responsible stewardship given to each individual. And if, as seems likely, consent is not forthcoming, then coercion involving some kinds of sanction will be needed.

To avoid misunderstanding, we would emphasize that our objection is not to planning for the future as such, but to planning for a particular outcome in terms of distributive justice. For example, the authorities may react to a perceived injustice by making plans for particular institutional changes or other partial remedies which will help to prevent the injustice recurring in future. Thus if a problem of youth unemployment is found to be partly due to inadequate training in skills at school and further education, then there is no objection to planning to remedy this deficiency so as to prevent the problem recurring. Much of the planning envisaged by social democrats has these characteristics.

Our conclusion is that the totalitarian characteristics of

communist régimes are not unrelated to the attempt to plan for distributive justice. Nor is it surprising that the attempt to play a divine role in respect of the lives of its citizens brings the state into conflict with Christians, who are unable to give the state the worship that it demands. The same criticism can be brought against any neo-Marxist or social democratic programme which seeks to implement some abstract ideal of distributive justice. But in social democratic programmes this emphasis is much less prominent, with a pragmatic approach to rectifying injustices.

Finally, we might criticize socialist programmes for their class bias. Is this not a case of the state stepping down from its God-appointed role of promoter of justice for all groups in society to a much more partisan programme on behalf of sections of that society? It ceases to be a minister of God, and becomes merely the most powerful faction in a society which is formally 'anarchic', *i.e.* without the rule of God's law. However we must distinguish those situations in which the authorities favour a particular group or class because they *are* that group, and those in which the authorities act on behalf of a particular group because they would not otherwise be justly treated by society. An example of the first was Amin's blatant favouritism towards Muslims, and particularly members of his own tribe, in Uganda. An example of the second could be the treatment of widows and their dependants in Britain. In much socialist analysis these distinctions are blurred. Marx was moved by the exploitation of the workers that he observed in nineteenth-century capitalism, and that gave him the moral basis for his espousal of the working class. However in later socialist analysis the cause of the working class is championed simply because they are that class.

5. Property

Socialism is frequently criticized for its abrogation of the rights of property. *Principles 3* and *8* of Chapter Two are relevant here. *Principle 3* states that stewardship of resources and personal talents implies a responsibility to determine their disposition. Each person is accountable to God for his stewardship. *Principle 8* reminds us that personal stewardship does not imply the right to consume the entire product: the rich have an obligation to help those poor who cannot provide for themselves by work. In the previous chapter we drew attention to the distinction between this concept of stewardship and the Roman Law doctrine of private property which accepts accountability neither for the disposition of resources, nor for the use of the product of those resources.

Socialism clearly does interfere with the exercise of private property rights. Our concern is whether it also prevents the exercise of responsible stewardship in the biblical sense. We need to make distinctions between property rights in one's own person, property rights over consumer goods, and property rights over the means of production.

None of the socialist programmes envisages the abolition of the first two rights. The individual in a socialist system can normally decide what work he is going to do, what career he will pursue, and what goods he will buy, including such capital items as private houses. (It is true that more radical communist systems have been proposed, but these are outside the mainstream of socialist thought.) The range of consumption goods may be limited deliberately by the planning authorities who make no provision for some goods considered to be of low priority. But this is not necessarily any more restrictive than the range of goods offered by a capitalist system at the same stage of development.

It is in the area of property rights over the means of production that socialist systems are most distinctive. Some socialist programmes are more radical than others: the communist system does not permit private ownership of the means of production (though in practice this may be relaxed in some sectors, especially agriculture associated with small producers). The social democrats, at the other extreme, encourage a privately-owned productive sector, reserving social ownership for major public utilities and natural resources. However the scope of social ownership is not at issue here. The question is whether such ownership conflicts with responsible stewardship.

Within a socialist system individuals will continue to exercise stewardship responsibilities, *e.g.* in the control of a factory, in working a machine, or in tending a plot of land. They necessarily have to make a wide range of decisions, given that tasks and responsibilities within a productive system can only be assigned in a general form. Insofar as the staff and workers are concerned, there will be little difference in stewardship responsibilities between a factory located in a socialist system and that located in a capitalist society.

However, there *is* a difference at the level of the management of the firm. In a capitalist system the managers are able to decide the over-all direction of the firm, *e.g.* in which markets it will operate, and how its activities will develop. This freedom of action is restricted within a planned system. In effect the managers become agents of the planning board.[32] (How this operates is the subject of our next section, when we will discuss questions of efficiency.) The ideal is that stewardship is exercised *in principle* for others, to contribute to the well-being of the society.

But these arrangements may also effectively remove the stewardship responsibilities of the managers in respect of determining how resources are to be used. Much depends on how the 'instructions' are framed. At one extreme they could be very restrictive, detailing what is to be produced, how it is to be produced with particular inputs, labour and technology, and to whom it is to be sent. At the other extreme, one could imagine managers being instructed that society is interested in more than profit: it wants a safe and reliable product, produced under conditions which are fair to the workers, and with due regard to pollution or the use of natural resources. The first extreme is incompatible with the Christian concept of stewardship: the second is probably not. We need to consider in detail what precisely is involved in planning under the different socialist systems.

The discussion has avoided so far the fundamental questions about property. First, should the state *own* property? Second, under what conditions is it right for the state to abrogate the existing property rights of individuals in the means of production, *e.g.* by nationalization? These questions are in fact linked, and we will deal with them in turn.

The first question loses some of its polemical content if we rephrase it as follows. Is there any ethical objection to resources being allocated by planning, with stewardship being exercised by individuals in conformity with what the political authorities conceive to be the interests of society? We have already seen that this does raise ethical issues, but they are not issues about ownership *per se*. The rephrasing of the first question gives us a way into the second. We can now understand nationalization as removing the stewardship of certain resources from one set of stewards (the owners in a capitalist system) and entrusting those resources to a new set of stewards. Given the biblical emphasis on responsible stewardship we require strong reasons for abrogating an existing stewardship right and transferring it to someone else.

A number of possible reasons present themselves. Stewardship may not have been acquired by legitimate means, *e.g.* it was acquired by force. Stewardship is being exercised for purely selfish objectives, without regard to the detriment of others: the monopolization of a natural resource is an example. Stewardship may be incompetent: the individual is incapable because the resources are too large or too complex for his personal abilities. This case would be particularly strong in a situation where others are prevented from exercising stewardship by inadequate access to resources. A good example is afforded by land-owners in a number of Latin American countries who have shown their incapacity or unwillingness to use their land productively, and yet they exclude competent peasant farmers from access to land.

These reasons are those most frequently advanced by socialist writers to justify dispossession of existing property holders. However a general condemnation of all capitalist ownership under these heads is not justified. So, while we would not deny to the authorities the power to redistribute stewardship in particular circumstances, we would be cautious about accepting any general redistribution policy. We may well suspect that such a policy is motivated more by a desire to promote the interests of a new class against the old.

6. Planning

In the previous two sections, two fundamental biblical criticisms of socialist economic systems have emerged. First, we should reject any attempt by the political authorities to use economic planning to bring about some abstract ideal of distributive justice. Second, there is a danger that planning will destroy responsible stewardship. To evaluate these criticisms further we need to look at the scope of planning in different socialist systems.

It is convenient to explore at the same time the issue of the efficiency of planned systems, since a recurring theme in the criticism of socialism is that it generates waste and inefficiency. We saw in Chapter Three that the concept of efficiency in traditional economic analysis relies on utilitarian criteria which Christians would not wish to affirm. Efficiency is defined in the usual sense of *economic* efficiency, which is minimizing the use of resources to achieve given ends or objectives. The utilitarian definition sets no limits to human wants which require satisfaction. We might wish instead to consider the efficiency of an economic system in achieving rather different ends. Two examples may serve to illuminate this point.

In his work on famines, A. K. Sen[33] found that in a number of famine areas food was actually being shipped out of the area while the inhabitants were dying. The proximate cause of the famine was the inability of the poor to buy the food, because unemployment or underemployment or some other economic affliction had left them with insufficient means. In one sense the markets 'worked efficiently', moving foodstuffs from markets where effective demand was too small to areas where it was greater. But in terms of distributing food to those who needed it, it was clearly inefficient.

A second example is afforded by the experience of many visitors to socialist economies. They report adversely on the shortage of consumer goods, and the queues for them in the stores. However, their conclusions as to the 'inefficiency' of socialist systems are beside the point if in fact the shortages resulted from deliberate decisions taken by the planners. For example, the planners may have given low priority to consumer goods, and may regard rationing by queuing as more just than rationing by price, as a method of distributing the limited quantities. The same situation arose in Britain during the Second World War when resources were diverted to the war effort, reducing the supplies of goods to the consumer. It was an act of policy by the authorities which gave rise to the shortages. The 'efficiency' of the situation has to be evaluated in terms of the ends desired.

It is evident that a Christian should not be applying the same criterion for efficiency as is applied in economic analysis. The criterion of unlimited wants is contrary to biblical norms, which would lay stress on satisfying basic needs, and would not see an abundance of goods as contributing to human well-being. The concept of responsible stewardship *does* involve a requirement not to waste resources. But avoidance of waste does not require us to maximize the return from a particular resource regardless of other aspects. In particular we will wish to avoid any process which destroys or has some other irreversible effect on the natural order (*e.g.* atmospheric pollution).[34] Similarly, a 'technically efficient' system which treats the workers as less than fully responsible people is not acceptable to Christians.

The efficiency of planning was the subject of an intense technical debate in the economics literature of the mid 1930s.[35] The burden of the critics' argument was that a planned system lacked competitive markets in which prices could be set. Hence economic rationality was impossible, for there would be no independent valuation of different outputs. Hence, *a priori*, inefficiency was bound to result. Hayek[36] drew attention to the need for information in any planning system. Abandoning the price system implied a loss of information about the needs of society which could not be obtained by other means. He argued that the technical expertise required for planning a whole economy was unimaginable. The size of the problem in terms of the number of final and intermediate goods, and the production links between them, defied the calculating capacity of any group of planners. The problem was just too big to solve.

Lange[37] assumed the use of the price system for the distribution of consumer goods, and for making payments to labour. Intermediate goods were to be planned by the central planning board. He then showed that even in the absence of markets the planners could establish prices by a trial-and-error method. He particularly rejected the criticism that a planned system would require planning of each individual's work and consumption. The law of large numbers operates to give stable aggregates in consumption. Hence the planning board only needs to know the distribution of income, and average consumption patterns.

The debate of the 1930s gave rise to a substantial technical literature on the theory of planned economies, which has been stimulated by the experience of planning in socialist countries. Three models of the socialist economy have been developed:[38]

1. *The bureaucratic centralized model.* A central planning authority (CPA) is at the apex of a hierarchical system of planning and management. The plan specifies physical production targets by sectors which are then progressively broken down into sub-sectors and finally plant production targets. The internal consistency of a plan is determined by the method of material balances, *i.e.* by summing all the requirements for an intermediate good, and then adjusting the targets for the supplying sector. The planning proceeds by a process of iteration until a consistent plan is found. It may be that no detailed plan is feasible, in which case the sectoral targets have to be adjusted. For example, a plan for construction could require more cement than the cement sector was capable of supplying within the plan period. Final goods are allocated to consumers by a mixture of prices, rationing, and rationing-by-queuing. This system suffers from its information needs. In the USSR some 20,000 commodities are included in the central plan. Beyond this, detailed instructions have to be given to each plant about its production targets, and its sources of inputs.

2. *'Planometric centralist' models.* The economy is viewed as a huge input-output model, with flows between sectors

calculated on the basis of the technology in use. The model is solved on a computer, enabling the calculation of an optimal plan given the objectives fed in. Constraints on the system can be built into the model. The computer can also calculate implicit prices for inputs and outputs, which are given .to plants in place of physical targets. Each plant then has to meet financial targets calculated in terms of the plan prices. These prices need not be the same as the consumer prices, which may be adjusted to bring demand into line with the planned supply.

3. *Selectively decentralized model.* The computation involved in planometric models requires a very powerful computing facility. In the absence of such a facility, a rather less sophisticated planning system can be evolved. This involves the setting of provisional prices, the reporting back by the plants of their production intentions given those prices, the scrutiny of the replies for inconsistencies between sectors, and the consequent adjustment of prices until a solution is found. The system may even be extended to investment by specifying a rate of interest or profit on the installation of new equipment, and adjusting the rate to bring intended investment into line with the supply capacity of the capital goods sector.

Within these three options we may distinguish two types of decentralization. The first is information decentralization, in terms both of information flowing from the central planning authority to the firms, and vice versa. More information incurs three disadvantages: (a) errors in transmission; (b) errors in computation; (c) deliberate misinformation, *e.g.* the firm provides false information about itself to the CPA in an attempt to reduce the production targets determined for it. These disadvantages are all reduced as one moves from the bureaucratic physical planning model to the decentralized model, though the latter does not eliminate the possibility of deliberate misinformation.

The second aspect is the decentralization of decisions. The matter can be illustrated by consideration of the principal–agent 'problem'.[39] The principal (in this case the CPA) is seeking to ensure that the behaviour of the agents (in this case the managers of plants) accords with the plan. There are three solutions. In the first the principal gives the agent detailed instructions as to how he is to act. In the second, the principal lays down guidelines as to how the agent is to act, but leaves the detailed decisions to the agent. In the third, the agent is given performance indicators by which he will be judged (and to which incentives may be attached). It is then up to him to take decisions.

What determines the choice between these models of principal–agent relations? The interests of the principal and the agent will diverge, not least because the principal only has to *say* what he wants, while the agent has to exert himself to achieve those objectives. The agent thus will trade off the objectives for a bit less effort. This would appear to indicate that the first relationship — that of detailed instructions to the agent— will be the most advantageous. However two considerations militate against this. The first is the question of information and monitoring. The principal has to convey more information to the agent, and he has to know a great deal about the capacity of the agent. The activity of the agent will have to be monitored closely to see if he is obeying instructions. Given that information giving and receiving is costly (time-consuming), this is a reason for adopting the method of performance indicators linked to incentives.

A further consideration is the location of blame if things go wrong. If the agent is given detailed instructions, and performance is unsatisfactory, it is difficult in an uncertain world to know whether the instructions were at fault, or the conditions were unfavourable, or the agent did not make sufficient effort. The agent has no incentive to exert himself, as he can always shift the blame. If, on the other hand, the agent is evaluated solely on the basis of the performance indicators, he can be held responsible for failures. Applying this analysis to alternative relationships between the planning board and the firm, both decentralized information and decentralized decision-taking are likely to be favoured.

The principal–agent framework is also useful for understanding the question of incentives. All socialist systems have in practice retained the pattern of incentives found in market economies for workers below the level of management. Positive economic incentives are represented by wages, bonuses, and promotion prospects. Negative economic incentives are the threat of dismissal and the possible reduction in earnings. So the problem of incentives has to be located at the level of management.

The principal–agent theory predicts that a physical planning system will find it difficult to ensure that plant managers are efficient. This difficulty led the USSR to adopt the Liberman proposals in 1965.[40] Liberman emphasized the need to provide managerial performance criteria. The criterion chosen was profit, defined as revenue minus costs of production, where the prices of outputs and inputs are determined by the CPA and not by the enterprise. Incentives were then attached to profit performance. A more radical decentralization would involve enterprises financing themselves by loans from state banks, and thus being able to determine their own size. Prices would remain determined by the CPA.[41]

What determines the allocations made by the CPA as between sectors? In practice, planning boards have shown marked preferences for capital accumulation rather than consumption, and within consumption, for social goods rather than private ones. Typically 20%–30% of national output is allocated to capital accumulation, with priority given to the means of production. Up to 30% of total consumption is directed to social consumption goods— child care, education, provision for the elderly, housing, public transport. The effect of these priorities has been a restriction on the quantities of private consumption goods available, which has led to shortages and rationing. However there has been a trend for socialist planners to pay more attention to consumer demand in response to popular discontent.

This role of the CPA was criticized by Hayek.[42] In the absence of an ethical consensus concerning such allocations, it would be impossible to get anyone to agree on the criteria for the division between current and future consumption, and between private and social consumption. Hence, according to Hayek, planning cannot be 'democratic', and truly reflect the wishes of the people. Even in its own terms this criticism is curious, since democracy does not necessarily demand that *everyone* agrees to a particular course of action.

To complete our discussion we consider planning as a supplement to the market system rather than as a substitute for it. The Yugoslav system, and planning agreements, were described above. Unfortunately there is no substantive evidence as to the efficiency of such systems. The Yugoslav experiment has been the subject of considerable debate in the economics literature. It is an interesting case as it enables comparisons between different régimes of economic organization: full capitalism, central planning, limited sectoral planning, and market economy with labour-managed firms. Unfortunately it is not easy to disentangle the effects of organization from other factors affecting economic performance. The 'planning agreements' system has not been put into practice, though there is some experience of indicative planning in France.

The purpose of planning to supplement the market system was succinctly described by Durbin[43] as an 'extension of the size of the unit of management and the consequent enlargement of the field surveyed when any economic decision is taken'. This principle is unobjectionable: but it avoids the question of how the decisions should be taken. One objection is that a 'bunch of civil servants' would not be capable of running a complex industry. This represents two separate objections. One is that it would be impossible to find civil servants with the skills required, which is absurd. The second is that the control mechanism and informational complexity would render the whole effort inefficient. This returns us to the problems of control and information that we have discussed above.

Some indication of the difficulties of creating control mechanisms can be gleaned from the experience of the UK nationalized industries. The 1967 White Paper[44] on the control of the nationalized industries tried to specify economic criteria by which management were to make decisions. The aim was to enable the managers to act independently, without constant recourse to the sponsoring ministry in Whitehall. A study in 1974[45] showed that this objective had not been attained. The economic criteria were not operationally effective, and successive governments had interfered with the decision-taking process. The assessment of the system was also made more complicated by the fact that several nationalized industries, notably coal, steel, and the railways, faced structural problems arising from excess capacity. Management problems were exacerbated by the strong trade unions existing in these sectors, and by the clear political impact of some decisions, *e.g.* pit closures and redundancies. On the other hand a number of nationalized industries with growing markets, especially gas, electricity, and telecommunications, had an enviable record of productivity growth in the 1960s.

The 1978 White Paper[46] recognized the difficulties of the previous system. It abandoned the attempt to set criteria for decisions that would include social costs and benefits, as opposed to financial criteria. It provided for political assessment of the consequences of the corporate plan for each industry. The provisions of this White Paper have been overtaken, in practice, by the programme of privatization initiated by the Conservative administration in 1981.

Having completed our review of the different types of economic planning, we now return to the questions we asked at the beginning of the section. In terms of the traditional concepts of economic efficiency, the performance of planned economies compares unfavourably with that of free market economies. They have grown slowly both in aggregate and in income per capita. Nor can their apparently more equal income distribution provide a compensating feature, since the distribution of goods depends as much on having contacts as on having the income to purchase goods. Nor do the planned economies have a better record on pollution and environmental protection.

The experience of state enterprises in the market economies has not been encouraging for those who believe that a socialist enterprise can be more effective than a private one. Financial losses, overmanning and low productivity, and poor consumer service in both price and quality are some of the more common criticisms.[47] Part of the perceived poor performance can be attributed to circumstances. Thus political interference to keep prices down, or to prevent the closure of uneconomic operations in politically sensitive regions, can explain some of the financial losses.[48] Difficult trading situations prior to nationalization have also been a problem in some industries. However, having made allowance for all these circumstances, there is still a question mark over the performance of state enterprises in general.

One reason for the inferior economic performance of planned economies may be the difficulties, outlined above, of providing managers with both a plan and sufficient incentive to carry it out. This relates to whether responsible stewardship is a possibility within a planned economy. Our discussion of the principal–agent problem indicates that there will be gains from providing a structure which gives managers a greater degree of responsibility. Highly centralized planning mechanisms are not only likely to restrict the exercise of responsible stewardship, but also are likely to be ineffective.

Our final question concerns the role of planning in ensuring the future in respect of some predetermined ideal of social justice, including distributive justice. Such a concept does lie at the root of much central economic planning in communist countries. Ideological priorities are determined by the communist party, and this has profound effects on the allocation of resources. On biblical grounds it should be firmly rejected. However, that ought not to lead us to condemn all activity which involves non-market or planned allocations of resources by the authorities. This can be a way of enabling activities which the community desires, and for which market provision is deficient. No utopian dreams of social engineering need be involved. The provision of general economic infrastructure, and welfare undertakings such as health and education, are examples. But the basis for social provision rather than private provision should be that it is more effective in meeting a perceived need, rather than any ideological commitment to state provision as part of a wider programme of achieving an ideal society.

This is much closer to the social democratic conception of socialism than to a communist or neo-Marxist programme. If it is agreed that social provision of a particular good is to be undertaken, then our analysis of the principal–agent problem suggests that decentralization of decision-taking is likely to be more effective than a close central control. That accords with our preference, on biblical grounds, for economic institutions which increase the scope for men to act responsibly.

7. Freedom

F. A. von Hayek's *The Road to Serfdom*,[49] published in 1944, has been one of the most influential critiques of socialism. In that book and his subsequent writings, Hayek has argued the case that freedom can only survive in a free market economy, and that socialism is *per se* inimical to it. This theme was restated by Milton Friedman,[50] and has become central to the modern critique of socialism. The biblical concept of freedom was discussed in section 3 of Chapter Two. The stress is on giving man space to act as a responsible steward. The freedom to act in the disposition of resources is balanced by an equal insistence on duties and obligations to others. The liberal concept of freedom was discussed in the last chapter; its deficiency is its insistence on rights without an equal stress on obligation. In a world of sinful men, the danger is selfish pursuit of personal objectives to the detriment of others. For the Christian freedom is not, and cannot be, an end in itself.

For many people the question, 'Does socialism restrict freedom?', has an obvious answer. The dramatic warnings of Solzhenitsyn,[51] and the experience of communist régimes in various parts of the world, serve as a grim reminder of the capacity of socialist régimes to oppress their people, especially if they are members of dissident minorities. However, that experience is not unique to totalitarian régimes of the Left. It has been the experience of fascist régimes in Europe, military régimes in Latin America, and of the majority of Islamic states. The first two have been associated with capitalist economic organization, though with varying degrees of state intervention in the market. Totalitarian régimes are by no means unique to socialism. However that does not exclude the possibility that socialism may be particularly conducive to such régimes.

This point is argued forcefully by Hayek.[52] The goals of

socialism are ideals of social justice, equality and security. These are to be sought by the creation of a planned economy (or in democratic socialism, by the creation of a substantial planned sector in the economy). So planning is not just rational decision-taking: it is the setting down of a plan for controlled social change. Since no complete ethical code is available, and since individual views of what should be done are likely to coincide in only a limited degree, democratic planning becomes impossible. Planning is delegated to experts, who have discretion to choose both the goals and the means of achieving them.

Hayek disposes of the defence of planning which argues that it applies to only part of life, which if implemented successfully would leave men free for higher things. He argues that there is no separate 'economic motive'. People are motivated by a desire for general opportunity, and by the desire for power to achieve unspecified ends. Almost all choices do involve economics in that the means are provided by our fellow men. So planning *would* impinge upon the range of possibilities. For example, the planner can restrict the range of choice of different consumer goods. He can control occupational choice by fixing qualifications and remuneration for each kind of work. The appearance of choice would be deceptive because there would be no scope for the individual to branch out on his own, to 'prove himself'.

Furthermore, as Friedman has pointed out, a socialist régime gives little scope for dissenters to obtain a hearing. There will be few wealthy patrons who can espouse a cause. Even if dissidents can raise the money, they may be unable to get their literature printed or purchase space in the media. Finally, since the only source of employment is the state, the planners dispose of a particularly powerful sanction against dissent.

What Hayek has shown is that government in a socialist planned economy has the potential to be totalitarian, but this is far from establishing that it has to be. The planning mechanism does affect the allocation of resources between different sectors of the economy, but it need not impinge on individual choices in consumption, work and leisure. In practice, there are few socialist systems which have attempted to influence such choices.

A similar response can be made to Hayek's point that a less privileged position for an individual in society is easier to accept when it is the result of chance, than when it is the outcome of the determination of some planning authority. Hayek extols the virtues of a system in which the authorities announce the 'rules of the game' beforehand, enabling each individual to order his life in the light of those rules, without *ad hominem* action by the authorities. But in practice, no socialist planning mechanism has ever determined the pattern of life of individuals, and there is a good reason (lack of information) why it should not do so.

However, the fact is that communist régimes are in practice totalitarian. The persecution of dissident individuals and religious believers is the norm rather than the exception. The reason is that the planning mechanism is being used to pursue political ideals. Planning, like terror, can be a tool of totalitarianism: it gives extensive powers to the authorities in determining the shape and future of society. A government which begins with the best of motives can quickly become a tyranny seeking its own ends if the means are available to it.

It is that ugly possibility which Hayek places before us and advises us to avoid. While we do not share Hayek's concept of economic freedom, it is evident that a biblical concept of responsible stewardship is also at risk from a totalitarian planned economy. We would be wise therefore to heed his warnings.

8. Work

In Chapter Two we outlined three biblical principles for man and his work (*Principles 4* to *6*). Man has a right and an obligation to work, which is the primary means of exercising responsible stewardship. Work is a social activity in which men should cooperate as stewards of their individual talents, and as joint stewards of the resources they use.

Various socialist ideals concerning work closely mirror these Christian precepts. For example, the socialist ideal for work is that it should be a good to be enjoyed by every person according to his ability. The alienation arising from the divorce of capital and labour, and the concept of competition, is to be replaced in socialism by an ideal of cooperation. The objectives of work should be controlled by the workers themselves, or at least determined in their interests, rather than by the bourgeoisie pursuing their own interests. However it is debatable whether these ideals are in practice attained more fully in socialist than in capitalist systems.

Such evidence as exists on centrally planned economies suggests that they have been reasonably effective at maintaining high levels of employment. Individual freedom of choice of occupation and of place of work is now followed in all Eastern European socialist countries, though membership of the Communist Party implies willingness to be directed. Communist governments have however resorted to direction of labour during periods of crisis, for example in China during the Cultural Revolution. In theory the weapon of unemployment to ensure discipline is replaced by a disciplinary code administered by the trade unions, as an arm of the Communist Party.

The hope that socialist production would reduce alienation and induce a new attitude to work has proved singularly disappointing. The alienation of workers in capitalism is matched by an equal alienation in the 'state capitalism' of centrally planned economies, and of nationalized industries in social democratic systems. The alienation arises partly from a divorce between workers and professional management, and partly from the direction of the enterprise by a bureaucratic planning authority. The response has been an increasing reliance on material incentives, perhaps linked to enterprise performance, where the socialist ideal would be reliance on the moral incentive of working for the common good.

The basic defect of such a system is that it does not provide conditions under which workers can operate as responsible stewards. They need to be able to participate in decision-making on issues concerning their work and future livelihood. The Yugoslav experiment in workers' management merits careful consideration in this respect. The operation of such firms has been described by Vanek.[53] The enterprise is formed and owned by a group of workers. A workers' council within the firm recruits managers and key personnel, and approves the enterprise plan. This plan specifies the distribution of the firm's income between personal incomes, welfare (social consumption), capital and reserves. Personal remuneration is based on predetermined rules, the values being related to the success of the enterprise.

Vanek reached the following conclusions about the actual behaviour of such enterprises. The short-run behaviour of the firm is directed to cost-cutting, with prices based on costs. Survival and growth of the enterprise are the long-run objectives. Adjustment to changed business conditions, and the search for growing markets, are the major content of the annual plans. There is an emphasis on accumulation of assets which are related to the welfare of the enterprise, not just for production, but also for collective consumption.

Management is important in the provision of enterprise and initiative. Successful management is not frustrated by the workers' council. The trend is to workers' involvement by representation on the council, rather than general referenda or meetings of workers, especially in large firms. Income differentials within such firms seldom exceed the ratio 3:1, though differences *between* enterprises can be as large as 7:1, since remuneration depends on the success of the enterprise. The enterprises have proved well suited to expanding markets, but firms with declining markets have been reluctant to release workers (they cannot be dismissed). The lack of an active labour market makes it difficult to transfer resources. There is a substantial literature which suggests that the Yugoslav system is inefficient in the allocation of resources. However, Vanek rejects this conclusion on the grounds that the objectives assumed in such models cannot capture the reality of the Yugoslav firms.

A degree of worker participation in the management of firms has also formed part of the programmes espoused by the neo-Marxists, and by some social democrats. It was given added impetus by the publication of the Bullock Report.[54]

There is however a subtle difference of emphasis between the workers' *control* espoused by neo-Marxists for the operations of state enterprises (to match worker involvement in the planning process), and the less radical concept of worker participation or 'industrial democracy' of social democrats, including the Bullock Report.

Evidence on worker participation has been summarized by Wall and Lischeron.[55] They look at three aspects: the demand for participation, the effect of participation on worker satisfaction, and employee response to worker participation schemes. It emerges that there is strong desire among workers for participation in decisions affecting the immediate work environment of the individual. The evidence is scanty on desire for 'distant' participation: generally there is no demand for worker control though some involvement in higher decision-making would be welcome. A difficulty with this evidence is that workers may have very little idea as to what distant participation would involve, and find it difficult to express views on the subject.

Wall and Lischeron are cautious about accepting the conclusions of empirical studies that participation in immediate decisions has improved worker satisfaction. For example studies that depend on turnover rates and absenteeism are not measuring satisfaction *per se*, and such indicators can reflect other factors in the situation which are difficult to allow for in the analysis. The same is true for experimental studies which show higher productivity. On more distant participation, the evidence from Israel and West Germany is unambiguous that employee response to the opportunity for influencing company policy has been minimal. The schemes have been imposed by legislation and are not always well suited to the conditions of a particular enterprise. Worker directors have proved to be ineffectual, and this has been perceived by the workers themselves.

Three points are stressed. First, workers prefer a system in which the responsibility of control is shared by workers and managers rather than worker control *per se*. Within that system, control should be biased towards workers at the immediate level and towards managers at the strategic level. Second, worker participation should be direct, and not via an intermediary body such as a trade union. Third, participation must be taken in conjunction with other variables such as the degree of trust and openness between the personalities involved in decisions, the problem-solving strategies adopted, the means of resolving role conflicts and the communications within the enterprise. A formal participation scheme without progress in these other areas may increase worker frustration and alienation, not reduce it.

To conclude, socialist ideals for work are close to the biblical principles outlined in Chapter Two. The analysis of socialist experience illustrates the difficulties of putting these ideals into practice.

9. Inequality

The existence of material inequality has been a pivot in the moral criticism of capitalism in socialist writings; achieving greater equality has been an important objective of socialist programmes. Our biblical principles 7 and 8, on the other hand, do not speak of equality as an ideal. Instead they affirm a man's right to a minimum basic standard of life, those basic needs to be met primarily through useful work, and place an obligation on the rich to help the poor who are unable to provide for themselves. Stewardship of resources does not imply the right to consume the entire product of those resources.

A number of these biblical themes find a precise parallel in socialist ideals. Indeed, the Judaeo-Christian intellectual inheritance is almost certainly the source. Socialists have emphasized the need to eradicate absolute poverty, the state in which men do not have the minimum conditions for human existence. They have drawn attention to the need for equal opportunity, for each person to have adequate conditions for exercising their abilities. They have denied that those who have great resources also have the right to consume the proceeds of those resources, regardless of the condition of their fellow men. They have extolled the ideal of a classless society as 'one in which men will be separated from each other less sharply by variations in wealth and origin,

than by differences in character'.[56] The biblical assertion
that a man's life does not consist in the abundance of his
possessions is mirrored by Marx's criticism of commodity
fetishism, and his dream of a society where goods will be so
abundant that man will no longer be dominated by the need
to produce. He will be creative rather than hedonistic.

It remains to be seen whether socialist programmes have
been a means to achieve these ideals. There have been three
relevant elements in socialist programmes. The first is the
reduction, or abolition, of property incomes. In communist
societies with all the means of production socially owned, the
surplus after paying the workers returns to the state (or
planning board) to be re-invested or to be used in socialized
consumption (welfare programmes, *etc.*). Depending on the
degree of centralization in the planning process, this allocation may be determined centrally or even at the firm level (in
the Yugoslav system).

In those socialist societies where an extensive privately-
owned sector still exists, the aim has been to restrict the
accumulation of large wealth-holdings by taxes on capital
and especially on inheritance. Now there is nothing in biblical teaching that requires us to deny to individuals the
stewardship of great resources, so long as they exercise that
stewardship fruitfully and unselfishly. Thus a socialist programme aimed at property cannot be justified without the
presumption that large accumulations of wealth will not be
wisely administered.

The ideal of equal opportunity is that each individual
should have equal chances of developing his own abilities,
and that access to all positions of responsibility should be
based on capacity to undertake them. Questions of class or
family background, or of family wealth, should not enter
into determining a person's education or work responsibilities.

The means of achieving these objectives are mainly the
educational system. A positive step is the provision of education as a public good; more radical measures include the
banning of private education, by means of which the rich can
obtain privileged facilities for their offspring. In addition,
appointments to positions of responsibility are to be made on

the basis of open competitions with the selection criteria made public. A further step would be 'positive discrimination' in appointments in favour of applicants from backgrounds where they have had difficulty in developing their talents. Within the framework of equal opportunity it is admitted that differential rewards may remain great, given that individuals have very different gifts. The difficulty with all this, as Crosland[57] shrewdly observed, is that it results in the creation of a meritocratic élite which is just as keen to protect its own class interests as the capitalists and property owners. It was this 'new class' that Milovan Djilas castigated in the development of communist societies.

The third element concerns social consumption goods. A range of goods and services is provided free, on the basis of need, rather than by purchase. Examples are medical care, education, legal advice, housing, public transport and recreation and entertainment. Access to certain minimum facilities is given on an equal basis to each member of the society. When linked with cash benefits (*e.g.* to families, unemployed persons, the retired and the chronically sick) these form a major step to the provision of a minimum standard of life for all citizens.

There is no doubt that this is consistent with the biblical provisions in the Law for the poor and disadvantaged. Naturally these goods and services have to be paid for, and the source varies from diversion of enterprise surpluses (in communist countries) to taxes on income and profits in socialist mixed economies. Programmes of this kind are always subject to a risk of waste, and of fraudulent claims in respect of financial benefits. However the existence of such difficulties should not surprise us. But they cannot be put forward as a reason for abandoning such programmes, given reasonable safeguards in administration. The needs of the many should not be ignored because of the dishonesty of the few.

Finally, we should stress again that the biblical criteria are addressed to the question of redressing inequality, especially poverty. There is no concept of economic equality as an objective. Each person should have access to resources so that he can exercise his stewardship and provide for himself.

The provision of a 'safety net' to maintain each person at a minimum level is secondary within this system. For example, the primary emphasis in the Law is on every family having access to land. The provisions for wage labour, and for the poor to share in the harvest, are secondary. A Christian will find more to support in programmes that provide employment and access to resources, than in those that are seeking economic equality in consumption by redistributive taxation and transfer payments, essential though these may be as a safety net.

10. Conclusions

In the previous sections we have examined six areas in which socialism has distinctive features — the role of the state, public ownership of productive assets, planning to replace or supplement markets, restrictions on economic freedom, the organization of work and policies to promote equality. Each has been evaluated in the light of the biblical principles derived in Chapter Two.

It is not easy to draw general conclusions, not least because of the diversity within socialism. This diversity is most significant in respect of the role of the political authorities. In the communist system, the state is seen as the instrument for achieving ideals of social justice in the future, exercising its power through the planning mechanism. In social democratic systems on the other hand, the authorities see their role as creating a framework within which independent firms and other economic institutions can act responsibly, as providing a focus for communal endeavour which would otherwise fail for lack of organization or participation, and as reacting to perceived injustices that the system may throw up. We may conclude that a communist system is definitely incompatible with biblical criteria, but that a social democratic system need not be.

A particular focus of our analysis was whether or not a planned system gave sufficient scope for the exercise of individual stewardship responsibilities, in the sense of determining the disposition of resources. Socialist analysis has helped us to see that the market system is not the only way by which resources may be allocated, nor is it necessarily the most effective. The examples of health, education and the church come immediately to mind in this respect. However, the danger of planned allocations, particularly as part of some comprehensive economic planning strategy, is that personal stewardship responsibility is effectively destroyed by the need to conform closely to instructions received. In practice, we suggested, the difficulties inherent in such detailed planning mean that even within a centrally planned economy individual managers will have considerable discretion. Naturally the scope for individual responsible action will be much greater in those systems which do not attempt detailed central planning for activities at the level of individual enterprises and institutions. We need to scrutinize carefully the form that 'planning' takes in different socialist systems. The more restrictive it is, the less it accords with the biblical notions of stewardship.

Our biblical principles cover two further areas— man and his work, and the distribution of income. In respect of the former, we found that socialist ideals were close to our biblical principles, in that work is viewed as a cooperative activity in which men exercise control over, and have responsibility for, the resources they use. Institutional arrangements which give the workers control over their firms, as in the Yugoslav experiment, are particularly good in this respect. But we also noted that in practice these ideals are seldom realized, partly because of the stifling effect of the planning system.

In respect of income distribution, we distinguished the socialist ideals of equality from the more limited biblical principles of access to resources for productive work for all men to provide for basic needs, and the obligation on the rich to help the poor. The question is whether a socialist system is seeking to establish some abstract ideal of distributive justice, or whether it is seeking those institutional arrangements which are conducive to avoiding poverty and relieving its worst effects where it occurs. On this criterion we may be reasonably content with some social democratic systems, but sharply critical of more utopian systems such as communism.

CHAPTER SIX
Macroeconomic policy

1. Macroeconomic analysis

The previous two chapters have been largely concerned with microeconomic issues, in particular the economic behaviour of the various actors in the economy—firms, households, and factor market institutions such as trade unions and financial intermediaries—given the pattern of incentives and controls that are provided by market capitalist economies and by socialist planned economies. The focus has been on an evaluation of these two systems in terms of the biblical criteria developed in Chapter Two.

Macroeconomic analysis makes the assumption that particular groups of economic actors can be treated analytically *as if* they all acted in the same way. Thus all firms are aggregated into the production sector, all households into the household sector, all financial institutions into the financial sector, and the different activities of government into the government sector.

This is by no means a straightforward procedure. First, the underlying analytic conditions which must hold for aggregation are very demanding.[1] Suppose, for example, that we are considering the consumption and saving responses of households to increased income. Then the aggregate response will only be a satisfactory '*as if*' constant if the responses of the individual households are identical, whatever their level of income. Alternatively, the assumption has to be made that the statistical aggregate gives consistent responses even if it is inadequate to reflect the behaviour of individual households.

Second, there is the question of what are the appropriate weights to use in aggregating the output of the economy.[2] The obvious weights are values derived from prices. But market prices may be distorted by indirect taxation, may not reflect the social value of the output, and will change over time. Since much of macroeconomic analysis is concerned with comparing performance in the economy over time these problems are not trivial. But without aggregation macroeconomic analysis would be impossible.

The advantage of aggregation is that it permits attention to be focused on the links between sectors, and on the behaviour of the economy as a whole. Households supply resources, especially labour and financial capital, to firms, and receive wages and profits. Households use part of their income to buy the goods that firms have made. Another part of the income is saved in the financial sector. Firms borrow from the financial sector to finance their capital investment. The government enters the picture by levying taxes, and through its own expenditures. The system can be extended to an open economy by incorporating exports and imports of goods and services and international flows of money capital. The total stock of money (defined as cash in the hands of the non-bank public, and demand deposits at the commercial banks)[3] is an important variable in the system.

The complete system is used to determine changes in the level of national income in the short and long term, the rate of wage and price inflation, the behaviour of the exchange rate for foreign currencies, and employment and unemployment. A change in government policies (such as a tax change) or other changes outside the system (such as the growth of overseas markets or an oil price shock) can be traced through the model to estimate the effects on these variables, the choice of which presumably reflects underlying value judgments as to their economic and political importance. We will consider the question of the evaluation of macroeconomic objectives in the next section and ask whether they are consistent with the biblical principles of Chapter Two.

Section 3 discusses various technical issues. The development of macroeconomic theory and policy has been closely related to the development of the discipline of econometrics. First, there is the identification of relationships between macroeconomic aggregates, such as the determinants of the demand for money or the determinants of the demand for new capital goods by the production sector. The search is for relationships which are sufficiently stable over time to give confidence that underlying causal mechanisms are being satisfactorily modelled. The second aspect is the quantification of these relationships: it is not difficult to predict that an increase in income will generate an increase in consumption. But that is of little help if we wish to identify the effects of, for example, a reduction in income tax. Will a one percentage point reduction in the income tax rate increase consumption by 0.2 or 0.7 percentage points, and how quickly will that change take effect?

The third aspect is the development of large-scale computer models[4] of the whole economy that can be used to simulate the response of the system to changes in government policies. These consist of a complex system of equations which models the behaviour of various sectors, including quantitative responses to changes in economic variables. The accuracy of these predictions depends critically on whether the underlying economic theory is correct (do firms really behave in this way?) and whether the quantitative estimates are correct (will a 1% drop in interest rates increase business fixed investment by ½% or 4%, and how quickly will this increase occur?).

Section 4 describes schools of thought about macroeconomic policy. Different schools are to be distinguished not only by disagreements on technical issues, but also by their visions as to the kind of society which would be desirable. The focus returns to the evaluation of the different economic systems of Chapters Four and Five.

2. Evaluating macroeconomic performance and policy

Not *all* the traditional objectives of macroeconomic policy—full employment, price stability, stable exchange rates and growth in both the short and long term— can be justified within the utilitarian framework usually adopted in normative analysis. Our task is to look at these objectives from the standpoint of the biblical *Principles* set out in Chapter Two.

That everyone should have opportunities for work is clearly consistent with *Principle 4*: man has the obligation and the right to work. However this does not mean that any work is acceptable however it is organized. No doubt full employment could be ensured by a system of slavery. So we should qualify the work objective by reference to principles concerning the nature of work. We also need to recognize that not all work needs to be paid employment or self-employment. Remunerated work is, of course, the first defence against poverty for families (see *Principle 7*), and that needs to be a feature of any satisfactory economic system. But there is much work done for which no remuneration is paid—parents looking after young children, housework, do-it-yourself, gardening, voluntary work in the community. From the biblical viewpoint this is just as much work as forms of employment, and is accorded the same 'status' of requiring the exercise of responsible stewardship. Just because someone is unemployed does not mean that they are not working, or that they should not be expected to use their time productively. How this might be organized is another question.[5]

The objective of full employment is linked in the textbook analysis to the desire to maximize the level of national income. If some resources are unemployed, then real output is being lost, and the community is not as well off as it might otherwise be. This is a straightforwardly utilitarian objective, and we might be tempted to reject it for the reasons explained in Chapter Three. In a rich economy where the citizens are well provided for, our biblical principles would give no weight to increasing national income to increase consumption. But in a poor economy, where incomes are insufficient to provide for basic human necessities, there is much in favour of policies which will provide necessities by raising basic incomes.

Precisely the same distinction applies to a consideration of the growth of economies via capital accumulation and productivity growth. Whether growth is an acceptable objective will depend on the circumstances of the economy under consideration. This will be further discussed in Chapter Eight, where we will consider the argument that growth is essential for social and political stability. But for the moment we make the provisional judgment that the maximizing of national income over time is not a major Christian priority unless there are other elements involved, like the reduction of unemployment or the relieving of poverty.

A third objective of macroeconomic policy is price stability, or the absence of inflation. Textbook analysis has some difficulties in explaining why this should be given such prominence. If inflation is no more than a change in the nominal prices of goods, with all relative (or real) prices remaining unchanged, then as Friedman[6] has pointed out, the only social costs are those of creating the additional money stock required for a higher price level. Neither printing bank notes nor increasing bank credit is a costly process in terms of real resources, and one wonders why this should be regarded as a serious social detriment. However, the argument runs, the unpredictable effects of inflation on prices are more serious. Relative price changes, which should motivate shifts in resources in a market economy, are masked by much larger shifts in absolute price levels. Those who lend and borrow money are uncertain about the real returns and costs. This uncertainty reduces saving and investment below the levels which would prevail in a more stable environment. (There is, incidentally, very little hard evidence to substantiate these alleged effects of inflation.[7])

A more 'apocalyptic' concern about inflation is that, if uncontrolled, it may lead to a loss of confidence in money as a medium of exchange, with a subsequent flight from money into goods, and an eventual collapse of the market economy. The Weimar Republic, and the experience of hyperinflation in Latin American economies, are often cited as examples of the disastrous consequences of unchecked inflation.[8] If we discount this extreme scenario and concentrate on the problem of the more moderate inflation levels experienced by most advanced Western economies over the past fifteen years, then the *efficiency* effects of inflation are probably quite small.

There are, however, considerations with more moral teeth: that inflation redistributes income from the weak to the strong and that inflation involves theft. The two aspects are not unrelated.[9] Consider first the issuing of new paper money by the authorities. If a new paper note is issued by the authorities they are able to obtain goods and services to an equivalent *real* value: however subsequent inflation induced by issuing new paper money (so the story goes) devalues the purchasing power of that note. Furthermore all other holders of government debt will suffer similar losses on their holdings due to inflation. The action of the authorities is 'theft', because those who are holding government liabilities (such as paper money and bonds) are deprived of a part of the real value of those holdings.

This is a correct description of the outcome if there is an element of deception; that is, if those who hold government liabilities have no idea that paper money is being issued or that the consequence will be inflation. If they *are* aware of these matters, then no deception is involved: they do not have to accept government contracts, nor do they have to hold government bonds. In practice, if they tender for contracts, they will adjust the terms under which they are willing to supply. So, too, holders of bonds will expect higher nominal interest rates to compensate for inflation. Holders of paper money will economize on those holdings to the point where the positive *convenience* of holding cash just compensates for the inflation-induced losses.

Similar arguments apply to contracts between citizens, which are also supposed to have redistributive effects. Thus any contracts for lending and borrowing which are fixed in nominal terms (*e.g.* deposits and loans by building societies) effectively make lenders worse off and borrowers better off during the periods of inflation. Of course, if this is well understood by both parties, then the problem can be avoided, either by adjusting the nominal interest rate, or by index-linking the contracts, thus maintaining their real values.

We conclude that it is *unexpected* inflation which can have redistributional effects. Fully anticipated inflation cannot. An oddity about the moral argument is that it is often deployed by monetarists against inflationary actions by governments.[10] But as we will see in the next section, it is modern monetarist theory which claims that inflation as a result of government monetary policy is fully anticipated. Hence monetary policy has no real effects on the economy, and the monetarist moral argument against inflation thereby collapses.

Evidence on the redistributive effects of inflation is generally insubstantial. However there is some evidence which suggests that recipients of social welfare benefits may be particularly affected.[11] First the uprating of benefits tends to lag behind the rise in prices. Second, even where benefits are uprated in line with inflation, the movements of the retail price index may underestimate the rise in the prices of those goods and services which are important in the household budgets of low income groups.

The fourth objective of macroeconomic policy can be stated alternately as either a stable external value for the currency (under flexible exchange rates), or as long-run equilibrium in the balance of payments (under fixed exchange rates). It is not immediately obvious why such technical conditions should constitute an objective of policy; it may be best to view them as intermediate objectives, necessary conditions for achieving other ends. For example, under the fixed exchange rate régime of Bretton Woods, which lasted until the early 1970s, an economy which reflated in order to reduce unemployment often found itself constrained by a balance of payments deficit which its reserves could only sustain for a short while. It then had a choice: either to stop the reflation or to devalue its currency. Devaluation was frowned upon by the international financial community, and was thought to be unpopular with voters. Hence governments generally put reflationary policies into reverse as a balance of payments 'crisis' appeared.

Under flexible exchange rates, the case for a stable value of the currency relates to the effects of volatility.[12] A fall in the exchange rate provides incentives for exporters and import-competing industries, but also raises domestic costs of imported goods and materials. An appreciation brings down costs, but is a disincentive to domestic producers. The problem with *volatility* is that while currency markets adjust very quickly, the shifting of resources in and out of export activity, for example, is necessarily much slower. An exporter can sign what looks to be a profitable export contract, only to find that currency changes lead to losses. While it is possible to make forward contracts in foreign exchange markets to reduce exposure to such risks, the transactions costs may be high. Our conclusion is that the balance of payments or exchange rates are rightly understood as 'constraints' on the conduct of macroeconomic policy, rather than as 'objectives' in themselves. Their evaluation requires no ethical criteria.

Whatever our evaluation of the objectives, we need to consider the prior question as to whether the concept of macroeconomic policy is valid on biblical criteria. The mere existence of the government in an advanced economy will have extensive macroeconomic effects. Even those libertarians who will only admit a minimal state recognize that the behaviour of the state in taxing and spending is not entirely neutral.[13] Furthermore, there is general agreement that the government has to oversee the operations of the central bank in the issue of new paper money, and in the regulation of credit markets. Only Hayek has argued that this is unnecessary, and should be left to private enterprise.

It is one thing to accept that the government has responsibilities which have consequences for economic performance: it is quite another to suggest that the government should use the leverage which it thereby obtains in an attempt to direct the future course of the macroeconomy. It is this second aspect which has motivated macroeconomic policy-making in the post-war period. Leaving until the next section the *technical* question as to whether an economy can be controlled in this way, we need to discern whether such a policy is, in principle, acceptable.

The debate on this issue is an extension of the discussion in the previous chapter on the role of the government in planning. The case against is that it represents an attempt to control the future, and thus substitutes human agency for divine providence. While it would be possible to try to use macroeconomic policy in this way, it is probably more appropriate to evaluate it as a rather less powerful instrument of policy. If it is a fact that market economies are subject to instability (which is disputed, as we shall see in the next section), then macroeconomic policy could have a dual role.

The first role is to create a more stable economic and financial environment, making it easier for economic actors to exercise responsible stewardship. This is on a par with the creation of an appropriate legal framework. But the analogy is *not* exact, because to create stability it will be necessary for the authorities to make forecasts of the future course of the economy, and to make discretionary adjustments to policy instruments. The second role involves the authorities in reacting to instability and the perceived injustices which result. For example, suppose that widespread unemployment emerges in the economy, and the cause is traced to deficient aggregate demand (again a diagnosis which is hotly disputed in the technical literature), then the use of macroeconomic policy to overcome the deficiency in demand could be the authorities' response to a perceived injustice. Our conclusion is that these two roles for macroeconomic policy are consistent with the biblical view of the responsibilities of the authorities as set out in Chapter Two.

There are two further ethical issues to be discussed briefly here. A feature of recent developments in the economies of Western Europe has been a steady increase in the share of the public sector in national income and output.[14] The reasons for this are complex. A part is due to governments taking on wider responsibilities for the public provision of services. Another element is that public services themselves have become increasingly complex and expensive: the provision of health services is a case in point. A third element is the growth in the number of unemployed and retired people with subsequent demands on the social security system.

The objections voiced to this growth in the public sector are that it takes away from individuals the responsibility to provide for themselves and their familes, and that it can only be financed if taxation is at such a level that the incentives to act as responsible stewards of talents and resources in the private sector are impaired. This objection can be countered in two ways. The first is that responsible stewardship of resources *can* be as much a feature of public sector as private sector operations, as we saw in Chapter Five. Compare, for example, the roles of head teachers in private schools and state schools. While the latter could be made subject to such rigid control that they had no room to act responsibly, the analysis of the principal–agent problem suggests that this is unlikely to happen. Second, at least part of the public sector reflects the authorities performing an enabling role as a focus and institutional framework for responsible com-munal endeavour. The citizens may prefer public provision of schools, health services and social security, financed from taxes, to a haphazard and unequal provision by private markets, private insurance or private charity.

Even if these two counter-arguments are accepted, the objection does raise valid concerns about a large public sector in a mixed economy. There needs to be constant review to ensure that particular programmes are providing an effec-tive framework for responsible communal endeavour. There is always the danger either that they will become instruments of social engineering, or that they will become highly politicized vote-winners. Governments are seldom totally disinterested parties in public expenditure pro-grammes.

A final ethical issue concerns the financing of the opera-tions of the authorities. The particular question is whether a state should aim to meet all its expenditures from taxation, or whether a budget deficit is acceptable. The focus here is on deficits *per se* and not on their macroeconomic con-sequences. A government deficit can, in principle, be finan-ced in one of two ways: by printing money, or by issuing bonds. Issuing bonds essentially requires future taxation to pay the interest and eventually to repay the principal in the bonds. Taxation is deferred, but not avoided. Given that at least part of government expenditure is in investment activities which will generate wealth and a higher national income stream in future, the bond financing option appears not only acceptable, but even desirable. Those who will benefit in future also pay for the investment, rather than calling upon current tax-payers.

Financing a deficit by printing money raises different issues. Although money has the appearance of a government liability ('The Bank of England promises to pay the bearer on demand the sum of . . .'), once issued a bank note simply becomes part of the money stock. If it is right for the authorities to take control of the supply of money as part of their task of creating the financial environment for a mixed economy, then there is no objection to financing deficits by issuing money, so long as this is done responsibly. It is the standard method for increasing the money stock according to the needs of the economy. Of course, if it is done irresponsibly it can have adverse effects, such as unanticipated inflation. We conclude that there are no valid moral objections to government deficits in themselves.

3. Technical issues in macroeconomic analysis

Before we look at schools of thought in macroeconomic policy, we need to recognize that part of the divergence of views which we will outline arises from genuine disagreements over how the macroeconomy operates. There is no consensus on either the causes of unemployment and inflation, or the effects of fiscal and monetary policy. These disagreements reflect much more fundamental divergences on the correct framework for analysing the macroeconomy. As explained in Chapter Three, appeals to the evidence are not decisive where competing frameworks or paradigms are involved. Each paradigm believes that the facts can be shown to be consistent with its own interpretation of how the economy works. In what follows we will make no attempt to explain the full subtlety of these disagreements, let alone resolve them.

We begin with the problem of unemployment. The level of unemployment is the product of two factors: the flow of new people into unemployment (either because they have left their jobs or because they have reached working age, but there is no job to go to), and the average length of time that a person remains unemployed. For example, in an economy where workers change jobs very frequently, and take a short break between jobs, the unemployment rate would be high, but it would scarcely be regarded as a problem. However if a high level of unemployment reflects people being out of work for a long time, then there is likely to be greater public concern.

The key element in the unemployment rates of the Western economies in the last twenty years, and in particular in Britain,[15] has been the growth of long-term unemployment, with individuals being out of work for periods of time measured in years rather than weeks or months. This long-term unemployment is concentrated on young workers, on manual workers with few skills, on workers in the older industrial and manufacturing centres, and on members of ethnic minorities, and has been the major concern of policy-makers.

The major disagreement about the causes of long-term unemployment is between those who see the main problem on the supply side of the economy, and those who point to a failure of aggregate demand.[16] Supply side analyses emphasize four factors.[17] The first is the level of labour costs relative to the value of output. Labour costs can rise in a number of direct and indirect ways. The most obvious direct route is an increase in real wages obtained by trade union bargaining. Minimum wage legislation in non-unionized sectors can have the same effect. Employment taxes, to finance social security programmes, represent another element in the cost of employing labour. Costs are indirectly increased by the presence of restrictive practices in the labour force, by employment protection legislation and by equal opportunities legislation. For example, if employment protection makes it difficult to lay off labour, then the implicit cost of hiring an additional worker is higher, and firms will be cautious about expanding their labour force.

A second factor is the slow growth of output per worker. If productivity is growing fast, then higher direct and indirect labour costs can be paid for out of the greater output. But if productivity growth is low, then the outcome is higher prices, lower sales and output and hence probably less employment. Why productivity growth should have been relatively low in the 1970s is something of a puzzle.[18] One explanation is that the relatively depressed state of the world economy led firms to cut back on physical investment, and on research and development expenditures for innovation.

The preceding argument is often stood on its head in popular analysis of the effects of technical progress. The fear is that technical progress will destroy jobs, as machines displace workers. While sudden technical advance may indeed lead to a rapid reduction in the workforce in particular sectors, a consideration of the long-term evidence is more reassuring. The past forty years have seen unprecedented technical advances, yet unemployment has only recently emerged as a serious issue. The explanation is simple. Technical advance can result in the same labour force producing a great deal more output, or in a reduced labour force producing the same output as before. Until the last ten years the former was the case, with the result that real incomes grew. So an explanation must be sought as to why recent experience has been different.

A third factor is structural changes in the world economy. The last twenty-five years have seen a relaxation of barriers to world trade, both tariffs and non-tariff barriers. They have also seen the growth of industrial production in many Third World countries, particularly in the newly industrializing countries such as Taiwan, Korea and Singapore. We will consider these developments further in Chapter Seven. The liberalizing of trade has meant that some sectors within an economy have had to contract, while others have grown, in response to comparative advantage in different sectors. This is not necessarily a smooth process, and gives rise to the 'adjustment problem'. For example, if an advanced industrial economy finds its steel industry under pressure, steel workers will be laid off. The compensating growth may come in a completely different sector, for example, computing software. Given that the skills from one industry do not match with the other, unemployment in the traditional industries is likely to be persistent.

A fourth factor advanced to explain unemployment is more controversial. The argument is that the registered unemployed include a significant number who have no intention of working, even were jobs available.[19] The reason given is that the level of benefits available to the unemployed is sufficiently generous that they have no incentive to take a job. The problem is made worse by the existence of a 'poverty trap' at low income levels. Working a bit harder, or getting a slightly better job, makes little difference to income, because as income rises so entitlement to social security benefits is reduced. So there may be little incentive to the unemployed to get a first job, hoping to use that as a springboard for something better.

The alternative explanation for unemployment is that associated with Keynesian economic analysis.[20] The simplest form of the argument is that when aggregate demand is not growing, then firms are reluctant to take on labour as they can see no prospect of making a profit. They are also reluctant to invest. The Keynesian multiplier theory points to the second-round consequences of these decisions by firms. The unemployed have low incomes, hence their consumption will be lower than it would be if they were employed, and so aggregate demand will be lower. There is an element of self-fulfilment in the expectations of firms. If they expect low demand, then demand does indeed turn out low because of their own actions. If on the other hand they are optimistic, then demand will grow as a result of their investment and employment decisions.

The textbook analysis of Keynesian models saw the problem as the outcome of special features of macro-economic markets, such as inflexible wages, insensitivity of fixed investment to interest rate changes, and 'sticky' interest rates in bond markets ('the liquidity trap'). The more recent re-interpretation of Keynes has concentrated on problems that arise from the decentralized nature of the price system.[21] Prices may be 'wrong' for the system to attain full employment equilibrium, but there may be no incentives for economic actors to adjust those prices, because their own expectations are fulfilled at the 'wrong' prices. Furthermore, a decentralized market economy has a particular difficulty in getting the right amount of investment for future outputs, in the absence of future markets. Suppose, for example, that consumers start to save more, with a view to consuming more later. Firms receive a signal that current demand for consumer goods has gone down. They do not receive any direct signal that future output demanded will be greater. At best, they may infer this from evidence on higher savings. But they may doubt whether demand for their particular product will be higher in future.

Unfortunately it is very difficult to distinguish these different explanations of unemployment empirically, since there is little agreement as to what is an appropriate method. This difficulty is all the more disconcerting in that we need to know the cause before we can prescribe the cure. Thus supply side causes indicate policies to get the labour market to work more effectively. Reducing the powers of trade unions, cutting the costs of employment (such as pay roll taxes) and reducing social security benefits for the unemployed make up an appropriate, if painful, strategy. Measures to increase training and retraining in appropriate skills are also emphasized. A Keynesian policy, on the other hand, sees the problem as arising basically from inadequate aggregate demand. This was the rationale for macro-economic policy in the 1950s and 1960s, which involved the authorities manipulating demand by changes in their own expenditures and by changes in taxation. Confidence that the government would keep demand growing became an important part of the economic environment within which firms took their decisions about employment and investment.

The analysis of inflation generates an equally diverse set of views as to its causes. The monetarists, who correspond to the group with a supply side analysis of unemployment, see inflation as the outcome of budget deficits leading to expansion of the money stock.[22] The labour market is in equilibrium at a real wage determined by the supply and demand for labour. Any measured unemployment is due to the supply side imperfections previously discussed. Given those imperfections, the labour market settles at a 'natural rate of unemployment'. The outcome in the labour market determines not only employment, but also the level of national output, at the 'natural rate'.

Suppose now that the authorities expand the money supply at a faster rate. In the older monetarist story, this could have a temporary effect on output and employment, as prices are bid up for output, but wages lag behind. Eventually, however, wages catch up, and employment and output fall back to the natural rate. The whole of the increase in the rate of growth of the money supply is translated into inflation.

Recent developments in macroeconomics, the so-called New Classical economics, have taken the argument further. If workers can perceive what is happening to the money supply, they will base their expectations of the price level on those perceptions and wages will be adjusted up immediately. As there is no lag in adjustment, so there can be no effects on employment and output.[23]

The concept of 'rational expectations' is central to this interpretation.[24] Suppose an economic actor, in this case a worker, has to make an estimate of future price inflation. One naïve estimate would be to presume that current inflation rates will continue. A slightly less naïve method would involve looking at recent inflation trends and extrapolating. But the really intelligent thing to do would be to predict the economic situation by applying the 'true' economic model. The New Classical model makes the assumption that workers do just that. Hence any expansion of monetary demand is translated directly into wage and price increases. Workers cannot be blamed for inflation: they merely aim to keep their wages in line with a rising price level.

This analysis has to be modified for the case of an open economy with flexible exchange rates: monetary expansion in the domestic economy leads to a depreciation of the currency in foreign exchange markets. The domestic prices of traded goods rise, and the prices of non-traded goods and wages move into line. The mechanism is slightly different, but the final message is exactly the same.

A Keynesian interpretation of inflation would differ from the monetarist and New Classical view in two respects. First, it would argue that expansion of aggregate monetary demand could result not only in a higher inflation rate but also in some fairly persistent gains in real output. Second, Keynesians see a role for cost–push pressures in wage setting. Some of these come from trade unions pushing for wage increases which exceed productivity growth. Some, such as commodity price increases, are external to the economy, particularly the effect of large increases in oil prices engineered twice by OPEC in the 1970s. These pressures on costs and prices are subsequently 'validated' by governments which expand aggregate monetary demand in order to avoid a deficiency in real demand. The causation is therefore precisely the reverse of that assumed by the monetarists.

The contrast between monetarist and Keynesian analyses of inflation carries forward into their analysis of the effectiveness of monetary and fiscal policy. Keynesians believe that such a policy, if used judiciously, does have effects on real demand, output and employment, though they accept that any attempt to expand the economy too fast will result in inflation. Monetarists, on the other hand, believe that fiscal policy cannot affect real output, and that monetary policy only affects the price level. Their view of fiscal policy is that a deficit financed by issuing debt will be matched by an equal and opposite increase in savings by the private sector in order to finance the *future* tax liabilities implied by issuing debt.[25] Even if this did not happen, any increase in demand by the public sector can at best 'crowd out' private consumption, since total aggregate supply is fixed at the 'natural rate' of output.

While in principle these differences of view over the workings of the macroeconomy should be resolved by appeals to the evidence, in practice this has proved extremely difficult. The reason is that a macroeconomy is an extremely complex system, where many things are happening more or less simultaneously, and causal mechanisms can only be imperfectly observed.

4. Schools of thought in macroeconomic policy

We can distinguish at least five schools of opinion in respect of macroeconomic policy. At the risk of some caricature they can be ranked from the political Right to the political Left, and linked up with the analysis of Chapters Four and Five. At the extreme Right, the libertarian view is that macro-economic policy is a delusion and a snare. If one shares Hayek's view of the economy as a spontaneous order,[26] then attempts to control its outcomes over time are misguided. Governments cannot, in principle, achieve control: if they try, they are likely to make matters worse by introducing instability. Not even the money supply should be a concern of the authorities.

The next three schools are, in order, monetarism, moderate Keynesianism and ultra-Keynesianism. Monetarism corresponds to market capitalism without the libertarian ideology. Moderate Keynesianism is the position taken by social democrats. Ultra-Keynesianism is closer to the neo-Marxist analysis of the economy. These three will be described in more detail below. The final 'school' is the equivalent of the fully planned economy. This follows the libertarian view in dispensing with macroeconomic policy, but for a completely different reason. Given that the economy is planned at the microeconomic level, macroeconomic policy is irrelevant.

In considering programmes for macroeconomic policy, we have in mind the problems of unemployment and inflation which have characterized the Western economies in the past fifteen years. Macroeconomic policy has developed very much in response to these problems. As the problems change, so we would expect the policy prescriptions to vary. But the underlying philosophy of policy in each of the programmes is likely to be maintained.

(a) Moderate Keynesianism

The intellectual origin of Keynesianism is J. M. Keynes' work *The General Theory of Employment, Interest and Money*, published in 1936. There is still a great deal of disagreement about the correct interpretation of this seminal work, with an influential group of commentators arguing that Keynesianism as it developed in the 1950s and 1960s was a perversion of Keynes' original contribution.[27]

The Keynesian position can be summed up in the sentence: *markets work but they need help*. Keynesians accept that the operations of private enterprise in markets are an efficient method of allocating society's scarce resources. However, two imperfections require action. First, many industrial markets are dominated by large oligopolistic firms, which confront monopolistic trade unions in labour markets. The outcome is all kinds of rigidities and inflexibilities, so that the economic system is slow to react to shocks and stimuli. Prices and wages are not very flexible and outputs adjust slowly. The second imperfection is that a capitalist economy is not good at allocating resources over time, because of lack of information. Investment and savings decisions taken on the basis of private information are inadequate, because firms and persons can only operate on the basis of their 'expectations' (hunches, guesses) about the future state of the economy. Because of these imperfections, judicious intervention by the authorities is necessary, not to replace markets, but to help them out.

That intervention involves two elements. First, the regulation of aggregate demand by fiscal and monetary policy. Fiscal policy involves the tax and expenditure decisions of the government. A reduction in income tax, for example, will stimulate consumer expenditure, and the government can add to demand directly by its own expenditure on goods and services. Monetary policy seeks to influence the spending behaviour of households and the investment of firms, by affecting the terms under which they can obtain credit. The objective is to keep aggregate demand growing smoothly at the same rate as the underlying growth in productive potential of the economy, and to avoid booms and slumps. This has a threefold effect: it prevents the emergence of unemployment; it provides a stable environment in which business has the confidence to invest; and it helps to stabilize the external balance and the exchange rate by ensuring that the economy does not consume more than it produces.

For a long time, Keynesians also thought that fiscal policy and monetary policy were sufficient to deal with the problem of inflation. Their argument was based on an empirical 'trade-off' between the rate of wage inflation and the level of unemployment. Less demand in the economy would lead to a reduction in the output of firms, which in turn would lay off workers. The growth of unemployment would lead workers to accept lower wage settlements. Firms' costs, and hence prices, would grow more slowly and the inflation rate would fall. In the late 1960s however it was thought that this mechanism had broken down, and there was therefore more interest in direct intervention in the labour market by means of an incomes policy.

For Keynesians, the problems of the 1980s are seen to be the outcome of the instability of the world capitalist system. The first shock was the breakdown of the Bretton Woods system of fixed international exchange rates in the early 1970s. A second was the oil price rise from 1974 onwards, which created severe balance of payments problems for most of the Western economies. A third was the attempt by Western governments to solve this problem by cutting aggregate demand at home. The effect was a fall in aggregate demand and a downward revision by businessmen of their expectations, leading to a cut in investment. The result was a downward spiral of output and employment into the worst recession since the 1930s.

The Keynesian policy prescription[28] would be for gentle expansion of aggregate demand via tax cuts and public expenditure to give business sufficient confidence about future demand to stimulate investment and new employment. However, it is dubious whether this could be achieved in one country alone. Any expansion would be likely to generate a rapid growth of imports and hence a deterioration in the balance of payments. The best solution would be for all the Western economies to reflate simultaneously, thus reviving world trade and world demand. Insofar as reflation brought about a renewal of inflationary pressures, the Keynesian prescription would involve incomes policy (preferably a permanent institution) to curb the power of trade unions seeking excessive wage settlements. A vigorous anti-monopoly policy would also encourage competition and keep prices down.

An important part of moderate Keynesian prescriptions is that fiscal policy should be aimed at reducing the level of unemployment.[29] For example, public expenditure in labour-intensive programmes such as construction and urban renewal will be more effective in reducing unemployment than tax cuts which give the same budget deficit. Tax cuts tend to benefit those in work, and the better off, who are more likely to save an increment of their disposable income, or spend it on imported goods. Fiscal policy may also be used to improve the chances of employment for the unemployed. The labour costs of firms can be reduced by reductions in taxes on employment (payroll taxes, social security contributions). Marginal employment subsidies for new employees drawn from the pool of long-term unemployed are also advocated.

Moderate Keynesians are committed to the welfare state. Their analysis of the market economy includes the observation that people may, through no fault of their own, be unable to earn sufficient to maintain a reasonable standard of life. Unemployment, prolonged illness and old age may be the cause of poverty. So moderate Keynesians would seek to provide a safety net of cash benefits and other benefits in kind (such as medical care), paid for by progressive taxation on the better off.

(b) Monetarism

The fundamental proposition of monetarism is that *markets work best if they are left unhindered and uncontrolled*. Problems arise when governments attempt to intervene, or when markets are monopolized. The policy implications are best seen in contrast with Keynesianism.

First, employment and output are determined both in the long run and in the short run by the individual decisions of entrepreneurs, workers and consumers. Hence attempts by the authorities to influence the level of aggregate demand are doomed to failure. Fiscal policy has no demand effects since government expenditure 'crowds out' private sector activities without increasing output or employment. Monetary policy has no lasting real effect. In an open economy an expansionary monetary policy spills over immediately into greater demand for imports. The exchange rate depreciates and the prices of all traded goods (which are determined in world markets, not domestic markets) adjust by the full amount of the devaluation. Indeed people may come to understand this process so well that they will make it the basis for their expectations of price changes and adjust prices directly. The result is domestic inflation.

The policy outline would therefore be simple.[30] Government involvement in the economy would be reduced to the minimum and confined to goods and services that are genuinely public (such as national defence, which could scarcely be provided by private markets). These would be financed by taxes that would interfere as little as possible with the functioning of private markets. A fixed rate for the expansion of money and bank credit would be determined so that the money supply increased no faster than was required by the growth in the output of goods and services in the economy. Preferably control of the money supply would be removed from government, since governments are tempted to finance expenditure by monetary expansion, rather than by the less popular means of raising taxes. Finally, a vigorous anti-monopoly policy directed as much at trade unions as at firms would be pursued.

It is pertinent to ask how monetarists explain high unemployment levels. They argue[31] that this is mainly the consequence of factors increasing the 'natural rate' of unemployment, such as the level of social security benefits available to the unemployed, taxes on employment to finance these benefits, the existence of monopolistic trade unions in labour markets, the implementation of minimum wage laws, and extensive legislation giving rights to workers. Their policy prescription is to deal radically with all these factors, increasing the incentives for the unemployed to look for work (cutting unemployment benefits), decreasing the costs to firms of taking on workers (cutting payroll taxes and reducing workers' rights) and reducing the power and privileges of trade unions.

Some monetarists will also point to the long period of

inflation experienced in the 1970s as a causal factor in unemployment. This inflation built up inflationary expectations among workers. Time is needed for more 'realistic' attitudes to be established in wage bargaining and this was hindered by the trade unions. It also takes time for private initiative to move into the gaps left by the reduction in public activity, though this will occur in the long run. In the meantime, some unemployment of resources is regrettable, but inevitable.

(c) Ultra-Keynesianism

The ultra-Keynesian school is convinced that private markets are incapable of solving macroeconomic problems. *Markets do not work without a great deal of help*, and in many circumstances it may be better to replace them with alternative mechanisms for resource allocation. Markets should be retained only as servants of the allocative process, not as masters of it.

This ultra-Keynesian position shares with Keynesians the analysis of the fundamental defects of the capitalist system. Inflexible product markets dominated by large firms, and the lack of information to guide investments, are the problems. But the proposed solutions are more radical. Growth needs to be 'planned', with the authorities taking a view on which sectors are to be developed. The 'instruments' of planning include the nationalization of industries (with coordinated investment planning in the whole of the public sector), planning agreements with large private sector corporations to make them more responsive to national needs, and control of the financial sector to direct resources to investment in particular sectors.

With this foundation for long-run growth, the authorities should use fiscal and monetary policy in Keynesian fashion to maintain full employment. Any balance of payments problems would be dealt with by import controls as well as devaluation. Inflation is put down to external cost–push factors (*e.g.* the oil price rise), and to the pricing policies of big firms, rather than to trade unions. Workers are thought to seek a target real wage growth in line with the long-run growth of productivity, and cannot therefore be blamed for inflationary pressures.

The policy prescription for the Western economies is focused particularly on unemployment.[32] The problem is perceived to be deficient demand, as in the Great Depression. The solution is to expand aggregate demand by a mixture of tax cuts and increased government expenditure on social goods such as health and education. A flood of imports would be avoided by import restrictions, so that demand would be directed towards domestic producers. Employment and productivity would both rise in the boom, enabling the real wage aspirations of the workers to be met without causing a wage explosion. A strong emphasis would be put on policies to promote new industrial development. These would include investment programmes for public sector firms, planning agreements with major private firms, and the creation of a state investment bank.

5. Assessing the alternatives

Evaluating the alternative macroeconomic policy prescriptions outlined in the previous section is difficult. There are three elements involved: technical issues as to how the economy functions, priorities with respect to achieving goals in respect of employment and inflation, and long-term vision as to the appropriate ordering of the economic system. We look at these in turn.

Section 3 has outlined some of the disagreements on technical issues with respect to the genesis of inflation and unemployment, and the effectiveness of monetary and fiscal policy. Unfortunately, for the reasons outlined in Chapter Three, a resolution of these disagreements by means of empirical research is not forthcoming.

One possibility is that there may be no definite answer, however good the analytic tools. For example, the behaviour of economic actors can change in response to changed circumstances. A part of those circumstances could be the very economic analysis that is attempting to elucidate the situation. For example, trade union negotiators have probably changed their bargaining behaviour in the light of better information about the effects of exchange rate changes on future inflation rates, and about the effects of tax changes on take-home pay.

More fundamentally, behaviour can be affected by the nature of the economic system which the authorities are seeking to promote. The investment behaviour of the private sector is likely to be quite different under monetarist and ultra-Keynesian policy régimes. In the monetarist economy the entrepreneur has to utilize private information. In the ultra-Keynesian economy, information is available about investment plans for the public sector and large private sector firms. The task of the entrepreneur is to sift this information to establish the significance for his own business. He may also be under pressure in the form of exhortations from the state investment bank.

It is possible to argue that all three policy options would work eventually, if they could be implemented given technical and political constraints. The 'eventually' indicates that the time path for any one objective, such as increasing employment, could differ markedly from one policy to another. Thus a monetarist programme gives a priority to tackling inflation and to supply side policies. The expectation is that these will create a climate of business confidence, and that economic growth and falling unemployment will follow. Keynesian and ultra-Keynesian programmes give priority to job creation, and are not so concerned about reductions in inflation. Keynesians propose to deal with inflation by incomes policies; ultra-Keynesians believe that expansion of the economy will bring its own solution to the inflation problem.

Given our evaluation of objectives in section 2, we might be tempted to conclude that on ethical grounds a Keynesian policy is to be preferred to a monetarist one, because our biblical criteria give a higher priority to employment than to price stability. However, that would be a mistake. The reason for the monetarists' preoccupation with inflation is that they see no other way to create employment. Expansion of aggregate demand will not create new jobs: monetary stability and supply side policies will. The fact that the latter operate slowly is a matter of regret, but nothing can be done about it.

In section 2 we also examined the ethical implications of the concept of macroeconomic policy. We concluded that macroeconomic policy could have appropriate roles in maintaining a stable economic environment for responsible stewardship, and in responding to perceived injustices, such as unemployment. But we were less happy with macroeconomic policy which was part of a scheme to control the future path of the economy. On these bases we might criticize monetarism for its unwillingness to respond rapidly to unemployment. To which criticism the monetarist will reply that within his understanding of the economy, there is nothing that can be done *rapidly*. At the other extreme, the proposals of the ultra-Keynesians might be thought to go too far in the control of the future, given our biblical criteria for action by the authorities.

The third element in assessing the three policy programmes is the realization that implicit in them are different options for the shape of the economic system, and society. The monetarist vision is of a free enterprise economy with private provision of goods and services insofar as private markets can be sensibly created. The role of the government, and its expenditure, would be sharply reduced. Public expenditure would be met from taxation. The government would provide an environment in which private markets could flourish. There would be an emphasis on law and order, the protection of private property rights and a legal framework for the enforcement of contracts. The welfare state would be reduced to an ultimate safety net. For most citizens social provision would be replaced by private insurance for health and unemployment, and by private saving for retirement. A vigorous anti-monopoly policy would police the behaviour of firms in private markets. Reduced taxes on income and capital, made possible by the reduction in state expenditure, would create an incentive for a small business sector that would keep large businesses competitive. National trade unions would disappear as major influences in the labour market. Wage bargaining would take place at a local level with reference to local conditions.

The moderate Keynesian solution implies a more corporatist vision of society. It accepts an economy dominated by large corporations, national trade unions, and a powerful central government, which have competing claims. The objective would be to bring them into joint decision-making so that the long-run behaviour of the economy could be regulated. However, this would require the major institutions to be cohesive and to have control over their constituent parts.

The ultra-Keynesian carries this view to its logical conclusion. The groupings in the moderate Keynesian scenario are unlikely to agree on the conduct of economic policy, since their interests are conflicting. This could be 'solved' by a socialist government with its roots in the trade union movement and with substantial control, via nationalization, of the productive sector.

In both the Keynesian policy models, the state would continue a large measure of involvement in social security, pensions, health and education, providing much more than a safety net. Equality both of opportunity and of outcomes would be as much an objective of policy as economic growth and stability.

The critical evaluation of these options takes us back to the analysis of market capitalism and varieties of socialism we looked at in Chapters Four and Five. As we explained at the beginning of section 4, monetarism is the macroeconomic counterpart of market capitalism, Keynesianism of the social democratic analysis and ultra-Keynesianism of the neo-Marxist analysis. While it is possible to advocate monetarist policies without also advocating the market economy, or ultra-Keynesian policies without believing in the rightness of a degree of planning, it is not plausible. In practice, there is always a link between the macroeconomic policy and the long-term vision.

Leaving aside these choices between macroeconomic policies, with their different long-term visions, is there common ground on which Christians might agree? Three points are implicit in our biblical analysis, and have particular relevance to the issues of this chapter. The first two points are a reflection of *Principle 4*: man has the right and the obligation to work, and *Principle 7*: that basic needs of food, clothing and shelter are primarily to be met by productive work. By these standards long-term unemployment is a grave social evil, and not to be tolerated or accepted as a permanent feature of the economy.

Second, it is wrong for people to be *idle*, even if paid employment is not available. Social security payments to the able-bodied unemployed should be made dependent on their participation in some useful activity, whether it be do-it-yourself, retraining or education programmes, or work in the community[33].

Our third point stems from our biblical conviction that the authorities have responsibility to do justice in society. If an economy is characterized by mass unemployment, many citizens do not have the opportunity to be responsible stewards in work. It is just as much the responsibility of the authorities to seek solutions for unemployment, as it is that they should prevent civil disorder, and punish thieves. *How* they might set about that task has been the subject of the chapter, and on that Christians may legitimately disagree.

CHAPTER SEVEN

Rich nation, poor nation

1. International issues: widening the perspective

The previous chapters have dealt with economic issues as they affect a single society. From a conceptual viewpoint, the international economy is an extension of the market capitalist system from a single economy to a group of interacting economies. The analysis of Chapter Three therefore can be carried over in all substantive respects. However, there are new issues for consideration. The first is disparity of living standards between countries, which is described below. A second set of issues refers to the effects not only of free trade, but also of impediments to trade, such as tariff barriers and trade restrictions. These are the subjects of sections 2 and 3. In section 4 we consider international capital flows, including direct investment by multinational companies. In sections 2 to 4 we will concern ourselves mainly with economic description and analysis, though pointing to the issues for moral evaluation.

Because the subject-matter is so immense, we shall restrict ourselves to the 'North-South problem': economic relations between the rich, advanced industrial economies which comprise the 'North', and the poor nations of the Third World, or 'South'.

This example is chosen because it has generated the most debate in Christian circles.[1] (The choice in no way implies the absence of other examples. Arguments for and against free trade, the regulation of international financial markets, restrictions on international migration, and the choice between floating and fixed exchange rates all merit evaluation, but they are only touched upon obliquely in what follows.) In section 5 we will outline policy issues including proposals for a new International Economic Order between North and South. Evaluation is the subject of section 6, which also deals with the responsibility for international economic policy.

The influential World Development Report,[2] produced annually by the World Bank, divides the world economy (excluding the communist bloc countries) into three broad groups.[3] The thirty-six low-income countries had a total population of 2,390 millions in 1984. They include large economies such as India and very small ones such as Lesotho. They are all characterized by having an annual income per capita of less than $380 in 1984. The average for the group was $260. The second group comprises sixty-five middle-income countries of which the largest are Nigeria and Brazil. With a combined population of 1,188 millions, and an average income per capita of $1,250 per annum, they are considerably better off than the low-income countries. Finally, the third group, which includes the USA, Europe, Japan and Australia, has a combined population of 733 millions, and income per capita of $11,430 per annum.

These figures can be expressed as multiples of the income per capita of the low-income countries. The middle-income countries' income per capita is five times that of the poorest group, and the high-income countries' income per capita is a staggering forty-four times as great. An alternative way of putting it is that the rich one-sixth of the world's population disposes of nearly four-fifths of its income. We follow the usage established by the Brandt Commission, and refer to the high-income economies as 'North', and the middle- and low-income economies together as 'South'.

The growth picture is scarcely more encouraging. Few would doubt that the past twenty years have seen unprecedented efforts to promote development in the Third World. National income has indeed grown at very high rates. But in the low-income countries income per capita grew at only 2.8% p.a. over the period 1965–84, and

3.1% p.a. for middle-income countries. This compares with 2.4% p.a. in the industrialized countries. So there was little reduction in the disparities.

While the GNP per capita figures are useful for global comparison they should be used with caution for a number of reasons. The exercise of converting them to dollar measures depends critically on the exchange rates used, which are not always good indicators of the relative costs of living in different countries. Further, there is a certain relativity about what constitutes a reasonable standard in different cultures.[4] Another difficulty is that much production in the South is for subsistence. The output is not marketed, and its value is notoriously difficult to estimate. So the data may be unreliable.

The use of per capita figures may also mislead. Most of the poorer countries have a very high proportion of children in their populations. Insofar as the children live with their parents and share housing and other family possessions, their per capita *needs* are probably less. Finally, we should note that averages are not necessarily good indicators. It has been noted[5] that although the GNP per capita in Brazil grew at a rate of 2.5% p.a. in the period 1960–70, the share going to the poorest 40% fell from 10% to 8%. This suggests that we need to take note of inequality of incomes within the Southern economies.

Statistics, however described and interpreted, do not make the most interesting reading. But the message of the World Development Report indicators is overwhelming. A very large proportion of mankind lives in conditions of great personal deprivation. By comparison the inhabitants of the industrial countries live in prosperity and luxury.

2. International trade and inequality

The world trading system is an extension of the market system from a single economy to a large group of interacting economies. As we shall see in section 3, this extension is subject to a number of restrictions created by authorities in those economies. Ignoring these for the moment, we concentrate our attention on the implications of an international market economy.

The first implication concerns the determinants of the structure of production in different economies, and this makes up a major part of the subject matter of international trade theory.[6] The second implication concerns the kind of income disparities which we noted in the previous section. In a market system, income depends on ability to supply products or services to the market. Consumption then depends on income, or purchasing power. Our task is to ask why the economies of the South lack the capacity to earn higher average incomes, when compared to the economies of the North.

The concept of comparative advantage focuses on the rate at which an economy can increase its output of one good by giving up production of another, presuming that resources are fully employed. The application to international trade and specialization is best illustrated by an example. Consider two countries, A and B, both of which can produce potatoes and wheat. Let us suppose that in country A an extra ton of potatoes can only be grown by giving up two tons of wheat, but that the reverse is true in country B. Then country A has a comparative advantage in growing wheat, and B in growing potatoes. Both parties could gain if A concentrated on wheat production and B on potatoes, and they then traded to obtain the good they did not produce. In aggregate there will be more output of both potatoes and wheat than if the countries produce on their own.

The argument is silent about the absolute efficiency of production in both countries. For example, better soil and climate could make farmers in country A more productive than farmers in country B in producing both wheat and potatoes. In that case the country A farmers will be better off than those in country B. But that has no significance for the previous argument, which relies solely on comparative, or relative, efficiency.

The theory is incomplete without some explanation of the determinants of comparative advantage. Much prominence is given in the literature to the Hecksher–Ohlin theory, which states that a country will specialize in those goods for which it has a favourable resource endowment. A country with an abundance of labour will have a comparative advantage in the production of labour-intensive goods, it will specialize in their production, and it will export them. Empirical work on this hypothesis came up with a 'paradox': Leontief[7] looked at the imports and exports of the US, and found that imports were, on the whole, capital-intensive, and exports labour-intensive. This was exactly the reverse of what might have been expected. The paradox is resolved if a longer list of factors of production is considered, particularly the presence of natural resources, and the degree of skill of the labour force (human capital, reflecting the effects of investment in training).[8]

One of the least appealing features of the textbook Hecksher–Ohlin model is the assumption of a common international technology available to all countries. Most new technology is developed in the North, and is not freely available. Quite apart from patent protection and industrial secrecy, many economies in the South lack the technical skills required to transfer the technology. A lag in the spread of new technology is therefore to be expected. These observations have given rise to the technological gap theory of trade.[9] New technologies are applied first in the North, and give rise to exports. Later, as the techniques become well known, production can be transferred to locations in the South, which have a comparative advantage. These economies begin to export to the North, which in turn moves on to newer processes and products.

Recent developments in trade theory have incorporated increasing returns to industry scale to explain the phenomenon of regional concentration of industrial development. A region or economy with a larger capital stock in a particular sector will have lower unit costs than its competitors with smaller capital stocks, which both lowers costs further and expands supply in that region. The implication is that any economy which can get ahead in the race for industrial development will be able to consolidate its position over time. Such a model may have implications for Southern industrial development in the face of the established industrial sectors of the North.[10]

We now consider the implications of trade and specialization for international disparities in income levels. The initial focus of attention is on capacity to produce. Differences of resource endowment clearly contribute to disparities. At one extreme, Kuwait and the United Arab Emirates are distinguished by a higher income per capita than the USA, based on their ability to produce petroleum. In the same part of the world, the Yemen has no resources, is almost entirely desert, and falls into the lower middle-income group of nations. But Japan has developed despite a lack of natural resources, and despite geographical restrictions on the supply of agricultural land. Singapore and Hong Kong have industrialized, again without either resources or fertile land. Equally, a number of African and South American countries are known to be rich in resources, but these have not so far stimulated development.

One reason is that resources are of no value without the human skills and the capital necessary to make use of them. Human skills are basically developed by education, and access to education is restricted in the South to a level well below that in the North. In low-income countries only 23% of adults are literate, only 80% of children of primary school age regularly attend school, and less than one-third of children receive secondary education. In middle-income countries there is virtually complete coverage of primary education and nearly two-thirds of the adult population are literate.[11]

Estimates of the capital per man in the South compared to the North are not available, since the information is difficult to obtain. However, energy consumption is a proxy measure.[12] Very approximately, in 1984 energy consumption per capita was four times greater in the middle-income countries than in the low-income countries, and seventeen times greater in the high-income countries.

Another ingredient determining the ability to produce is knowledge. Griffin[13] has drawn attention to the geographical concentration of R and D (research and development) expenditures in the North. 98% is undertaken in the advanced industrial countries, 78% in the USA alone. The expenditures themselves are heavily biased towards defence, and technologically advanced products such as aircraft. Very little is done on problems arising from production in the South. It is scarcely surprising that technical progress makes a greater contribution to growth in the North than in the South.

It is possible to argue that the disparities give the South scope for improving their position by catching up technologically with the North. However, technology tends to be very specific to the production conditions of the North and many have doubted whether it is either feasible or wise simply to transfer it to the South. Because of the technological progress in the North, it is able to pay higher returns to skilled manpower. As a result there is a considerable movement of professionally qualified people from the South to the North.[14] The consequence for the South is a deterioration in their prospects of development.

There is a further set of factors affecting the capacity of an economy to produce, which tends to be neglected in the technical economic analysis. These factors are the underlying culture, the economic system and good government. One reason for their neglect is the fact that some of their effects are difficult to quantify, but it would be foolish to ignore them for that reason. Cultural factors are perhaps the most difficult to analyse. In Chapter Two we spelt out the biblical view of man as responsible steward of the created order, exercising that stewardship through work. In Chapter Four we referred to the Weber thesis that it was precisely this framework of thought that gave rise to capitalism in Britain.[15] This may be contrasted with a Hindu view of the same question. The Hindu is not concerned with material prosperity, but with the development of the inner life. A rigid caste system which has the effect of keeping the poor in their poverty is tolerated because there is the possibility of reincarnation into a more privileged caste. The outcome is poor communities which, in J. K. Galbraith's graphic description,[16] resist development because of cultural accommodation to poverty.

The second factor is that of the economic system. There is considerable evidence to suggest that economic growth has been faster in those Southern economies which have favoured capitalist development, compared to those which have adopted a framework of economic planning.[17] This evidence has to be treated with caution, since in comparing economies sufficient allowance must be made for other factors that might affect economic performance. For example, planned economic development has often been advocated for large-scale projects (*e.g.* irrigation projects requiring the construction of major dams and other works) in regions where markets function only in a rudimentary fashion. However the lack of development of markets also reflects a general lack of human skills in the use of resources, which makes economic planning a difficult exercise. But the alternative to a poor performance with planning may well be that the project is not undertaken at all.

Another element in the comparison of performance is the degree to which market economies have achieved faster growth, but without that growth trickling down to the poorer section of the community. The evidence on this point is mixed.[18] On the one hand, Taiwan has achieved a measure of equity with its rapid growth. On the other, growth in Brazil in the 1960s and 1970s was not accompanied by any perceptible improvement in the distribution of income. However, even this example is not quite what it seems at first sight. Morley[19] has shown that there was in fact considerable mobility *within* the income distribution during the period. The same people did not necessarily remain in poverty over the period. But new concentrations of poverty were created, especially by migration from the countryside to the cities.

The third factor is good government. It is obvious that the absence of civil strife is a precondition of economic development. The effects of civil war in Lebanon, Ethiopia, Sudan, Mozambique and Kampuchea in recent years have been to destroy a large part of those economies, with serious refugee problems and famine as a result. However, even if there is peace, development can be seriously hindered by corrupt and incompetent administration. Corruption is a particular problem in those economies where the authorities are involved in the planning and regulation of the economy, or in major development contracts. The award of licences or

256

ECONOMICS TODAY

contracts comes to depend on bribery and contacts in the bureaucracy, rather than on rational criteria.

Corruption can also be a problem for market economies, where contracts between businesses depend on bribery, or where the administration of commercial law is corrupt. The effect of administrative incompetence is that scarce resources are wasted or misdirected. A Southern economy often lacks sufficient trained administrators to bring major projects to a successful outcome. The problems of corruption and incompetence may help to explain the poor performance of those Southern economies which have relied on economic planning to any great extent.

These three factors of culture, economic system and quality of government are important precisely because they have an impact on the efficiency of the economy. A country may have natural resources and sufficient skilled labour and capital, and yet fail to prosper. The economy of Argentina is currently a case in point. Similarly an economy without natural resources may be able to prosper so long as the other conditions for economic growth are present. Obvious examples are Japan, Hong Kong and Singapore. The uneven pattern of world development cannot be explained solely in terms of natural resources, the supply of economic factors of production and the uneven spread of technology.

A general source of disparities between North and South identified by some analysts is a long-term trend for the relative price of goods produced by the South to fall in international markets. This possibility has occasioned much dispute since it was first asserted by Prebisch[20] in the early 1950s. His argument was that the world income and price elasticities of demand for primary commodities tended to be low. So the world market would grow slowly and attempts by the South to sell more would depress the price. He predicted that over time the South would find its primary commodity exports were purchasing less and less in terms of manufactured products.

Empirical analysis has produced a mixed verdict on this general hypothesis.[21] Early studies gave it strong support, since they took as their starting point the high prices of commodities that prevailed during the Korean War. Taking a starting point further back, in the 1920s, analysis suggested that there was no long-term general decline in the terms of trade. However, much depends on which commodities a country is exporting. Over the period 1960–80 the low-income countries did suffer a deterioration in their terms of trade, largely because of their reliance on agricultural export crops. The middle-income countries, particularly those producing metals and oil, saw their position improve.

Past experience need not, of course, be a good indicator of future trends. Those who are pessimistic about the long-term market for Southern commodities in the North point to the increasing share of services in consumption in advanced economies, and to the accelerated replacement of traditional materials by synthetics in the aftermath of the oil price rises.

What then are the consequences of an uneven pattern of world development? The obvious corollary is that those who produce little of value (because they lack the capacity to produce) will also have low incomes, and so consume little. This point has been illustrated dramatically in a study by Sen[22] of the great Bengal famine of 1942–4 during which three million people died. The official version was that there was a dramatic fall in the availability of food. However, this is not borne out by the data. Food supplies in 1943 were indeed 5% lower than in the previous year, but they were 13% higher than in 1941. In 1941 there had been no famine. So what was the explanation? It seems that over the period 1940–43, the price of grain rose much faster than the wages of labourers. There was no shortage of food: but the poorest section of the community lacked the income to purchase it. So they starved. Sen also quotes the case of Bangladesh in 1974. Floods reduced the demand for agricultural labour. The result was famine, *before* the harvest failed.

Precisely the same point has been made by Jones[23] in the context of world food supply problems. He points out that all the problem of malnutrition in the South could be solved with perhaps 2% of the world cereal harvest. The difficulty is to get it to the people who need it. They tend to be those with low incomes. So when world production dips a little they are the marginal consumers who are pushed out of the market by higher prices. The situation is eased if the North increases food production or decreases consumption, since that will moderate the price increases: but that still does not give the poorest section of the world community the income that they would need in order to make purchases.

The principle is the same in every case. Consumption is possible only if one has income, and income is determined by the resources that one puts onto the market. So those who have little to offer must expect to consume little: that is the essence of the international market system. Note that we are not assigning malevolent motives to anyone in reaching this conclusion. Economic actors are merely reacting to world price signals, and adjusting their behaviour accordingly. The rich are probably quite unaware of the consequences for the poor.

3. Barriers to trade

Barriers to trade exist in all the economies of the North to prevent the access of goods from the South. Many Southern economies are thereby prevented from earning incomes on products for which their resources give them advantages in production. The irony of the situation is that it exists after thirty years of devotion to free trade on the part of the North. A sequence of negotiations under the General Agreement on Tariffs and Trade has enabled world trade in manufactures to grow extremely rapidly.[24] To an extent the South has shared in that growth, registering high growth rates of both output and exports. However, there are signs that this growth may be jeopardized by increased protectionism on the part of the North.

What are the products in which the South has a comparative advantage in manufacture? A wide variety of studies[25] has found two features to be important. The South tends to have an advantage in the production of labour-intensive goods such as textiles, clothing, footwear and leather, particularly where these are linked to local resources. However, since 1965 the Southern economies have diversified production into a much wider range of products, including electronics and electrical machinery, other machinery and transport equipment, basic chemicals and iron and steel products. The common feature of these is that they are products which are late in the product cycle. Either the technology or the product is completely standardized. The economies of the South often have sufficient skilled labour to produce such goods, even if they do not have the ability to innovate. This is particularly true of a select group of Newly Industrializing Countries (NICs), including Hong Kong, Taiwan, Korea, Singapore and Brazil, which account for some 60% of Southern manufactured exports to the North.[26]

The reaction of the North to this increasing manufacturing export potential of the South has been broadly negative, particularly since 1973.[27] For example, the Kennedy Round of tariff negotiations under GATT, 1968–72, brought down average tariffs to the range 5% to 11% within the North (the EEC tariff went down to 10.0%). But textiles, footwear, clothing and food products were specifically excluded. It also promoted the Generalized System of Preferences (GSP), whereby the North grants tariff reductions on designated imports from the South on a non-reciprocal basis. This was finally implemented by the USA in 1976, having been implemented earlier elsewhere. However, there are specific exclusions: textiles, leather products, footwear, wood and paper products, certain categories of electrical and electronic equipment, furniture, toys and miscellaneous light manufactures. The subsequent Tokyo Round 1973–9 resulted in further cuts in tariffs of about one-third, though many of the same restrictions applied. Tariffs in respect of goods of particular interest to the South remained higher than average, and the pattern of escalation of tariffs within sectors (much higher against finished goods than on raw materials or semi-manufactures) persisted.

The Tokyo Round also failed to make progress on a variety of non-tariff barriers to trade such as technical requirements for products and special rules for customs valuations.[28] Also of importance are 'voluntary export restrictions' and 'orderly marketing arrangements', which operate effectively as import quotas, but outside the rules of GATT. The evidence is that all these non-tariff barriers have increased substantially in importance since 1980, offsetting any advantages from tariff reductions. The effect has been retardation of the growth of Southern exports in the sectors most affected.[29]

A specific example of the restrictions imposed on Southern exporters is the Multifibre Arrangement.[30] This was originally negotiated in 1974 as an orderly marketing arrangement for Southern clothing and textile exports to the North. However, it has rapidly become a restrictive instrument. Under the Third Multifibre Arrangement, 1982–6, Common Market quotas actually reduced the import levels for Taiwan, Korea and Hong Kong. Other leading exporters have seen the growth in their quotas reduced sharply. Since one response of the South in the past has been to diversify production to goods outside the restrictions, the new rules introduced very low trigger levels for further quota restrictions to be applied. The USA, in its own bilateral agreements on textiles with the South, has frozen quotas. New quantitative restrictions have come into force (in addition to tariffs) on footwear, steel, television sets and shipbuilding. And there is a rising chorus of demands for protection on a wide range of products of interest to the South.

The implications of these restrictions are very serious; not so much for those economies in the South which are already major exporters of manufactures and can diversify reasonably easily as quotas become restrictive, but particularly for the poorer economies which are looking for markets for their exports as they begin tentatively to industrialize. These include some of the poorest countries such as Bangladesh and Sri Lanka.

However, the most glaring example of Northern protectionism is the area of agriculture.[31] We will take the example of the EEC Common Agricultural Policy, the purpose of which is to ensure security of supplies, to stabilize markets, to keep prices at a reasonable (undefined) level, and to provide a fair (undefined) standard of living to those involved in agriculture. In practice, the policy has been geared to European self-sufficiency in food and the protection of small farms. To achieve this result, livestock farming in Europe has been protected, at a high cost to consumers. So imported meat, poultry, eggs, dairy produce and sugar are kept out. Instead Europe imports cereals to feed its livestock.

The inefficiency of producing food this way is well known. The gross ratio of food consumed (as inputs to the process) to food output has been calculated at 30:1 for beef, 20:1 for pork, and 12:1 for chicken. In a more rational world, Europe would import these products from other countries (including the South) where livestock farming could be based on natural pastureland. The South would be able to use the income so generated to import the cereals that they need from the USA and Western Europe. The main livestock operation remaining in Europe would be dairy farming for milk, for which there is sufficient pastureland available in Europe.

An objection is that it makes no sense to import food for Europe from the South which already has insufficient food. But malnutrition results from lack of income rather than inadequate food supplies. Production would give people in the South the incomes they now lack. For example, the EEC protection afforded to sugar beet has had detrimental effects on the sugar producers of the Caribbean. Without markets for their sugar, many sugar workers are now unemployed. A sugar worker cannot live on sugar cane alone.

The reason for protectionism in the North is not hard to find.[32] It has attracted much attention as the adjustment problem. The difficulty arises because the impact of Southern competition tends to be felt most in a few industries, notably textiles, clothing and footwear, though the list is likely to grow. Import penetration leads to the closure of factories and the displacement of workers. In many countries the impact will be concentrated regionally. So pressure for protection for those employed in the industry is not surprising.

But there are a number of reasons why Northern governments might be advised to resist such pressures. First, the costs to consumers are often high.[33] They are denied cheap sources of supply. Second, imports are only one of a number of factors that generate changes in employment patterns over time. Technical progress, changes in tastes and trade with other Northern countries are others. Every competent study has shown that the employment effects of Southern imports are truly negligible by comparison with these. One can only suspect that changes arising from the South's exports are singled out for attention because the South has no powerful voice.

Third, one presumes that the earnings of the South from new exports will be spent. Most economies are extremely short of foreign exchange, and are likely to spend any increment on imports to help their development. They are already an important export market for Northern manufacturers. They could be even more important. The conclusion is that workers in the North will have to switch jobs, not, in aggregate, lose them. And everyone could be better off.

Fourth, protection of jobs in the North has a much greater effect on employment in the South. Lydall[34] calculated some orders of magnitude for twelve manufactured product groups of particular interest to the South. Displacing one worker in the EEC in these sectors would generate on average two jobs in a middle-income country and 4.6 jobs in a low-income country. The comparable figures for the USA are 2.8 and 6.5 jobs respectively. These are merely the direct employment effects. Multiplier effects of the expansion of activity in the South made possible by their additional earnings of foreign exchange could increase these impacts by between two and five times the figures quoted. Thus in a very poor country the effect could be as high as twenty additional jobs for one worker displaced in Europe or the USA.

4. Capital flows

Capital flows from the North are an additional source of savings for development in the South, and provide foreign exchange which would not otherwise be available. The three main components are official flows in the form of aid, direct investment associated with the operations of multinational companies (MNCs), and portfolio investment. Portfolio investment includes direct lending to Southern governments and institutions by international commercial banks. Between 1960 and 1980 there was a major change in the composition of external capital.[35] At the beginning of the period about 66% was official flows and some 20% was direct investment. By the end of the period these had fallen to 41% and 16% respectively: but portfolio flows, which were small in 1960, had by 1980 reached 31% of the total. The causes of this change in the composition of capital flows, and the resulting 'debt' problem of the 1980s, will be considered below.

The definition of aid is a transfer of resources on concessionary terms. Our focus here is on capital, but aid can take the form of supplies of goods, including armaments, capital equipment and food. About 60% of aid goes to low-income countries, and about 25% to the least developed countries within that group, particularly in Sub-Saharan Africa. In the 1980s aid has amounted to about 0.35% of GNP of the advanced industrial economies. It is channelled via a variety of routes. Government to government or bilateral aid, which accounts for about three-quarters of all aid, has a high political profile, and may be used for purposes other than economic development. Multilateral aid passes through a number of intermediaries, of which the most important is the International Development Association of the World Bank.

Aid may be linked to specific investment projects, though the emphasis in the 1980s has switched to programme lending for use in broad development programmes, *e.g.* in agriculture. An evaluation of aid by Cassen *et al*[36] found that most aid programmes are successful in achieving their development objectives, and give a reasonable rate of return on the capital invested. On the criterion of relieving poverty, performance was less satisfactory, but the reason may lie as much with the domestic policies of the recipients as with the aid programmes. 'Failures' of aid are greatly overstated, according to Cassen *et al*. The highest failure rates of projects and programmes occur in the most difficult environments, especially Sub-Saharan Africa. 'Donor failure' is linked to the use of aid for political or commercial purposes of interest to the donor, to poor technical design of projects, and to failure to learn from past mistakes. 'Recipient failure' arises partly from the use of aid for political prestige, and partly from the inability of recipients to provide complementary finance from their own private or public resources.

The second major source of external capital for the Sout is provided by multinational corporations. These are no easily categorized according to product, since many hav diversified their operations. But it is possible to distinguis an older group, in cars, pulp and paper, aluminium, zin petroleum, copper and lead, whose grip on world marke has diminished over the past twenty-five years. The newe multinationals tend to emphasize high technology product (*e.g.* computers, pharmaceuticals, transport equipment The control of world markets by this newer group i growing.

The origin of the multinationals was in direct investmer abroad by firms that sought opportunities outside thei national markets. Three distinct reasons for direct inves ment have been explored in the literature.[37] The first relie on the advantages from vertical integration. The typical cas is a firm that uses as an essential input a resource that available only in another country. Firms search out supplie and then make the necessary investments. In this way the can ensure their supplies, and benefit the country in whic the resource was found by supplying the requisite capita technological skills and entrepreneurship.

The second reason for going multinational arises fro labour supplies available in the South. Given the high wag costs in the developed nations, firms have found it advan tageous to move the more labour-intensive parts of thei production to low wage countries. This is the phenomeno known as sourcing. Control over the production and ma keting is retained by the headquarters of the multinationa but production itself may take place at a large number c locations with only final assembly taking place in the majo markets.

The third reason is particularly applicable to firms usin advanced technology. Suppose such a firm has developed new product that represents a considerable technic advance. It now wants to gain the maximum, internationa market for the product. One way of doing this could be vi exports. But that is likely to be unattractive, for two reason National markets, particularly in the South, are likely to b heavily protected. Further, for many differentiated products, the marketing of the product is essential to its success. This means that it must be adapted to meet local conditions of use. Both these factors weigh in favour of dispersed production, and hence direct investment. The alternative is to license the technology to a national firm. But that will not always work: the local firm may lack the entrepreneurship to exploit the market to the full.

A defence of the role of multinationals in the South would emphasize the following points.[38] Multinationals are ideally suited to provide for development. They have access to funds, so that they can undertake large projects. They may also be able to mobilize additional aid from their home countries to provide for infrastructure investment. They can provide entrepreneurship and managerial skills that are lacking in many economies of the South, and their presence can help with the training of a local labour force. They can bring with them valuable technology and experience of making new products which the South could only acquire otherwise by research and development expenditures that they are in no position to undertake. Finally, with their marketing experience, multinationals can do much to improve the distribution network in a Southern economy.

However, there are other aspects of multinationals that give pause for thought. First, the arrival on the scene of a highly efficient multinational producer will tend to eliminate indigenous firms. Local firms will sell out to the multinational. But inability to compete will stunt the growth of local enterprise, and in particular local savings may diminish as profitable opportunities are not available to national entrepreneurs. Second, a local industrial élite will be prepared to bring pressure on national governments to provide the necessary infrastructure for development. Multinationals on the other hand will provide a total investment package, and will be less interested in government action on education, health and other public services.

Third, decisions about the level of production in a particular country will be taken at the headquarters of the multinational, and the welfare of that country will not necessarily be taken into account. For example, a multinational with sources of materials in a large number of countries may react to a recession in demand by closing down completely in one or more countries, rather than reducing output equally across all countries. Another possibility is the manipulation of transfer prices between different sections of the company. To avoid local taxation, or restrictions on remission of profits abroad, the multinational may arrange for its subsidiary to charge a low price for its supplies to other parts of the company, or it may charge its subsidiary an excessive price for the use of technology. For example, pharmaceutical firms are often accused of charging very high licence fees to their subsidiaries in the South.[39]

Fourth, multinationals are frequently criticized for bringing the wrong sort of development to the South. They have little interest in making appropriate mass produced products, since local competition would quickly compete away the profits. So they concentrate on sophisticated consumer durables that will be purchased only by an élite. But it is not merely a matter of appropriate products. Multinationals tend also to bring their production technology with them. That technology, having been developed in high wage countries, tends to be capital-intensive and labour-saving. It is not appropriate to the conditions of a Southern economy. The problem is compounded by the generous incentives to foreign capital that many economies in the South have used to attract foreign investment. The multinational is given little incentive to devise technology that is adapted to low wage conditions.

The third component of the capital flow to the South is private portfolio lending. Up to 1970 this constituted a relatively minor part of the total flow. All this changed in the mid 1970s.[40] The oil price shock of 1973–4 generated surpluses for the OPEC countries which were largely saved and recycled to the main financial centres. Non-oil producing Southern economies were simultaneously faced by balance of payments problems which official financing was inadequate to resolve. They turned therefore to the commercial banks who were seeking investment outlets for the OPEC savings. Many of the larger Southern economies— notably Mexico, Brazil, Argentina, Venezuela, South Korea, the

Philippines and Indonesia— appeared to offer a reasonable prospect. They had very little sovereign debt, and their economies were growing quite strongly. The second oil price rise of 1979 initially provoked a similar response: but the pattern of the 1970s was not to be repeated.[41]

The recession in the industrialized countries deepened in 1982, thus affecting the demand for exports from the South. Simultaneously, real interest rates which had been low or even negative in the inflationary 1970s suddenly became positive and large. Finally, the dollar, in which currency most of the debt of the Southern economies was denominated, appreciated sharply and continued to appreciate until 1985. Debt service ratios which relate interest and amortization charges on the debt to export earnings in a particular year rose from about 15% in the early 1970s to 25% in 1982.

At this point, Mexico called a moratorium on its debt repayments, claiming an inability to pay. The impact on portfolio capital flows was immediate: to the major debtor countries they fell to about nothing in 1983, and scarcely one-tenth of their 1981/2 level in 1984 and 1985. The debtors were no longer creditworthy, and the banks stopped lending.

The crisis arose because the debtors were unable to refinance their debts. The responsibility for this state of affairs has been attributed to both the banks and borrowers. It is argued that the banks followed a 'herd' instinct in lending to Southern economies, and that they should have rationed credit much more strictly in the 1970s, noting that the accumulation of debt was likely to give the borrowers a strong incentive to default if conditions became adverse. The borrowing economies are blamed for continuing to borrow heavily in the early 1980s even when it became apparent that the world recession was deepening, and for not taking action to stem capital flight when the crisis supervened.

Wherever the blame for the situation is attributed, the debtor countries have been left with stark policy alternatives: either they cut domestic activity, reduce imports and use a higher proportion of export earnings to pay debt servicing, or they default in whole or in part. The former policy is possibly not sustainable politically over a number of years, unless the terms of the debt servicing become less onerous (falls in real interest rates, and depreciation of the dollar, for examples), and some interim arrangements are made for refinancing at least a proportion of the debt as it falls due.[42]

5. The New International Economic Order

The New International Economic Order (NIEO) is a series of proposals for change in international economic relations enshrined in resolutions of the General Assembly of the United Nations in 1974. Within the United Nations the proposals were associated with the South, united for this purpose in the Group of 77. This Group was formed by Third World delegates at successive United Nations Conferences on Trade and Development (UNCTAD) since 1964: its membership now consists of well over one hundred Southern countries.

The starting point for the proposals is the failure of conventional development programmes to make much progress in alleviating poverty in the South in the past thirty years. The proposals can be examined under seven heads, which we will examine in turn.[43] If in what follows we are critical of some of these proposals, this should not be taken as lack of sympathy with the desperate situation that prompted them. There is, however, little point in supporting proposals that are unlikely to be effective.

An immediate reservation can be expressed about the whole package of proposals. By focusing on injustices in the international economic order, proposals of the NIEO divert attention from failures of domestic economic policy and administration. It is arguable that internal causes of poverty and lack of progress in development in the South are just as significant as international economic problems, if not more so. The NIEO encourages Southern governments to believe that they are victims of the international economic system and therefore not at all responsible for their circumstances. So they fail to face up to the realities of sensible domestic policies. An issue to which we will return in section 6 is whether the North should make progress with international reforms, or indeed any form of assistance to the South, conditional upon reforms within the Southern economies.

The first element in the NIEO proposals is that priority in international aid and development effort should be given to the poorest countries. These countries are characterized by very low income per capita (less than $200 at 1984 prices), very little manufacturing and high rates of illiteracy. They are located in Central Africa, to the south of the Sahara, and in a belt which stretches from the non-oil economies of the Middle East across South Asia into East Asia. They depend largely on agriculture to support their populations, and suffer from difficult environmental conditions. Not surprisingly, their lack of potential for development does not make them attractive for private development finance, or even for loans from international development agencies. Returns are too uncertain, and results may be achieved only in the very long term. But the needs of the population are acute. The call is for much more financial assistance on concessionary terms, and for development of production techniques specifically for the difficult environmental conditions.

A second priority of the proposals is an attack on world hunger by giving greater attention to questions of food supply. Malnutrition is estimated to affect some 800 million people. The majority of these people are located in low-income countries that do not have the capacity to import food when domestic production is insufficient. During the 1960s and early 1970s, grain stocks in the United States were allowed to run down as a result of policy changes by the United States Government. These stocks had previously been used to stabilize world markets for grains. The effects of the policy were first seen in 1972 and 1973, when droughts in Africa and poor harvests in the Soviet Union led to a steep rise in wheat prices. The consequence was that many poor countries were literally priced out of the world markets, with serious food shortages as a result. The Group of 77 has therefore proposed, and argued for, a reserve stock to be maintained, with finance provided by the major developed countries. The countries of the South lack the financial capacity to undertake the task themselves, and private stock-holders have shown themselves unable to cope with the task.

A third area of concern of the NIEO is with trade in commodities. Many Southern economies are highly dependent on exports of commodities (agricultural and mineral) to earn foreign exchange. For some of these commodities there has been a long-term decline in price relative to prices of manufactured exports from the North, though this depends on the particular commodity and the time period over which comparisons are made. More immediately, commodity prices have been subject to sharp falls in 1980–82 with deleterious effects in the exporting countries: one calculation is that the loss of foreign exchange to commodity-exporting Southern economies in 1980–84 was 63% of the total value of their commodity exports in 1980. Moreover, Southern countries have noted that their share in the commodities market is limited to primary production. Processing, marketing and distribution are the preserve of Northern firms, whose activities are protected by tariff and non-tariff barriers to trade which inhibit Southern producers from competing.

The NIEO proposals to deal with the perceived problems fall under three headings. First, although it is generally agreed by analysts that little can be done to affect the long-term shifts in relative prices, there is a degree of optimism that a group of Southern producers could emulate OPEC by forming a cartel to restrict output and raise prices in the short term. But the prospects are not good. Natural fibres, such as cotton, already face severe competition from synthetics in the North. Attempts at producer cartels for cocoa, coffee and tea have not been too successful in the past.

The second proposal is for effectively financed International Commodity Agreements with a view to holding stocks and stabilizing prices. However, detailed analysis[44] suggests that the gains from stabilization may be quite small and that the conditions for a scheme to succeed are quite stringent. So there is probably some value in proposals to improve compensatory financing for countries suffering from short-run declines in export earnings due to price fluctuations.[45] The third proposal consists of various measures to enable producer countries to begin processing and distributing their commodities, with access to consumer markets in the North.

A further emphasis in the proposals for NIEO is in the area of industrialization. The share of the Southern economies in world manufacturing output, and trade in products, increased slowly during the 1970s. But much of this growth has been limited to a small group of eight countries, often referred to as the Newly Industrializing Countries, which include Brazil, Korea, Taiwan and Singapore. But their growth has been curtailed since the latter half of the 1970s by increasing protectionism in the North, which was described in section 3 above. The Group of 77 have not been slow to point out the inconsistency of this, since the North has systematically sought to reduce barriers to trade between its own economies through the conferences of the General Agreement on Tariffs and Trade. The same countries have been deaf to Southern requests for more liberal trade policies in respect of their potential exports.

A fifth area of concern of the NIEO proposals is that of the activities of multinationals. The proposals focus on mechanisms for effective international control, and on the transfer of technology. The former objective is being met to some degree by an internationally agreed code of conduct, to strengthen the bargaining position of host countries, and by international cooperation in the area of corporate taxation.

The Group of 77 has always been highly critical of the institutions and international agreements that constitute the international monetary order. The 1944 Bretton Woods agreement set up the International Monetary Fund (IMF) to regulate international monetary relationships. The agreement was directed particularly to the needs of the advanced industrial economies, each of which agreed to maintain a stable value for its currency in return for the right to obtain short-term finance from the IMF should it suffer a temporary setback in its balance of payments. The Group of 77 contend that the IMF was created by the North and that its policy has been dictated by the North.

This criticism has been focused on the issue of 'conditionality'.[46] Every IMF member has the right to a certain level of financing without conditions: however further finance is only available on 'high conditionality', which implies an agreed programme to achieve balance of payments adjustment. The programme typically includes monetary and fiscal restraint to cut imports, devaluation to switch expenditure and limits to short- and medium-term foreign borrowing to prevent capital inflows undermining the adjustment. Critics complain that in practice the restrictive policies are overdone, that adverse income distribution effects are ignored, that large nominal devaluations can spark inflation, and that the adjustment period is too short. Another complaint is that all balance of payments problems are treated as if they resulted from profligate fiscal and monetary policies.

The resulting policy prescription is not appropriate to problems arising from external shocks (*e.g.* a collapse in export prices) or from fundamental disequilibrium. In the first case compensatory financing is more appropriate; in the second, assistance for adjustment in the long term is required. These issues are sharply debated.[47] What makes the issue of 'high conditionality' particularly important is that IMF approval for a stabilization programme is often a prerequisite for borrowing from other sources. A country in balance of payments is therefore in a weak position to resist IMF conditions.

Finally, the demands for a NIEO have included a solution to the problems of Southern capital requirements.[48] Since the early 1970s the amount of aid (Official Development Assistance) has fallen far short of the development needs of the South. Those economies have turned to private loans to finance development programmes. The consequence is the current debt crisis described in section 4: so private lending will certainly not provide for the needs of the 1990s.

The problem with aid has not only been its quantity, but also the terms on which it is offered. The complaints are: that not enough aid is available for flexible use in broad development programmes (*e.g.* in agriculture); that aid is often tied to purchases in the donor country; that too much aid is given unilaterally, rather than multilaterally, thus making its continued availability subject to the changes in the foreign policy of the donor; foreign policy of the donor; and that the flow of aid is not sufficiently predictable to enable a country to plan for development even in the medium term (up to five years ahead). The Group of 77 have therefore asked not only for more aid, but also that those questions concerning the *form* of aid should be dealt with.

These seven proposals for a New International Economic Order were endorsed, in substance if not in detail, by the Report of the Brandt Commission: *North–South: a Programme for Survival*, published in 1980. The aim of the Report was to motivate world leaders to take action. To this end two groups of arguments were advanced. The first is that failure to act might result in some disaster which would engulf the North as well as the South. The second is arguments from mutual economic interest. We will consider these briefly in turn.[49]

The particular disasters which are foreseen are war, irretrievable ecological damage and the collapse of the international economic system. As far as the threat of war is concerned there is no evidence at all that recent wars have been linked to issues of international economic justice, or even world hunger. Most conflicts, like those of South-East Asia, have been inspired by ideological or racial conflicts rather than development issues. The brutal fact is that the poor who die from starvation are usually *rural* poor, with little voice in democratic political affairs, let alone international affairs. The urban poor are generally kept fed by anxious governments keen to avoid trouble.

Ecological damage is envisaged by the Report as a second potential disaster, and references are made to the indiscriminate use of forests for fuel, especially in the poverty belts of Africa and Asia. But some might argue that this is a reason for discouraging Southern development in order to keep the total strain on the world ecosystem at a tolerable level.

The third potential disaster is a collapse of the world economic system triggered by a Southern default on their debt. While there is no doubt that this *is* a serious problem for the international banking system, it seems probable that it will be resolved by rescheduling of debts and by requiring these countries to adopt restrictive internal economic policies.

The 'arguments from mutual economic interest' are given more attention in the Report itself, but it is doubtful whether they are sufficient to convince Northern leaders. For example, the proposals for stabilizing commodity prices might well bring gains to the South. But the gain to the North, who would be expected to finance the operation, would be minimal. Major commodity users in the North already operate privately in established commodity markets, and do not need to be looked after. Besides, as we noted above, there is considerable doubt about the efficiency of such schemes.

Similar difficulties arise in the arguments for the lifting of protection from Northern markets to allow in Southern exports. The nature of the adjustment problem was described previously. The problem for governments in the North is pressure from localized and specific industry groups. It may be difficult to persuade electorates of long-term benefits, when the immediate impact of lifting protection is localized unemployment in the affected industries.

The third argument from mutual economic interest is the proposal for a Keynesian style reflation of the world economy to offset the world recession. This would be achieved by *giving* the South foreign exchange to continue with their development plans. The expenditures, it is argued, will feed back to the North, with consequent stimulating effects.

Monetarists claim that such financing of the South would be inflationary, and should therefore be avoided at all costs. It is ironic that the Brandt Commission made a Keynesian proposal at a time when a majority of Northern governments were pursuing monetarist policies. Even if Keynesian policy won wider acceptance, it is not obvious what is to be gained from an indirect reflation via the South, with uncertain consequences, rather than a direct reflation of the Northern economies in the conventional manner. Our conclusion is that arguments from mutual interest are unlikely to be persuasive for Northern governments.

6. Evaluating international economic relations

In the previous sections we have set out various aspects of international economic relations between North and South. We have also described the demands for a New International Economic Order which have come from the South. In this section we provide a brief commentary, using the evaluative criteria which were developed in Chapter Two.

It would be simpler if we could focus our discussion solely on the international aspects, ignoring questions about the appropriate framework of development within the South. But a set of issues relating to the domestic economies of the South is likely to be an important component of any understanding of low incomes. The proximate cause of poverty in the South is that people do not have access to resources, and having nothing to work with, they produce nothing and thus have no income.

This situation can be faulted on at least three of our biblical principles: *Principle 2* reminds us that *all* people are called to exercise responsible stewardship of resources and talents, *Principle 4* that work is the means by which such stewardship is to be exercised, and *Principle 7* that this is the primary means by which basic needs of food, clothing and shelter are to be met. However our evaluation will depend on the reasons for people not having access to resources. For example, in many Latin American countries much rural poverty is linked directly to landlessness, even though landowners are by no means using all their land productively. Other causes of poverty include civil disorder, corrupt or inefficient governments, and negative elements in the prevailing culture. More controversially, an inappropriate choice of economic system or economic policies may result in misallocation or misuse of resources, leaving some people without a means of livelihood. Alternatively, lack of access to resources may reflect difficult environmental conditions, the absence of natural resources and a lack of education and technical knowledge.

The last set of problems may be alleviated by assistance from outside the economy, and thus, within our Christian

framework, implies responsibilities for people in rich economies. The nature of these responsibilities finds expression
in the question of international aid. We need to distinguish
two types of aid. The first is aid in the form of gifts to a
particular group who are victims of famine or disaster. While
this is an essential response in the short term, it can create a
problem of dependency in the longer term. The people
come to rely on gifts to save them when troubles come. The
second type of aid avoids this problem. Its aim is to develop
responsible stewardship by providing the basic resources of
land, equipment and knowledge, so that the people involved
can be independent and provide for themselves. The most
effective aid of this kind will often come not in the form of
cash or goods, but in the form of dedicated expertise.
Development workers need to be people who can evaluate
development potential, design a viable project and then set it
up with the full involvement of the people it is designed to
help, so that in due course they can withdraw leaving a viable
self-supporting community.

Problems arising from patterns of landholding, negative
elements in the culture, inappropriate economic systems and
policies and corrupt or inefficient administration can in one
sense only be dealt with by action *within* a Southern economy.
The principles which might be applied have already been
considered in Chapters Four to Six. However the international dimension enters again with the concept of 'conditionality'. Let us suppose that a particular Southern economy
suffers to a greater or lesser degree from all the causes of low
incomes that we have listed above. Would it be appropriate
for aid from the North for development projects and programmes to be made conditional on action within the economy to deal with other shortcomings? It is not implausible to
imagine a donor making aid contingent upon land reform,
less regulation of markets, and even political reforms or the
removal from office of corrupt or inefficient ministers or
bureaucrats.

Such 'political interference' is probably implicit in much
bilateral aid: continuing 'good behaviour' by the government
of the recipient country is necessary to maintain the flow of
aid. It has not been an explicit feature of the multilateral aid

administered by the World Bank, though Southern governments suspect that the World Bank favours the use of markets rather than planning in development. We have already seen that 'high conditionality' is important in the short-term lending of the IMF, and that too has been resented by some Southern governments as unwarranted interference in their internal policy.

Conditionality raises important questions about the locus of responsibility for the poor in the South. Our analysis of Chapter Two quite unambiguously assigned responsibility for the domestic economy to the polical authorities of that country. The political authorities are answerable to God for how they have discharged their responsibility, as judged by our Christian principles for economic life. To enable each citizen to be a responsible steward of resources, so that each can provide for himself and his family, and to see that the rich do not evade their responsibility to aid the poor who cannot provide for themselves, are the relevant principles to be applied here. It is not obvious that it is the responsibility of any outside authority to intervene or to bring pressure to bear, even if the political authorities are failing egregiously to fulfil their responsibilities.

However that does not mean that donors of aid are obliged to give regardless of the internal circumstances of the recipient country. If they have good reasons to believe that aid will be wasted or diverted by a corrupt administration, and that little will reach those who actually need it, then wisdom dictates that aid should be withheld. Similarly, IMF conditionality may be justified as prudent behaviour by a bank which wishes to ensure that loans will be repaid. The difficulty is to define what might constitute good reasons for withholding aid, and what are reasonable conditions to attach to loans. Donors and lenders perhaps need to err in the direction of being generous to recipients and borrowers, and being sensitive to the difficulties that many Southern governments face in governing their countries.

A second set of issues arises directly from the involvement of countries in the international trading and financial system. Given the difficulties that this creates for some economies of the South, such as instability of foreign earnings and pressures from lending institutions like the International Monetary Fund, some have advocated that low-income countries should withdraw, partially or completely, and pursue their own development behind closed economic borders. We do not accept this approach for the following reasons.

First, there are *gains* to be obtained from international specialization and trade. In practice many of the objections to export development are not objections to exporting in itself. For example, agriculture for export in the tropics has sometimes been associated with large-scale capitalist development. The problems which result can be traced to the pattern of ownership, not to trade itself. If large-scale operations are required (and frequently they are not), then some form of cooperative enterprise involving a dispersal of ownership and rewards is feasible. Second, many of the smaller economies of the South have a limited range of resources. A desire for economic independence may severely restrict the scope and speed of development. Given the scale of the problems in many Southern economies, rapid progress is essential, even if it brings other costs.

Two of these costs were identified above, in section 2. One is the instability of export earnings for economies which depend on commodity exports. The second is the effect on the poorer countries of short-term fluctuations in the price of foodstuffs relative to incomes in those countries. The result can be a sudden deterioration in the economic situation of a poor economy for reasons entirely outside its control, with disastrous consequences for its citizens. Such instability does nothing to encourage responsible stewardship: on the contrary, it can give rise to apathy and despair among those affected. The proposals of the NIEO for smoothing the wilder fluctuations in commodity prices by maintaining stocks can therefore be interpreted as an attempt to create a framework for stewardship, and to avoid some perceived injustices. Whether they will in fact *work* in the way envisaged by the Group of 77 is still in doubt. But our concern here is with an ethical evaluation of the objectives, not with the practicality of the proposals.

In section 3 we discussed the problems caused for the

South by protectionist policies in the North. The ethical implication of these policies is that they greatly restrict the capacity of Southern economies to be responsible stewards of their resources within an international market system. In effect, the goods which the South is capable of producing, the North refuses to buy.

The other side of this argument is the adjustment problem in the North if protection is removed. Workers in the same sectors in Northern economies will have to move to other occupations, presuming that alternative occupations are available. As explained in section 5 above, in the long run both Southern and Northern economies should gain once the adjustment has occurred. But the adjustment is not painless to those most directly affected. Geographical or occupational immobility may involve some workers in extended periods of unemployment. We have already noted that industry lobbies are likely to exert powerful pressure on governments not to remove protection, and the consumer lobby for lower-priced imported supplies is likely to be weak. A government may weigh the immediate costs, both economic and social, of adjustment more highly than the promised long-term gains.

This is but one example of international economic policies that may involve costs for a Northern economy, at least in the short term. Another is the transfer of aid to the South, where that aid is financed by taxation in the North. The issue that must be addressed is whether a Northern government is justified in acting in this way to favour the citizens of another country for which it has no direct responsibility.

The biblical position, spelt out in Chapter Two, is that the political authorities have the responsibility for their citizens, and for the economic institutions within their jurisdiction. They are to encourage economic institutions within a framework of law, to react to perceived injustices and to provide an institutional framework for responsible communal endeavour. But who is responsible for international justice? International bodies such as the United Nations have no real power to pursue international justice except by licence from their members. Why then should Northern governments pursue international policies that may be detrimental to the self-interest of some or all of their citizens?

The answer to this puzzle is perhaps provided by O'Donovan's defence of the Just War theory.[50] He suggests that a national government should conduct its international affairs on the basis of what would be required of it by a justice-seeking world authority, if such an authority existed. Morally, then, a government should act on the basis of international justice even to the detriment of the economic interests of its own citizens. This principle provides a context for considering such policies as Official Development Aid, commodity stabilization programmes, and the removal of protectionist trade barriers in the North. Where there are human beings living in great poverty in the South, without provision for their basic needs of food, clothing and shelter, then there is an obligation on those who are better placed in the North to help directly. Christians in the North have no reason to hold back from pressing their governments to be generous in providing immediate relief which is paid for from general taxation.

But Northern responsibility goes beyond immediate help. An international authority which applied the *Principles* of Chapter Two would seek to ensure that every person in the South had access to resources with which to work, and a framework of international economic relations within which they could exercise responsible stewardship (*Principles* 2 to 5). This is no more than an extension to the international sphere of the principles that should guide the political authorities in the pursuit of economic justice at home. In practical terms that means continuing aid for the development of the South to give access to resources for poor people, and a willingness to open Northern markets to those products in which the South has comparative advantage. While such policies may involve costs for the North, these pale into insignificance compared to the immense gap between rich and poor countries that is revealed by international comparisons. The North can and should be able to afford such policies.

CHAPTER EIGHT
Economic growth

1. Introduction

Economic analysis in the 1960s was remarkable for its concern with the process of economic growth in the advanced industrial economies. That analysis was sustained by the adoption of growth as an objective of policy. Keynesian policies had proved effective in maintaining aggregate demand in line with the growth potential of the economy, so attention could be switched to understanding the determinants of that potential. Growth would not only enable individuals to enjoy a higher personal standard, but also would give scope for improvements in public services and social security. Poverty could be alleviated by transfers out of increased national income rather than redistribution of a given national income.

The economic analysis of growth is notable for the sharp disjunction between theory and empirical studies. The former concentrated on abstract analyses of the conditions for steady state growth in a market economy, and of the determinants of the growth rate.[1] The resulting models may be useful for illuminating the process of growth, but tell us little about the causes. For example, in the neoclassical growth model we find that the growth rate is determined by the growth of the labour force and the rate of labour-saving technical progress. But these two determinants are taken as exogenous.

Empirical studies were more eclectic, though the emphasis

was on supply side factors.[2] The most detailed studies were those of Denison, who disaggregated the sources of growth, taking account of the skills of the labour force, intersectoral shifts in labour and other resources, and the contribution of economies of scale and technical progress. The most significant finding of this study, and many others, was the relatively slow growth rate in the USA and UK relative to other OECD countries, especially Japan and West Germany. This was explained by appeal to such factors as technological 'catching up', transfer of resources out of low productivity sectors such as agriculture, high investment in manufacturing stimulating productivity growth, and export success.

Our major concern in this chapter is with the desirability of economic growth as an objective of policy. Two doubts have been expressed. The first is that the experience of economic growth has not brought the gains in terms of human satisfaction or happiness that were expected. Suggestions as to why this might be the case will be explored in the next section. The second doubt is that the physical resources of the planet are finite, so that exponential growth must sooner or later come up against natural resource limits.[3] An immediate fear is that the rate of exploitation of natural resources, and the destruction of the natural environment, are proceeding at such a rate that economic growth is not sustainable even for the foreseeable future.

To avoid misunderstanding, we note that the first of these doubts applies only to the developed North. The 1960s and 1970s were a period of great efforts for development in the South, where the problem was to provide a minimal standard of life. Economic growth in these circumstances is a moral imperative. However even Southern economies might wish to avoid some of the less pleasing aspects of the advanced economies in their development. The second doubt, concerning the exploitation of natural resources, applies equally to the South as to the North. Destruction of the natural environment for short-term income gains stores up a legacy of inadequate resources for future generations.

2. Why has economic growth proved so disappointing?

There is no shortage of secular critics of economic growth in the advanced economies. In this section we will look at the arguments of four of these critics — Thurow, Mishan, Scitovsky and Hirsch.[4] In each case these critics make some effort to stand outside the traditional framework of analysis. It is appropriate therefore to begin with the evaluation of growth within that framework.

There are two arguments to be considered. The first is that consumers seek to maximize their consumption of goods and services, subject to income at the level of the household, or subject to the capacity to supply through production and trade, at the level of the whole economy. Growth relaxes the constraints on consumption, and thus generates higher welfare or satisfaction. This utilitarian approach was discussed in Chapter Three. We recall that difficulties arise for evaluating social welfare gains in situations where economic growth does not bring increases in consumption for all. If there are losers as well as gainers, then the evaluation requires an appeal to an explicit social welfare function.

This argument should not be taken to imply that a higher growth rate is *per se* better. The consumers are seeking to maximize a stream of satisfaction or utility over time. It might be possible to achieve a higher growth rate by cutting current consumption, and investing more. But that need not maximize intertemporal utility if current consumption is severely reduced. The economic theory of optimal growth is therefore concerned with the choice and implementation of *optimal* growth paths for the economy. This choice raises, as mentioned in Chapter Three, questions about provision for future generations. It is not obvious that personal desires to provide for one's descendants will be a sufficient mechanism to ensure proper provision.

The second argument owes more to the liberal defence of the market economy. Economic growth, by relaxing the constraints on individuals, enhances their range of choices. Poor people may be so concerned with the daily struggle to maintain an adequate standard of life that they have little opportunity for making choices. By contrast, a rich person can make choices without constraints. Such choices need not be hedonistic. A rich person may prefer to live simply, and to give money away to charity or to pursue some eccentric but expensive hobby. Even if people do choose to be hedonistic, they can be so in a discerning way — they may enjoy fine wines, good cuisine, and visiting exotic and luxurious places. How they choose to spend their income is irrelevant: the gain from economic growth is that their freedoms are greatly enhanced. While this aspect could be incorporated in welfare economics, it usually is not.

In contrast with this benign description of the consequences of growth, a feeling that all is not well is one which has been widely reported.[5] For example, evidence from consumer attitude surveys in the United States suggested that there was no great increase in satisfaction as consumer income per capita rose. Easterlin[6] reported on surveys undertaken between 1946 and 1970 when real incomes per capita rose by some 62%. The proportion of the population who reported themselves to be 'very happy' with their lot in life fluctuated between 40% and 53%, but without any discernible trend over time. There was, however, a very slight decline in those reporting 'not very happy'. Furthermore, there is considerable evidence to suggest that what matters to consumers is their relative income, rather than the absolute levels they have achieved.[7]

There is however a measurement problem. Some of the apparent discrepancy between indicators of growth and of satisfaction may arise from a failure to include in measures of national income a sufficiently wide definition of what generates consumer satisfaction. For example, national accounting procedures do not include the value of leisure and non-market activities, such as housework and do-it-yourself. On the other hand, expenditures on travel to work by private households, and on defence, police and road maintenance by government, are included, although they are purely instrumental to other activities and not final goods as such. These observations led Nordhaus and Tobin[8] to recompute US national income excluding these latter 'goods', but including leisure and non-market activities. They also included estimates of the disamenities (or external costs) of living in urban areas. These computations of 'measurable economic welfare' suggested a much lower rate of growth of income per capita in the USA in the period 1947–65 than that given by conventional net national product measures.

But the critics argue that it is not just a question of measurement. While most of them concentrate on the consequences of economic growth for human satisfaction, Thurow[9] has drawn attention to the *process* of economic growth. He argues that economic changes are essentially zero sum. Even if the *net* gains from a particular change are positive, the gross gains and losses are so much greater that the appearance is zero sum. A particular example is the argument for adjustment policies in the North in the face of import competition from the Newly Industrializing Countries, as described in the previous chapter. Although the removal of protection will probably give a net gain in national income, the losses in the particular industries affected may be severe. Hence, industry representatives will demand from governments protection to ensure income security.

Thurow's point[10] is that a democratically elected government like that of the USA finds it difficult to make the distributional judgments implicit in gains and losses arising from economic change, whether that change is exogenous or policy-induced. They accede to requests for protection: but once protection has been granted, it is difficult to reverse since it is protecting someone's current income. The outcome is a growth of regulation and restrictions imposed by the government, which in the long run are inimical to further economic growth, and impair the very freedom of choice which is supposed to be a fruit of growth.

E. J. Mishan's book *The Costs of Economic Growth*[11] was first published in 1967. He can therefore claim to be something of a pioneer in this field. His attack on economic growth as an objective of policy has two aspects. In the first he draws attention to the undesirable consequences of economic growth in the form of externalities. The second is a critique of the arguments for growth from consumer sovereignty, which he describes as a 'myth'.

The theory of externalities has been an important part of welfare economics since the work of Pigou[12] in the 1930s. Production and consumption activities may have consequences for others, either benefits or costs. The traditional examples are those of a beekeeper, whose bees are a benefit to the owners of nearby orchards, and of a factory producing smoke which has adverse effects on people living in the neighbourhood. These side-effects are unintended and are not accounted for in any market. Thus the beekeeper cannot charge for the services of his bees. Nor are people compensated for living in a smoky environment.

How to deal with these problems has exercised the ingenuity of numerous economists. One route is to create property rights where none existed before. At an abstract level, the pollution problem could be solved by giving the inhabitants of a particular area a property right in unpolluted air. Then any polluter would have to pay for the right to pollute. Another route, which applies to the beekeepers/fruit growers example, is to 'internalize' the externality by integrating beekeeping and fruit growing in one operation. Then the owners of the integrated activity will seek an optimal balance between bees and fruit trees so as to maximize the joint returns from the fruit and honey.

A third route is to regulate either by taxation or by quantity controls. Thus, in the pollution case, the authorities could monitor emissions and charge firms according to the amount of damage that they do to the environment. In principle, a properly constructed tax could maximize net social welfare, by ensuring that at the margin the social cost of further pollution was equal to the social benefit of further output from the polluting activity. Alternatively, the authorities could decide how much pollution was tolerable, and then issue licences up to that amount. The licences would be sold to the highest bidder, ensuring that the output produced within the pollution limit had the highest market value.

All these technical solutions are well known to Mishan: indeed he has been a distinguished contributor to the literature on them. However, he is not hopeful that they provide the answer to the problems. First, he sees economic growth, and in particular growth in urban areas, as creating more and more serious problems of externalities. This is partly the effect of congestion: as people live closer together certain externalities, such as noise, become more acute. Second, he argues that technical solutions are pursued in a context where radical alternatives are ruled out. The prime example for him is the use of private cars in urban areas. Solutions are sought to ameliorate the situation created by heavy traffic. The possibility that the quality of life would be higher *without* the private car is not considered. The private car having been invented, we have to live with it. Third, externalities become so pervasive with economic growth that any effort to deal with them by regulation would involve an unacceptable extension of government into every day.

Other economists have taken issue with Mishan over his pessimism. Beckerman is representative of those who make three points in reply[13]. First, the rate of growth of an economy reflects the desire of consumers to save and provide for the future. There is no question of pursuing growth for its own sake. Second, Mishan's objection is not to growth as such, but to the wrong sort of growth. Externalities would exist in a static economy. They represent a misallocation of resources, and should be dealt with by way of the methods discussed above. The objective is not 'no pollution', but rather the level of pollution at which the social gains from the activity offset the social costs. Third, society in general and governments in particular have been sensitive to environmental issues, and this is reflected in both legislation and the activities of environmental lobbyists. Indeed, Thurow cites the success of environmental pressure groups in the US as a significant factor in slowing down the rate of growth. He suggests that there is a high-income elasticity of demand for a protected environment, so that lobbying on these issues tends to be a concern of the middle class. In the US he believes that they have been successful in holding up developments of mining, industry and nuclear power, as well as slowing down the building of new highways. The costs of development foregone have often fallen on lower income groups.

The second thread of Mishan's argument is that the doctrine of consumers' sovereignty is a myth. This doctrine assumes that the extension of the range of opportunities facing a person contributes to an increase in his welfare. But that rests on the presumption that the wants of consumers exist independently of the products created by industrial concerns. Suppose, alternatively, that the industrial system is actually want-creating and not want-providing. Then some deeper analysis is needed to decide whether the creation of new wants actually enhances welfare. Mishan believes, for example, that leisure is not increasing as fast as it should. People are continuing to work unnecessarily hard, in order to purchase sophisticated new products which bring little satisfaction.

Mishan's willingness to cut loose from consumer sovereignty enables him to extend his critique to a wide range of social phenomena. He is, for example, sceptical of 'progress' in technology and science. He accuses rapid communications of destroying local culture and regional variety, television of destroying values without putting anything in their place, and the media of succumbing to commercial pressures to peddle pornography. But the basis for this critique is never made explicit in his book. He denies consumer sovereignty as a valid criterion, but can only appeal to his own values to put in its place.

The critique of growth offered by Hirsch[14] is based on two elements that he perceives operating within the market system. The two elements are the 'neglected role of social scarcity' and the 'commercialization' bias. These problems are inherent in the growth process, but are not amenable to the same sort of corrective mechanisms as externalities.

The starting point for the analysis of social scarcity is the distinction between material goods, which are in principle reproducible, and positional goods, which are not. Material goods are the normal goods and services of an industrialized economy. Positional goods are such things as works of art, the beauty of the landscape, and jobs with considerable prestige attached. The significance of positional goods is that there is a high-income elasticity of demand for such goods. Hence one of the fruits of economic growth is intensifying demand for them, linked to inelasticity in supply.

Competition for positional goods may take one of three

forms. Works of art are typically competed for at auctions, being sold to the highest bidder. Who gets them depends on a person's relative position in the income distribution, and not on absolute income levels. Prestigious jobs are allocated by a screening process on the basis of more and more elaborate educational qualifications. A third method of competition applies particularly to areas of scenic beauty. As there is no means of allocating these goods in the market, they tend to become more and more congested, and the quality declines. The Mediterranean beach which is beautiful for a few tourists loses its charm when the beach is filled up with lots of bodies.

The outcome of these processes of competition, according to Hirsch, is consumer frustration. Growth in income brings the individual no greater access to positional goods, unless he manages to improve his relative position in the income distribution. Young people undertake longer training to get a job with more prestige, only to discover that others of their peers have done the same. The Mediterranean beach is no longer special if it has to be shared with all sorts and conditions of men. This frustration for the consumer is the problem of social scarcity. Hirsch sums up:[15]

> The choice facing the individual in a market or market-type transaction in the positional sector, in a context of material growth, always appears more attractive than it turns out to be after others have exercised their choice.

Hirsch's second main theme[16] is 'the commercialization bias'. He begins with an observation made by Linder[17], that affluence tends to make modern man more harried rather than less. The explanation is partly that increasing affluence generates a wider range of consumption activities which crowd into the leisure time of the individual, and partly that increasing productivity in the economy as a whole increases the relative price of personal services. The consumer therefore has to economize on his use of time, and simultaneously finds that he is substituting do-it-yourself for expensive personal services bought in. At the same time, increased competition for positional goods, with the personal striving to get ahead, requires the individual to work longer hours rather than shorter hours, thus effectively squeezing leisure time yet further.

Pressure on leisure time has other undesirable effects. One is the erosion of sociability. Time is too expensive and scarce for it to be 'wasted'. This applies as much to spending time with friends, as to giving time to voluntary work. People do not want to be involved. Being a Good Samaritan is too time-consuming.

The pressure to get ahead, in order to acquire positional goods, also strengthens the ethos of self-interest. The erosion of sociability and the growth of self-interest are contributing factors to the decline of social norms and conventions. The market is extended into new areas, with fully specified contracts replacing trust and a sense of mutual obligation. The discussion of this point by Hirsch leads into a third theme, which concerns the decline of the moral basis for capitalism. This theme was discussed in Chapter Four.

The final critic of economic growth to be considered here is Scitovsky. His book, *The Joyless Economy*,[18] suggests that economics has made a fundamental error in its assumptions about the psychological basis for human satisfaction. He makes a distinction between comfort and pleasure. At the risk of undue simplification, we may summarize the distinction by noting that the degree of comfort depends on the *level* of stimulation (*e.g.* work level, consumption, pleasure, interaction with other people) that the person receives, but that pleasure depends on *changes* in stimulation. For example, a person may feel pleasure at taking on an increasing work-load for a period, and will again feel pleasure when the task is complete and the pressure comes off. A period of foreign travel involving considerable challenge and discomfort will bring pleasure, only to be matched by the pleasure of returning home eventually.

Introducing these ideas in economics, Scitovsky makes two points. First, that economics concerns itself with the level of goods that are available for consumption. But these provide primarily for comfort, and he believes that demand for such goods is in fact satiable. An increased supply does little to make consumers feel more satisfied. Second, economics only registers those satisfactions which pass through the marketplace. It does not consider self-generated satisfactions, nor those which arise from non-market interactions with others.

He then goes on to apply his analysis in a critique of US society. He produces evidence which suggests to him that the US economy gives too great a weight to the comfort of the consumer, and too little to pleasure. Life is rich in material things, but also boring and dull. Despite their wealth, Americans are satisfied with more boring food, take fewer vacations, and spend less time socializing than Europeans. He traces the problem to the Puritan heritage of the USA. That heritage put an emphasis on work. A man was to find satisfaction in doing his work well, not in the consumption which that work made possible. Unfortunately, that ethic of work has not been able to survive the increasing mechanization of work, which makes pride in a job well done much more difficult to achieve. Human worth is now assessed in terms of money earned.

The consequence of this emphasis on work rather than consumption is that consumption is neglected as an activity. There is a preference for comfort, rather than stimulation. Yet consumption for comfort is so high in America that a huge proportion of the population is satiated.

It is difficult to do justice in a few paragraphs to these critics of economic growth. Any attempt at summarizing their position must inevitably be something of a caricature. However, we do need to evaluate their success in putting up a general case for placing less emphasis on growth as a goal of economic policy.

Their arguments can be arranged under four headings. The first is that the hedonistic model of utilitarian welfare economics (and to a lesser extent of choice theory) is not an adequate framework for expressing all the elements that go to make up human satisfaction. The equation of economic growth with an improvement in national welfare is therefore to be avoided.

The second theme is that of income distribution. Any interpretation of growth which fails to consider the pattern of gainers and losers is implausible. The zero-sum nature of much economic growth, and the stress by Hirsch on relative incomes in the competition for positional goods, suggests that the hope that growth will automatically increase the sum of human happiness is quite misplaced.

The third theme is that of disbelief that the market mechanism, linked to consumer sovereignty, produces acceptable outcomes. While some technical problems, such as externalities, may be solvable, others, such as the competition for positional goods, suggest a more fundamental difficulty. The instinct of the critics is usually to look for non-market solutions, or at least to call for substantial regulation of the relevant markets.

A further theme is explored in some depth by Hirsch, and given prominent mention by Mishan. This is the erosion of traditional values by the extension of the market-place. These writers see the intrusion of the market as corrosive of relationships of love, trust and mutual obligation.

Our judgment is that the critics have made a convincing case for treating with scepticism the claim that a higher level of Gross National Product in a market economy, or a higher growth rate of GNP, can be directly equated with an increase in welfare. However, from a Christian standpoint as outlined in the *Principles* of Chapter Two, it is arguable that their critiques do not go far enough. For the most part their critiques remain firmly within the utilitarian framework, where the happiness or satisfaction of the person is determined by the external circumstances which affect him or her. The implication is that a different set of goods could be made to yield greater welfare than the goods on offer.

The biblical material reviewed in Chapter One would make two criticisms of this assumption. The first is that man finds his highest satisfaction in relationships with God and with his fellow human beings, and not in things at all. Second, the provision of the basic necessities of life is essential to his survival: but ever-increasing personal possessions are described as potentially harmful in that they can become an idol. The many New Testament warnings concerning the dangers of possessions and possessiveness need to be taken seriously. Economic growth leading to ever-increasing consumption is not therefore an objective for the economy which a Christian can espouse.

That is not to deny that man has responsibilities in the area of economic life, however. He is called to be a steward of the environment with its natural resources, and of his own talents and abilities. He is to exercise his stewardship through work, and thereby to provide for his basic needs. Any surplus is to be used to provide for the needs of others, not to increase his own consumption. Economic activity is to provide the basis for life in community; it is not supposed to be its raison d'être. Jesus said: 'Watch out! Be on your guard against all kinds of greed; a man's life does not consist in the abundance of his possessions' (Luke 12:15).

3. Renewable resources and exhaustible resources

Our second task is to examine the economics of the exploitation of natural resources in the light of our biblical principles. We distinguish between renewable and exhaustible resources. The former present possibilities of biological regeneration, the latter do not. One fear is that the take of renewable resources may be increased to such a level that the species or ecosystem involved is threatened with destruction. Another fear is that the rate of depletion of exhaustible resources is so great that we are faced, in the foreseeable future, with exhaustion of these resources.

Sections 5 and 6 examine these fears in the context of a market economy. However, the criteria which we bring to bear on the question are not those of economic efficiency. Instead, we refer in section 4 to the biblical *Principles* outlined in Chapter Two which can be conveniently summarized by the concept of man as steward. We shall see that some of the problems of a market economy arise from the fact that no one person or authority is given the stewardship responsibility for a particular natural resource.

The biological model that underlies many cases of renewable resources is shown in figure 1.[19] The inverted curve relates the stock of a biological resource along the horizontal axis to the average change in stock on the vertical axis.[20] A typical example would be the population of a particular species in a geographical ecosystem. If the initial population Z_o is less than $\underline{Z}$, then mating probabilities are too low, and the chances of being killed by a predator are too high, for the population to reproduce itself. Over time the numbers will fall, and eventually the species will become extinct. If however Z_o exceeds $\underline{Z}$, then conditions are favourable for growth. Mating probabilities are sufficiently high for the population stock to increase, at an increasing rate up to $\hat{Z}$. As the stock increases beyond $\hat{Z}$, so the change in stock diminishes due to limitations on food supply. By the time the stock reaches $\bar{Z}$, there is a balance between gains in population due to reproduction and losses due to lack of food. Should the population by chance increase beyond $\bar{Z}$, then the losses will outweigh the gains, and there will be a tendency for the population stock to shrink back to $\bar{Z}$. $\bar{Z}$ is then the stable long-run equilibrium population for the species concerned, in the absence of any human interference.

A similar model is used for understanding a number of other cases. For example, the stock could be interpreted as vegetation cover. Below $\underline{Z}$ the vegetation is so poorly estab-

FIGURE 1

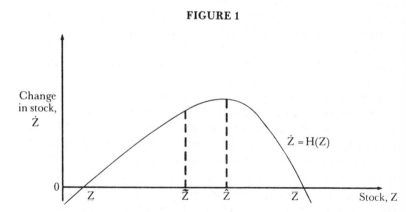

lished that reproduction is difficult and nutrients are leached from the soil. Hence the vegetation goes into irreversible decline. Between $\underline{Z}$ and $\bar{Z}$ conditions are favourable to an increasing density of vegetation cover, but as the stock increases beyond $\hat{Z}$, so growth slows due to crowding of the environment. The stable long-run equilibrium stock is at $\bar{Z}$.

The significance of this example, and that of animal species which preceded it, is that they give scope for farming the resource. Thus for any stock between $\underline{Z}$ and $\bar{Z}$, so long as the take is restricted to $\dot{Z}$, the natural change in stock, then the stock is preserved for ever. The level of intervention in the ecosystem will vary between cases. Whaling, fishing and the grazing of natural pastureland can take place without intervention other than catching the fish or putting the cattle on the pasture.

In other cases, farming will involve creating an ecosystem with the features indicated in figure 1. For example, consider planting an area with wheat. Define the stock as the quantity of wheat grain at the end of each growing season, which can be used either for planting or for consumption. If the stock is somewhere in the region of $\hat{Z}$, then the appropriate $\dot{Z}$ can be consumed, leaving sufficient seed to ensure renewal of the stock in the next period. However the attempt to maintain a higher stock, in the region of $\bar{Z}$, implies that the land is overcrowded and yields will be no more than is planted. Of course, no farmer would ever operate in this region, but it is the point to which a natural wheat ecosystem would tend. The declining stock below $\underline{Z}$ may be interpreted as negative yields due to the ravages of pests and diseases[21].

A final interpretation of figure 1 is in terms of pollution or waste disposal. The disposal of liquid effluent, which can be broken down by natural biological processes in rivers, is an example. The stock in this case is the level of dissolved oxygen in the water. The ecosystem, if left undisturbed, tends to an equilibrium at $\bar{Z}$. Below $\underline{Z}$ the oxygen level deteriorates until the river becomes dead. Between $\underline{Z}$ and $\bar{Z}$ the oxygen level can be maintained so long as the breaking down of the effluent does not require more oxygen than the surplus which the system is itself generating.

An exhaustible resource does not have any capacity for

reproducing itself[22]. However, we need to distinguish between resources that are destroyed in use and those which are recyclable. Petroleum and coal are examples of the former. Most metals, on the other hand, could be recycled. But the process of recycling usually involves at least some destruction of the stock. Hence it is appropriate to see recycling as a means of extending the period of use of the natural stock, rather than removing the prospect of it being exhausted at some future date. The same basic model can be used to consider pollution which builds up over time, and is not dissipated by biological means or by natural decay. We can imagine an initial stock of clean water or air that is progressively polluted, thus effectively reducing the stock.

4. Biblical teaching concerning the created order

The biblical understanding of the relationship between man and his environment is set out in key passages in the early chapters of Genesis. This biblical material was discussed in Chapter One, and from it we derived our *Principle 1:* man may use the resources of the created order to provide for his existence, but he must not waste or destroy that order. Here we recall some of the major emphases of that discussion[23].

Man is a steward of the created order, given authority over it, but ultimately responsible to God, who is the creator. That stewardship should be characterized by care, preservation and respect. Fruits and animals may be used for food as required, and that use will involve work and active husbandry. The ideal pattern of Genesis 1 and 2 has been distorted by the fall, but not destroyed. Relationships between man and the created order are difficult, not least because of the rapacity of man.

In the covenant with Noah there is an emphasis on respect for the natural order, which is itself included in the covenant. This emphasis is reflected in the Old Testament Law, with its inclusion of the ox and the ass in the sabbath rest, and the injunctions to allow the land a sabbatical rest. The inclusion of the natural order within the covenant is underlined by the inclusion of creation in our future hope. Thus in

Isaiah 11:6–9 animals are a part of the Messianic kingdom, and in Romans 8:21 Paul speaks of the whole creation awaiting freedom from its bondage to decay.

The application of these biblical principles to renewable resources is straightforward. If figure 1 is a fair representation of the biological dynamics, then any pattern of use which leaves the stock intact falls within the biblical principles. This can be achieved by consuming the quantity $\dot{Z}$ for any stock level between $\underline{Z}$ and $\bar{Z}$.[24] We might also prefer that the stock should be maintained in the range $\hat{Z}$ to $\bar{Z}$. Stocks in the range $\underline{Z}$ to $\hat{Z}$ will give the same consumption level, but with a lower stock. It might be objected that the 'natural' level of stock is, in fact, $\bar{Z}$: however the mandate to use plants and meat for food admits of some reduction of the stock below $\bar{Z}$ in order to create a biological surplus for consumption.

The maximum take, it will be observed, is when the stock is at $\hat{Z}$. If, for example, the initial stock is at $\bar{Z}$, and consumption is set at the value of $\dot{Z}$ which corresponds to $\hat{Z}$, then the stock will fall over time until $\hat{Z}$ is reached. However if the stock is in the range $\underline{Z}$ to $\hat{Z}$, and the rate of take exceeds the relevant $\dot{Z}$ on the curve, then the stock falls continuously. Once it falls below $\underline{Z}$ the situation is catastrophic, since the stock cannot be renewed biologically. It is therefore important to arrest the process before $\underline{Z}$ is reached, by reducing the rate of consumption.

There is the further possibility that by intervention man can improve the biological dynamics, increasing the surplus at every level of stock. This is the essence of farming and animal husbandry. The creation ordinance to till and to keep, and the reference to struggle against weeds in Genesis 3:18, suggest that active cultivation is encouraged. The danger is that ecosystems are very delicately balanced: increasing the biological surplus in one direction may lead to deterioration of the environment in another direction. The side-effects of fertilizers, pesticides and insecticides are a case in point. The destruction of soil by intensive cropping is another example. Agricultural systems need to be carefully scrutinized to ensure that they are conducive to steady state stocks in other elements of the ecosystem, and do not lead to the destruction of any of them.[25] This is a very stringent requirement by the standards of modern agriculture.

On the question of exhaustible resources, we can get little direct guidance from the biblical material, which refers exclusively to biologically renewable resources. We have to proceed by extrapolating our biblical principles.

One extreme position could be to stress conservation. If man is required to preserve the created order, then he should do nothing to deplete the environment which he hands on to his dependents. However this does not give sufficient weight to man's role as steward, given *dominion* over the natural order. A good deal depends on the view that is taken of human culture. If this is a proper activity of man in the image of God, then we may take a positive view of the human enterprise, including the artefacts that man has designed and made. A negative view, which is not without support in Genesis 1–11, is that human enterprise arises out of man's rebellion against God: it is in his artefacts that man seeks significance and security. We incline to the first view, while accepting that much human enterprise is indeed motivated by the second aspect.

Assuming that an exhaustible resource is going to be put to a good use, are we justified in depleting it and so depriving future generations? Our response is in the affirmative, but with a reservation. If a substitute does not exist, then it is presumptuous to believe that our needs are greater than those of a later generation. In practice, it is hard to find an example of a resource without a biologically renewable substitute. For example, the fossil fuels could, in principle, be replaced by wood and solar energy. Metals are more of a problem, but it is not impossible to conceive of a culture that uses no metal in its artefacts (and metals can be recycled to extend their availability over time).

We have not looked at the question of demand: it is arguable that much of the pressure on natural resources in our world arises from the greed of consumers in the advanced industrial nations. We will return briefly to this issue in our concluding comments. But for the next two sections we will presume that the level of demand for resource-using products can in fact be justified on the basis of human needs. Our concern will be whether a market economy will use resources in a manner consistent with our biblical principles.

5. Renewable resources in a market economy

In this section[26] we will be concerned with the market conditions under which a renewable resource may be exploited to extinction or may be preserved at a steady state stock in the long run. There are two cases to consider. The first concerns the behaviour of a whole industry acting together, which is fully aware of the biological dynamics illustrated in figure 1. The second is the problem of the 'common', where individual firms may be aware of the problems posed by renewable resources, but each has too little influence on the outcome to make it worthwhile to act on its own. The formal analysis of these cases is complex, so all we can hope to do is to sketch what happens.

To fix ideas we consider a fishing fleet in single ownership which is considering its policy for a fishing ground in which it is the sole operator. Assume that the price of the catch is invariant over time, and so are the costs of making the catch. If the industry's objective is to maximize the present value of its stream of profits over time, then it should reason as follows. Suppose the fleet makes an extra catch, and that the industry invests the proceeds in government bonds. Then it can enjoy a stream of interest payments at the rate on the bonds. Alternatively it can forgo the catch, thereby slightly increasing the stock Z, and thus making possible a slightly larger catch as shown by the function $H(Z)$ in figure 1. The value of the stream of incremental catches is, in effect, the return to the 'investment' that is represented by forgoing the catch now. An optimal policy will involve increasing the catch up to the point where the return on this investment equals the interest rate (that is, where the slope of the function $H(Z)$ equals the interest rate). The optimal catch will therefore involve a stock like $\bar{Z}$, which is less than $\hat{Z}$, which gives the maximum catch compatible with maintaining a steady stock. Increasing the stock may also make fishing less costly in real terms in future: if so, this return should be added to that of the investment in higher future catches.

Suppose however that the returns to forgoing the catch are small: an increase in stock only permits slightly higher catches in future, and there is no effect on costs. If these returns are less than the rate of interest, then it always pays the industry to make a catch now, rather than invest in future catches. The profit-maximizing policy is to run down the stocks as fast as possible within the constraints of the capacity of the fleet. The biological process is just too slight to make it worth waiting for it to produce a natural surplus. Unless the resource is given a value in itself, quite apart from its value in use, it will not be worth preserving.

If the industry consists of a large number of individual firms all seeking their own advantage, the situation may be even worse. This is the case of the 'common'. There are two separate problems for the allocation of resources. First, the firms can quickly destroy the stock of the resource. Even if they can see that this is going to happen, no one firm has an incentive to change its behaviour. The second problem is a classic externality problem. Each firm fails to take into account the effect of its own activities on the costs of other firms. The outcome is that at the margin the private returns are worth less than the full social costs.

The first problem can be analysed by considering the profit-maximizing behaviour of the firms. Given market demand for the resource, and given the costs of obtaining it, each firm seeks to maximize its profits. If the enterprise yields a surplus over costs, then more firms enter the industry until the surplus is eliminated by a fall in the market price as the supply increases. The equilibrium level of take depends on the level of stock in each period. A larger stock makes extraction cheaper (for example, the fish are easier to catch) and so the take will be larger. This relationship is indicated in figure 2 by the curves F_1 and F_2. The difference between F_1 and F_2 is that in the latter case the activity is more profitable: market demand is higher and/or costs are lower. So in equilibrium there will be more firms, and the total take will be larger.

If F_1 is the relevant curve, then the dynamics dictate that an equilibrium stock will be established at Z_e and the take in each period will be $H(Z_e)$. Suppose demand for the resource

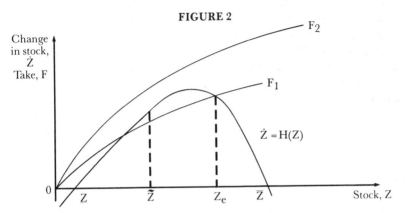

FIGURE 2

increases, so that the level of catch as a function of the stock is indicated by F_2. Then there is no intersection with the $H(\underline{Z})$ curve which represents the biological dynamics. The outcome is catastrophic for the resource. It is depleted at the rate indicated by the relevant points of F_2 until it is exhausted.

Unfortunately this outcome cannot be attributed solely to the ignorance of the firms concerning the biological dynamics. Suppose they are fully aware, and recognize that an optimal policy for the industry would involve a stock $\tilde{Z}$, and a take $H(\bar{Z})$. But for the individual firm the incentive to pursue the required reduction in its take is very weak. Indeed, if it believes that other firms will reduce their take, its individual incentive is to increase its own take. Unless the industry can reach an enforceable agreement between the firms to reduce the take to $H(\bar{Z})$, then the prospects are gloomy.

The second problem is that of externalities. In a range of industries involving the exploitation of common natural resources, the activities of any one firm affect the costs of other firms. In the fishing example, the crowding of boats in the fishing area makes it more difficult for any one boat to make a catch. The addition of animals to common pasture makes it more difficult for the animals already there to obtain fodder. Because firms do not take these additional costs into account, they expand their activities beyond the socially optimal point, defined as the level at which their take would be fixed if the firms jointly considered the matter. This is another feature of resource exploitation which could shift up the F function in figure 2, and thereby lead to depletion of the stock.

Leaving the exploitation of a biological natural resource to market forces may result in the destruction of that resource, possibly within a short time period. Such an outcome is inconsistent with the biblical requirement to keep creation. So we need to consider measures to regulate the relevant markets. First, we consider the externality problem. One solution is to do away with the common by creating exclusive property rights. Common pasture may be fenced, and each area allotted to a single owner. The externality is internalized: if the owner increases the number of animals on his pasture, then he affects no one but himself. But this solution is not always available: it is difficult to create exclusive fishing rights by area, for example.

A second kind of solution involves quantitative limits, with quotas being assigned to each firm. The problem here is that quotas permit the firms to earn large rents. It may be preferable, on distributive grounds, to auction the quotas to the highest bidders. The rents will be collected by the regulatory authorities rather than by the firms. A third solution is a tax on the activity designed to reflect the social costs which firms would not otherwise pay. Each firm will then find it in its own interests to reduce its activity.

A similar choice of measures is available for the problem of the excessive depletion of the stock due to maximization of profits. The fundamental difficulty is that no-one acts as the keeper of the resource, which is exploited for nothing. One solution is therefore to appoint a keeper who will charge for exploiting the resource at such a level that its long-term future is assured. Effectively the same result is achieved by a regulatory authority, which charges an equivalent tax, or which fixes quotas and sells them to the firms. Finally, if the problem is that the return to preserving the stock is less than the rate of interest, then simple tax incentives are of little assistance. Conservation will almost certainly require regulation by quota.

The interesting feature of these proposed solutions from the biblical standpoint is that they involve the assignment of stewardship responsibilities in a biological resource to some person or group of people. They make arrangements to regulate the use of the resource, and its conservation. Whether it is more effective to give incentives to these stewards by giving them *private* property rights in the resource is an interesting question. This solution will not give the desired result in the first case we examined.

The reality of regulation may be very difficult, particularly where the resource in question is internationally accessible. The problems are to secure agreement between the nations involved, and to police the agreement afterwards. Suppose, for example, that an international agreement stipulated that a particular resource should not be exploited for a time to permit regeneration, and that exploitation thereafter should be restricted. It is likely to be in the interests of a single participant in the agreement to renege, either secretly or openly. Unless there can be enforceable penalties for default, there is little prospect that agreement will be reached between the parties.

6. Exhaustible resources in a market economy

The biblical analysis gives us little guidance for dealing with the issue of exhaustible resources. Having concluded that the utilization of such resources is not inconsistent with man's stewardship of the natural order, we are left with no guidelines to answer the main question in the economic analysis of exhaustible resources — does a market economy tend to use up such resources too fast or too slowly? The difficulty is to define what is meant by too fast and too slow.

We need to consider the role that exhaustible resources

play in production. A fear commonly expressed is that once certain resources are exhausted the standard of life must drop dramatically. Extrapolations of present growth rates of consumption of exhaustible resources suggest that exhaustion is not a remote possibility, but might occur as soon as the lifetimes of our great-grandchildren. This gloomy scenario is however predicted on the basis of two assumptions which seem unlikely on the basis of historical experience. The first is that it is not possible to substitute produced resources for exhaustible resources in production. The second is that there is no technical progress of a resource-saving kind. If these assumptions are dropped, then the fear can be shown to be ill-founded. If we go further, we may consider future technologies which are based entirely on renewable resources (so long as we have not destroyed those resources in the meantime!). The range of products will probably look different from those we enjoy now, which are based on exhaustible resources, but there is no reason to think that the standard of life will be inferior.

We now consider the rate of depletion of a natural resource in a market economy. For a profit-maximizing industry the price of the resource will increase at the rate of interest. If the firm extracts a marginal unit of the resource, it can sell it for the market price in this period and invest the proceeds at the rate of interest. If the unit is left in the ground this period, it can be extracted next period and sold at the market price prevailing in that period. The firm will choose whichever course of action brings the higher return. At the equilibrium, therefore, the rate of appreciation of the price must be equal to the rate of interest. Assuming a positive rate of interest, the market price will increase exponentially over time.

The second feature of the equilibrium, presuming perfect foresight, is that the prices should be set to exhaust the stock of the resource over the relevant time period. For resources without substitutes, the relevant time period is infinite. More plausibly, there is a substitute, but with a higher cost. In this case, once the price of the exhaustible resource reaches that of the substitute, the switch will take place to the latter. The firm maximizes profits by ensuring that the time path of prices leads to depletion of the stock by the time the switch occurs. There is no point in leaving a part of it in the ground unused.

Three features of these price paths over time are of particular interest. First, the prices over time can be interpreted as increasing royalty or rent, due to the fact that the resource is in fixed supply. This becomes an important feature of the price as the prospect of exhaustion draws close. Where there is sufficient supply for the foreseeable future, then the competitive market price will be at the level of the costs of extraction.

The second feature arises if we remove, rather obviously, the assumption of perfect foresight. The price path will exhibit growth over time at the rate of interest. But the absolute level of the whole path may be 'wrong' if the resource is to be exhausted within the relevant time horizon. The fact that the price is wrong will not be immediately evident to the firms. For example, a price path that is too low will only become apparent when exhaustion approaches and there is no appropriately priced substitute. Alternatively, a cartel of producers may be tempted to fix a high price level, and find itself with some of the resource left in the ground when a substitute becomes available at a comparable price. It is, therefore, inappropriate to assume that markets will get the rate of depletion right.

The third feature is the role of the rate of interest. A higher rate of interest gives a higher weight to current consumption of the resource as against future consumption: a lower rate favours later consumption and therefore conservation. The interest rate reflects the willingness of the economy to defer consumption. But the market rate of interest, which motivates firms, may not be a particularly useful indicator of this role for interest rates. Capital markets are imperfect, and the interest rates are subject to manipulation by the monetary authorities. More seriously, a lower rate of depletion of a resource will probably benefit people who are not yet born. Yet their voice is only imperfectly heard in capital markets via the willingness of people to save not for themselves but to pass on assets to their children. A culture which gives a high priority to preserving family identity over the generations will probably perform better than one which leaves each generation to make its own way in the world.

These considerations suggest that a market economy will deplete resources too fast. Against this, it is argued that the pace of technical progress is such that we need not worry too much about future generations. Man has shown such inventive capacity, and made such technological strides, that there is the opposite danger of leaving resources in the ground only to discover later that they are obsolete. Taking no thought for the future is regarded as a virtue! But our biblical principles require us to think carefully before using up a resource. Even if we are sure that a substitute will be available, that is no justification for gobbling up resources just because they are there. We can never know how a future generation might have used an exhaustible resource, if we had not used it up. We should attach a considerable value to leaving resources untouched in the ground, and not presume to value them solely by their uses now and in the foreseeable future. We need perhaps to appoint keepers to regulate the use of exhaustible natural resources.

Our prescription of caution has particular force in respect of the production of certain chemical or radioactive wastes. Such wastes are not to any appreciable extent diminished by natural processes in the biosphere, there is no immediately available technology which would enable them to be rendered harmless, and the tolerance of the biosphere to such wastes in the long run is usually unknown. In these circumstances, the biblical principles of stewardship would seem to us to require an outright prohibition.

7. Conclusions

This chapter has considered doubts that have been expressed about the desirability of economic growth in an advanced economy. The first set concerned whether economic growth contributes to increasing human happiness in societies which have moved beyond the basic necessities of life. Various objections to the process of economic growth were considered: that growth inevitably involves distributional questions, since there are both gainers and losers; that economic growth brings an increase in unwelcome externalities which cannot easily be compensated by regulation or by the price mechanism; that growth brings with it a struggle for positional goods, which leaves people feeling frustrated, and a commercialization bias which destroys other social values; and that the hedonistic model of man, which presumes that more is necessarily better, ignores other insights into human psychology. Many of these objections are unsurprising to a Christian analyst. The idea that the pursuit of possessions brings increasing happiness is not consistent with the Christian understanding of man. Man finds his highest satisfaction in relationships with God and his fellow men, and not in things at all. Once a man has the basic necessities of life, then 'enough is enough'[27].

The second set of doubts concerned the exploitation of the environment and natural resources. The fear is that economic growth will lead to the destruction of renewable resources, and the exhaustion of non-renewable resources. The biblical material convinced us that the exploitation of renewable resources should be kept at a level which preserves the stock in the long run. Extinction of a species is not consistent with the biblical concept of stewardship. Economic analysis shows that an unregulated market economy does not have any mechanism to prevent the process of extinction, and, indeed, in a number of plausible contexts may actually generate such a process. The difficulty arises, in part, from the lack of a steward of the natural resource in question. Our biblical principles would suggest that a steward should be appointed to regulate exploitation, with explicit responsibility for keeping the resource in the sense of Genesis 2.

By farming, man intervenes in the ecosystem to increase biological yields, and thus the surplus for consumption. The injunction to till the garden in Genesis 2 is sufficient to indicate that some intervention is part of a positive stewardship of creation. However it is evident, on biblical criteria, that such intervention should not result in the irreversible deterioration of some element of the ecosystem. Yet in a market economy such deterioration could easily happen, when the pursuit of short-term gain is sufficient to induce the farmer to ignore the longer-term consequences.

While we could find nothing to indicate that exhaustible resources should not be exploited, we interpreted the concept of stewardship to involve a strong obligation to make provision for future generations. We concluded that markets are likely to err in the direction of using up such resources too rapidly. Exhaustible resources too need keepers.

We presumed throughout sections 3 to 6 that the demands which drive the exploitation of both renewable and exhaustible resources are justifiable on the basis of human need. In fact the pressure on resources which we witness in the world economy is largely a by-product of the demands arising from the high-income countries of the OECD nations.[28] The lifestyles which high incomes sustain are far removed from the basic requirements of food (and clothing) for which the created order is provided in Genesis 1, and to which Jesus refers in the Sermon on the Mount. A simpler lifestyle in these countries would greatly alleviate[29] the pressure on both renewable and exhaustible resources.

Postscript

The main theme of the book has been an exploration of a particular method of applying Christian social ethics to economic problems. In drawing the threads together it will be useful to focus attention on the method rather than on the detail of application.

The method can be summarized in the following diagram:

$$T \longrightarrow DSP \longrightarrow R$$

The starting point is the Christian *tradition* symbolized by the letter T. Our definition of T in Chapter One presumed the authority of Scripture. But this raises questions about how Scripture is to be interpreted. In practice, the scriptures need to be interpreted within a theological framework. This framework seeks to relate the elements of the biblical revelation in such a way that the weight and significance attached to each element can be more readily understood in the context of the whole. The possibility of constructing such a theology relies on a presumption that the biblical witness is itself consistent and a faithful record of the revelation of a consistent God. Our belief is that God does not act arbitrarily, so that by reading of his dealings with man in the Bible, we can discern consistent patterns in the relationships of God, man and the created order.

The task of interpreting Scripture is always an unfinished one. The theological framework, and our interpretations of Scripture, are at best provisional. Essential qualities for the interpreter are intellectual and spiritual humility, openness to the guiding of the Holy Spirit, and a willingness for misinterpretations to be corrected by other Christians.

From the tradition T, we derived in Chapter Two a set of *derivative social principles* (DSP). The DSP are intended to embrace, in a systematic fashion, ethical principles that are embedded in T. Some will be immediately evident: that is, they appear in T as unambiguous principles. Others will need to be teased out by considering what principles might lie behind some element in T which cannot be directly interpreted. This process of deriving the DSP is not, and cannot be, deductive in the sense that there is some strict process of logical reasoning that leads from one to the other. Rather we formulate our DSP in such manner as to correspond to, or at least, be consistent with, our understanding of T. The arrow from T to DSP in the diagram indicates the priority and ultimate authority of T in determining the shape of the DSP.

The DSP are always provisional. They are drawn out of T, but they do not carry the same authority as T, and they need to be open to correction and reformulation in the light of new insights in T. The Christian principles for economic life set out in Chapter Two are by no means final: it is our expectation that they will be revised, refined, added to and even deleted as they are discussed and evaluated by others with interest in this area of Christian social ethics. It is also probable that Christians will disagree about the DSP. If they share the same view of T then differences should, in principle, be resolvable, even though differences in interpretation can be acute. (Of course, if there is also disagreement about the content of T, then there is likely to be a wider scope for disagreement about DSP, and this cannot necessarily be resolved.)

The next stage in the diagram is the application of the DSP to *reality* (R). There are three elements in this: epistemological, ethical and prescriptive. The epistemological element was the subject of Chapter Three. Philosophy of the social sciences reminds us that R is complex, and that the positivist dream of allowing the 'facts' to provide their own evidential version of the truth about R founders on the logical difficulties of inductive reasoning which were first elegantly expounded by Hume. The DSP are highly significant in providing a framework for deciding which issues are significant for an understanding of R, and therefore which facts we need to consider.

The second element is ethical. In usual circumstances we may expect to identify a 'gap' between the DSP and R: the reality we observe fails to conform to the standards set out in the DSP. We expect a 'gap' because of the fallenness of mankind, and the pervasive influence of that fallenness in all endeavours and institutions. The task of identifying the 'gap' may be quite difficult: the application of the DSP is by no means purely mechanical. We will have to inquire deeply into circumstances and motives, and then make a judgment as to how the DSP apply. This critical task was attempted in respect of different areas of economic life in Chapters Four to Eight. Those particular evaluations are in no way definitive or final. Not only may the description of R be incomplete or inaccurate, but the judgments made on the relation of the DSP to R may also prove to be inadequate or misguided.

The third element, which is largely absent from Chapters Four to Eight, is prescriptive. How are we to respond to the 'gaps' which we identify between the DSP and R? The solutions we might propose are motivated by the method Jesus used in his teaching on marriage and divorce recorded in Matthew 19:3–9. In reply to a question about divorce, Jesus affirms the creation principles with a direct quotation of Genesis 1:27 and 2:24. A lifelong union of man and wife is, without doubt, God's ideal for mankind: this is the relevant DSP.

This affirmation brings the retort that Moses had permitted divorce. How could this be? Jesus replies that divorce is permitted because of their 'hardness of heart'. The difficulty is apparent. God has a creation pattern for mankind, but because of the fall (and the consequent 'hardness of heart') that pattern is not capable of fulfilment. Eden cannot be recreated. We must therefore look for a *second best* in a fallen world, while continuing to affirm God's first best. In each case we must seek to resolve the tension between God's ideal, which we capture as best we can in the DSP, and what is practicable in a fallen world. (We note, immediately, that our usage of 'second best' in this context is *not* the same as the second best of utilitarian welfare economics which we criticized in Chapter Three. However the principle of the second best, as a method of doing practical ethics in situations where DSP and R diverge, is not dissimilar.)

Even if the nature of the gap between the DSP and R is agreed, there may well be considerable disagreement about this prescriptive element. Prescription involves political and social judgment. There can be no definitive means of learning whether a particular proposal for reform will bring R closer to DSP than some alternative proposal. Indeed the notion of 'closer' may be impossible to define in complex situations. Christians should be particularly circumspect in their policy prescriptions, and cheerfully tolerant of other Christians who take a different line. (However that should not be used as an excuse for not exploring differences rigorously and carefully. Intellectual sloppiness is not a Christian virtue.)

To this point in our description of the method adopted in the book, we have traced the direction of thought from T to DSP to R. Two criticisms are frequently made of this procedure. The first is that it ignores an equally important interaction in the opposite direction. It is argued that the DSP are arrived at by a joint consideration of both T and R. For example, R will sometimes throw up new problems and issues with which our existing DSP are inadequate to deal. An example is the debate on experimentation with human embryos sparked off by the development of techniques of *in vitro* fertilization. We then need to go back to T, to look for new insights to inform and revise the DSP to make them more effective in dealing with the particular problem. Furthermore our experience of R may alert us to new meanings and applications, particularly of the DSP.

However, we need to distinguish this description of how we may in fact set about our ethical thinking (a process involving T, DSP and R simultaneously or iteratively) from the principle that T is normative, and ultimately determines our conclusions. In particular, we do not accept the criticism that T is always read in a particular social context, and that the context 'controls' the interpretation of T, the formulation of the DSP and the applications to R. Such a position is taken by many liberation theologians. In our view it is too passively relativistic. While we need to be aware of the constraints placed upon us by our social and intellectual milieu, our aim should be to transcend that milieu and to develop the mind of Christ. To do that we may need to ask for help from Christians who live in very different cultures from our own.

The second criticism derives from an unwillingness to accept that T is authoritative. Hence the rejection of any particular weight to be given to T in the formulation of the DSP, and in application to R. The difficulty with this position, in practice, is that it greatly weakens Christian ethical responses. If we approach R directly without any well-defined DSP, we run the danger of being fed 'facts' about R by non-Christian social scientists whose analysis is based on very different social ethical principles. Our evaluation of those 'facts' may then be limited to a pragmatic rather than a principled ethic. It is that particular danger that we have been at pains to avoid in this book.

It will be evident from this discussion of method in relation to the content of this book that the task of relating Christian faith to economic life presents an immense agenda for future work. We have already noted that our conclusions in the area of T, the DSP and R are at best provisional, and that we have not attempted the third, prescriptive, element in the relation of DSP and R. Our unwillingness to prescribe policy can be traced, in part, to the provisionality of our other judgments. However, there is the more fundamental limitation that our knowledge of R needs to be much more detailed than anything attempted in this book. The generalized (and idealized) descriptions of R which have been subject to critical scrutiny in Chapters Four to Eight may be adequate for indicating general lines of ethical enquiry, but they are insufficiently detailed and empirical for policy prescription. It can be intellectually exciting to conduct abstract debates about the advantages of socialism or capitalism, or about the limits to economic growth. But it would probably be more profitable now to apply our Christian social principles to detailed policy issues, including a careful empirical analysis of each issue, and a consideration of alternative policy responses that might promote a Christian second best.

Notes

Chapter One: Christianity and economics: biblical foundations (pages 11–57)

1. The contributions are too numerous to list here: but some will be referenced in the course of the book. Readers wishing to explore the diversity of the literature may find the following sample a useful starting point: Bob Goudzwaard, *Capitalism and Progress* (Wedge, Toronto, 1978); B. Griffiths, *Morality and the Market Place* (Hodder and Stoughton, London, 1982), *The Creation of Wealth* (Hodder and Stoughton, 1984); D. L. Munby, *Christianity and Economic Problems* (Macmillan, London, 1956); G. North, *An Introduction to Christian Economics* (Craig Press, Nutley, New Jersey, USA, 1974); R. H. Preston, *Religion and the Persistence of Capitalism* (SCM, London, 1979), *Church and Society in the late Twentieth Century: The Economic and Political Task* (SCM, 1983); J. F. Sleeman, *Economic Crisis: A Christian Perspective* (SCM, 1976); A. Storkey, *Transforming Economics* (SPCK, London, 1986); D. Vickers, *Economics and Man* (Craig Press, 1976); J. P. Wogaman, *Christians and the Great Economic Debate* (SCM, 1977), *Economics and Ethics: A Christian Enquiry* (SCM, 1986).

2. G. von Rad, *Genesis* (Old Testament Library, SCM, 1961); D. Kidner, *Genesis* (Tyndale Old Testament Commentaries, IVP, 1967); D. Bonhoeffer, *Creation and Fall: A Theological Interpretation of Genesis 1–3* (SCM, 1959); W. Granberg-Michaelson, *A Worldly Spirituality* (Harper and Row, 1984), especially Chapters 4 and 5.

3. J. Monod, *Chance and Necessity* (Collins, 1972), p. 110.

4. See D. M. Mackay, *Science, Chance and Providence* (Oxford University Press, 1978), Chapter 2.

5. C. J. H. Wright, *Living as the People of God* (IVP, 1983), Part One.

6. J. Hick, *Evil and the God of Love* (Fontana, 1968); H. Sylvester, *Arguing with God* (IVP, 1971).

7. D. Bonhoeffer, *op. cit.*

8. J. Ellul, *The Meaning of the City* (Eerdmans, 1970).

9. Critical analysis has suggested that the story of Cain and Abel, and the story of Cain's wanderings and the building of a city, form independent literary units. If that is indeed the case, then our discussion simply follows the line of thought of the editor, who so skilfully and thoughtfully juxtaposed the two.

10. This section owes much to D. Atkinson, *Peace in Our Time?* (IVP, 1985).

11. See L. Berkhof, *Systematic Theology* (Eerdmans, 1939), pp. 432–446.

12. C. J. H. Wright, *op. cit.*, Part One.

13. Apart from C. J. H. Wright, *op. cit.*, we have made extensive use of R. de Vaux, *Ancient Israel: Its Life and Institutions* (Darton, Longman and Todd, ²1965).

14. Presumably because a non-Israelite would have no land to work, and there was no developed system of free wage-labour.

15. Foreigners would be merchants, who required capital and had the means to make profits. The Israelite was expected to live off the land, and would not make profits. See section (e), below, in the text.

16. 1 Kings 16–22. This was a period of great prosperity and economic stability in Israel, though this is not evident from the biblical text.

17. See C. Boerma, *Rich Man, Poor Man and the Bible*, translated from the Dutch by John Bowden (SCM, 1979).

18. T. Hanks, *God so loved the World* (1983), cited by C. Wigglesworth, 'The Use of the Old Testament in Economics', *Shaft* No. 42, Winter/Spring 1982, pp. 7–10.

19. R. de Vaux, *op. cit.*, Chapters 2 and 11.

20. *Ibid.*, pp. 175–177.

21. J. Ellul, *op. cit.*, pp. 23–38.

22. A useful source for this section in its general aspects is D. Guthrie, *New Testament Theology* (IVP, 1981), especially Chapters 4 and 7.

23. J. H. Yoder, *The Politics of Jesus* (Eerdmans, 1972), Chapters 2 and 3.

24. M. Hengel, *Property and Riches in the Early Church* (SCM, 1974), Chapter 3.

25. It is curious that Hengel, *op. cit.*, does not discuss the parable of the talents. Moreover he explicitly dismisses the idea of stewardship as a Christian concept, attributing it to Judaism and borrowings from Greek sources.

26. M. Hengel, *op. cit.*, is again an important source. He traces a development from the radical attitudes to riches of Jesus and the early church, to a more pragmatic accommodating stance in the Pastoral Epistles.

27. Acts 5:4 makes it clear that they had every right, in the eyes of the apostles, *not* to hand over the entire proceeds of the land. Their offence was not holding back, but rather lying about it.

28. See R. J. Sider, *Rich Christians in an Age of Hunger* (IVP, Illinois, ²1984), pp. 91–92, for a discussion of this point.

Chapter Two: Christianity and economics: theological ethics (pages 58–89)

1. H. Richard Niebuhr, *Christ and Culture* (Harper and Row, 1951).

2. S. C. Mott, *Jesus and Social Ethics* (Grove Books, 1984), being an edited version of two articles, 'The use of the New Testament in Social Ethics', *Transformation* 1984, vol. 1, Nos 2 and 3. See also, by the same author, *Biblical Ethics and Social Change* (Oxford University Press, New York, 1982).

3. R. H. Preston, *Explorations in Theology, 9* (SCM, 1981), Chapter 5, 'From the Bible to the Modern World: A problem for ecumenical ethics'.

4. R. H. Preston, *Church and Society in the Late Twentieth Century: the Economic and Political Task* (SCM, 1983), especially Chapter 5 and Appendix 2.

5. *Ibid.*, pp. 104–105.

6. *Ibid.*, p. 106.

7. *Ibid.*, pp. 118–119.

8. F. D. Maurice, *The Kingdom of Christ* (1837), (reprinted 1960 by James Clark).

9. R. Clements, M. Schluter, *Reactivating the Extended Family: from Biblical Norms to Public Policy in Britain* (Jubilee Centre, Cambridge, 1986), Part II.

10. W. Granberg-Michaelson, *A Worldly Spirituality* (Harper and Row, 1984), is an

excellent example of the use of Scripture in this way.

11. See A. Richardson, *The Biblical Doctrine of Work* (SCM, 1973). For a very interesting popular discussion of the nature of work, see M. Moynagh, *Making Unemployment Work* (Lion, 1985), Chapter 5. Moynagh argues that work should be defined to include all useful human activity, and not just paid employment.

12. Brian Griffiths, *Morality and the Market Place* (Hodder and Stoughton, 1982).

13. *Ibid.*, pp. 92–93.

14. *Ibid.*, p. 100.

15. The distinction is helpfully made by D. Atkinson, *Peace in Our Time?* (IVP, 1985), Chapter 9.

16. The discussion here draws on the following: O. Cullman, *The State in the New Testament* (Scribner, 1956); R. A. Markus, 'Two conceptions of political authority . . .', *Journal of Theological Studies*, 1965; J. H. Yoder, *The Politics of Jesus* (Eerdmans, 1972); J. M. Bonino, *Revolutionary Theology Comes of Age* (SPCK, 1975).

17. N. T. Wright, series of four articles on Romans 13:1–7, *Third Way*, May and June, 1978.

18. St Augustine, *De Civitate Dei*, XIX, 14, 15.

19. G. B. Caird, *Principalities and Powers* (Oxford University Press, 1967).

20. This point is made by D. J. A. Clines, 'Social Responsibility in the Old Testament', *Interchange* 1976, vol. 20, pp. 194–207.

21. See R. A. Markus, *op. cit.*

Chapter Three: Economic analysis: methods and values (pages 90–144)

1. The caricature was well represented by the methodological introduction to R. G. Lipsey, *Introduction to Positive Economics* (Weidenfeld and Nicholson, [1]1966).

2. In this we follow two works on economic methodology which have been of great assistance in the preparation of this section: M. Blaug, *The Methodology of Economics* (Cambridge University Press, 1980); and B. Caldwell, *Beyond Positivism: economic methodology in the twentieth century* (George Allen and Unwin, 1982). We have also made extensive use of two unpublished works: A. J. Hartropp, *Economic methodology: a Lakatosian appraisal of the Keynesian-Monetarist-New Classical Controversy and a Critique* (University of Southampton PhD thesis, 1985); and A. B. Cramp, *Economics in Christian Perspective* (Institute for Christian Studies, Toronto, unpublished typescript, no date).

3. J. S. Mill, *A System of Logic* (first published 1843: citations are from *Collected Works*, vols. VII and VIII, edited by J. M. Robson, Routledge and Kegan Paul, 1973).

4. Notably D. Hume, *An Enquiry Concerning Human Understanding* (first edition 1748: edition cited here is that edited by L. A. Selby-Bigg, published by Oxford University Press, 1962). The contrasting of the views of Mill and Hume in this section is for expository purposes only. It should not be imagined that there was an actual debate between them on these issues! For a helpful discussion of Hume's position, see B. Stroud, *Hume* (Routledge and Kegan Paul, 1977), especially Chapters 2–4.

5. Hume, *op. cit.*, XII.I.119.

6. K. Popper, *Objective Knowledge* (Oxford, [2]1979), Chapter 1.

7. Compare W. H. Newton-Smith, *The Rationality of Science* (Routledge and Kegan Paul, 1981), Chapter 3. Newton-Smith argues convincingly that Popper's attempt to escape from 'inductivism' is a failure.

8. Mill, *op. cit.*, III.II.1.

9. *Ibid.*

10. K. Popper, *The Logic of Scientific Discovery* (Hutchinson, 1968), p. 252.

11. See the exposition in B. Stroud, *Hume*, Chapter 4.

12. The argument and the quotations in this paragraph are from Mill, *op. cit.*, III.XII.1.

13. This search for general propositions in the social sciences is evident in J. S. Mill, *On the Nature of Political Economy* (first published 1836: edition cited here is *Collected Works*, vol. 4, edited by J. M. Robson, 1967).

14. C. Hempel, P. Oppenheim, 'Studies in the Logic of Explanation', *Philosophy of Science* 1948, reprinted in H. Feigl, M. Brodbeck, *Readings in the Philosophy of Science* (Meredith Corporation, 1953). A very clear summary is given by B. Caldwell, *Beyond Positivism* , pp. 28–30.

15. W. Newton-Smith, *op. cit.*, pp. 28–34.

16. K. Popper, *Conjectures and Refutations* (Routledge and Kegan Paul, 1963), pp. 54–55.

17. An immediate objection to this way of stating Popper's point is that all theories, except the most trivial, contain some element of simplification, and must be false in some (hopefully unimportant) respects. We need some criteria for deciding what evidence would be sufficient to count for a 'falsification' of the theory.

18. P. Duhem, *The Aim and Structure of Physical Theory* (originally published in 1906: English translation by P. Wiener, Princeton University Press, 1954); W. Quine, 'Two dangers of empiricism', *Philosophical Review* 1951, reprinted in W. Quine, *From a Logical Point of View* (Harper and Row, 1961). A brief summary of the Duhem-Quine thesis, and the debate it has generated, is provided by R. Cross, 'The Duhem-Quine thesis, Lakatos, and the appraisal of theories in Macroeconomics', *Economic Journal* 92 (1982), pp. 320–340.

19. K. Popper, *The Logic of Scientific Discovery*, p. 50. For a critical analysis of Popper's views, see Newton-Smith, *op. cit.*, Chapter 3.

20. I. Lakatos, *The Methodology of Scientific Research Programmes* (Cambridge University Press, 1978); T. S. Kuhn, *The Structure of Scientific Revolutions* (Chicago University Press, ²1970). See also Newton-Smith, *op. cit.*, Chapters IV and V.

21. Kuhn, *op. cit.*

22. Newton-Smith, *op. cit.*, pp. 232–235.

23. The phrase is that of P. K. Feyerabend, *Against Method: Outline of an Anarchistic Theory of Knowledge* (New Left Books, 1975), p. 28.

24. See below, p. 319.

25. See M. Blaug, *op. cit.*, pp. 69–73.

26. J. S. Mill, *On the Nature of Political Economy* (1836).

27. M. Blaug, *Ricardian Economics. A Historical Study* (Greenwood Press, 1973); N. B. de Marchi, 'The empirical content and longevity of Ricardian economics', *Economica* 37 (1970), pp. 257–276.

28. See the discussion in M. Blaug, *op. cit.*, pp. 77–86.

29. L. Robbins, *An Essay on the Nature and Significance of Economic Science* (Macmillan, ²1935).

30. For a sympathetic sketch of neo-Austrian method, and useful bibliography, see B. Caldwell, *op. cit.*, pp. 117–124.

31. See a letter from Keynes to Roy Harrod, cited in M. Blaug, *op. cit.*, pp. 90–91.

32. We are thinking of the kind of theoretical work that is published in the *American Economic Review*, *Review of Economic Studies*, *Econometrica*, and the *Journal of Economic Theory*, among others.

33. F. Hahn, M. Hollis, 'Introduction', in Hahn and Hollis (eds), *Philosophy and Economic Theory* (Oxford University Press, 1979).

34. Hahn, Hollis, *op. cit.*, p. 4.

35. A. Deaton, J. Muellbauer, *Economics and Consumer Behaviour* (Cambridge University Press, 1980), Part One.

36. A point which has been made by, among others: G. Myrdal, *The Political Element in the Development of Economic Theory* (first published in 1929: translated by P. Streeten, Routledge and Kegan Paul, 1953); A. B. Cramp, *op. cit.*

37. F. Y. Edgeworth, *Mathematical Psychics: An Essay on the Application of Economics to the Moral Sciences* (1881), quoted by A. K. Sen, 'Rational fools: a critique of the behavioural foundations of economic theory', *Philosophy and Public Affairs* 6 (1976–7), pp. 317–344, reprinted in Hahn and Hollis, *op. cit.*, pp. 87–109.

38. J. R. Hicks, *A Revision of Demand Theory* (Oxford University Press, 1956).

39. A. K. Sen, *op. cit.*

40. The contrast with the approach of Becker, who has in recent years sought to apply economic models outside the domain of economic behaviour, is very marked. See, for example, G. Becker, *The Economic Approach to Human Behaviour* (University of Chicago Press, 1976).

41. R. D. Luce, H. Raiffa, *Games and Decisions* (Wiley, 1957); L. B. Lave, 'An Empirical Approach to the Prisoners' Dilemma Game', *Quarterly Journal of Economics* 76 (1962).

42. H. Simon, 'From Substantive to Procedural Rationality', in S. Latsis (ed.), *Method and Appraisal in Economics* (Cambridge University Press, 1976), reprinted in Hahn, Hollis, *op. cit.*, pp. 65–86.

43. M. Friedman, 'The Methodology of Positive Economics', in his *Essays in Positive Economics* (University of Chicago Press, 1953), reprinted in Hahn, Hollis, *op. cit.*; A. A. Alchian, 'Uncertainty, evolution and economic theory', *Journal of Political Economy* 58 (1950), pp. 211–221.

44. G. Becker, *op. cit.*

45. J. F. Muth, 'Rational expectations and the theory of price movements', *Econometrica* 29 (1961), pp. 315–335.

46. This discussion is based on D. R. Helm, *Enforced maximization; competition, evolution and selection* (unpublished D. Phil. thesis, University of Oxford, 1984).

47. See M. King, *Public Policy and the Corporation* (Chapman and Hall, 1977), Chapter 5.

48. S. D. Grossman, O. D. Hart, 'Takeover bids, the free-rider problem and the theory of the corporation', *Bell Journal of Economics* 11 (1980), pp. 42–64.

49. A third objection is that direct tests of the theory, by examining the takeover process and its consequences for the value of the firm and efficiency, have failed to find any strong evidence for an effective mechanism. So a key element in Friedman's *as if* argument that profit maximization is the appropriate assumption to invoke to describe the behaviour of firms fails on his own test by not providing a good prediction. See below, p. 319.

50. T. W. Hutchison, *The significance and basic postulates of economic theory* (Macmillan, 1938). See also B. Caldwell, *op. cit.*, Chapters 6 and 7.

51. P. Samuelson, *The Foundations of Economic Analysis* (Atheneum, New York, ²1965).

52. H. Schultz, *The theory and measurement of demand* (Chicago University Press, 1938).

53. M. Friedman, 'The methodology of positive economics' from his *Essays in Positive Economics* (University of Chicago Press, 1953), reprinted in Hahn, Hollis (eds), *op. cit.*, pp. 18–35.

54. *Ibid.*, p. 23.

55. See, for example, the discussion in B. Caldwell, *op. cit.*, Chapter 8.

56. D. Hendry, 'Econometrics: alchemy or science?', *Economica* 47 (1980), pp. 387–406; 'Monetary economic myth and econometric reality', *Oxford Review of Economic Policy* 1 (1985), No. 1, pp. 72–84. See also E. E. Leamer, 'Let's take the con out of econometrics', *American Economic Review* 73 (1983), pp. 31–43.

57. R. Cross, *op. cit.*, pp. 320–340.

58. This whole section borrows considerably from A. F. Holmes, *All Truth is God's Truth* (Eerdmans, 1977/Inter-Varsity Press, 1979) and *Contours of a World View* (Eerdmans, Intervarsity Press, 1983), Chapters 8, 9. I only hope that Professor Holmes accepts the truth of the adage that 'Imitation is the sincerest form of flattery'.

59. Holmes, *op. cit.*, Chapter 5.

60. For a discussion of the Christian view of history in the context of a survey of philosophies of history, see D. Bebbington, *Patterns in History* (Inter-Varsity Press, 1979), especially Chapter 8. It is a moot point whether God's providence in history can be used, as in the text, as justification for a belief in a providential order to be discerned in social behaviour.

61. The situation is the same for natural science: appeals to the doctrines of creation and providence make science possible, but are not a substitute for science.

62. A survey of the field is Y. K. Ng, *Welfare Economics* (Macmillan, 1979). An older and more sceptical view is given in J. DeV. Graaf, *Theoretical Welfare Economics* (Cambridge University Press, 1957).

63. A. Deaton, J. Muellbauer, *op. cit.*, Chapter 9, review of social welfare functions. Inequality is explicitly introduced as an argument by Atkinson's inequality index: A. B. Atkinson, 'On the measurement of inequality', *Journal of Economic Theory* 2 (1970), pp. 244–263.

64. See D. C. Mueller, *Public Choice* (Cambridge University Press, 1979), Chapter 9: this book was a useful source for much of the discussion of this section.

65. K. J. Arrow, *Social Choice and Individual Values* (John Wiley and Sons, 1951, revised edition 1963).

66. A. K. Sen, 'Personal utilities and public judgements: or What's wrong with welfare economics?', *Economic Journal* 89 (1979), pp. 537–558; Mueller, *op. cit.*, Chapter 10.

67. A. K. Sen, *op. cit.*

68. Ng, *op. cit.*, Chapter 3 gives a clear exposition, and references to the relevant literature. The three contributors cited in this paragraph are: N. Kaldor, 'Welfare propositions of economics and interpersonal comparisons of utility', *Economic Journal* 49 (1939), pp. 549–552; J. R. Hicks, 'Foundations of welfare economics', *Economic Journal* 49 (1939), pp. 696–712; T. Scitovsky, 'A note on welfare propositions in economics', *Review of Economic Studies* 9 (1941), pp. 77–88.

69. A. C. Harberger, 'Three basic postulates for applied welfare economics: an

interpretive essay', *Journal of Economic Literature* 9 (1971), pp. 785–797.

70. J. J. C. Smart, B. Williams, *Utilitarianism, for and against* (Cambridge University Press, 1973).

71. These contributions are collected in A. K. Sen, B. Williams (eds), *Utilitarianism and beyond* (Cambridge University Press, 1982).

72. B. Williams, 'A critique of utilitarianism', in Smart and Williams, *op. cit.*

73. R. M. Hare, 'Ethical theory and utilitarianism', in Sen, Williams (eds), *op. cit.*

74. J. A. Mirrlees, 'The economic uses of utilitarianism', in Sen, Williams, *op. cit.*

75. A. K. Sen, *On Economic Inequality* (Oxford University Press, 1973).

76. F. Hahn, 'On some difficulties of the utilitarian economist', in Sen, Williams (eds), *op. cit.*

77. R. M. Hare, *op. cit.*

78. F. Hahn, *op. cit.*

79. F. A. von Hayek, *The Constitution of Liberty* (University of Chicago Press, 1960); R. Nozick, *Anarchy, State and Utopia* (Basil Blackwell, 1974).

80. J. Rawls, *A Theory of Justice* (Oxford University Press, 1971). For discussion see D. C. Mueller, *op. cit.*, Chapter 12, and B. Barry, *The Liberal Theory of Justice* (Oxford University Press, 1973).

81. H. L. A. Hart, 'Rawls on Liberty and its priority', *University of Chicago Law Review* 40 (1973), pp. 534–555, reprinted in N. Daniels, *Reading Rawls* (Basic Books, 1974), pp. 230–252.

82. R. M. Hare, *Freedom and Reason* (Oxford University Press, 1963).

83. See E. Nagel, *The Structure of Science. Problems in the logic of scientific explanation* (Routledge and Kegan Paul, 1961), and the discussion in M. Blaug, *op. cit.*, pp. 131–134.

Chapter Four: The capitalist market economy (pages 145–175)

1. F. Hirsch, *The Social Limits to Growth* (Routledge and Kegan Paul, 1977), Chapter 10, examines this issue in some detail.

2. This assertion flows from the presumption that Adam Smith's economic analysis in *The Wealth of Nations* relies substantially on his social analysis in *The Theory of Moral Sentiments*. See A. W. Coats (ed.), *The Classical Economists and Economic Policy* (Methuen, 1971), for a summary of the arguments.

3. K. J. Arrow, 'Gifts and exchanges', *Philosophy and Public Affairs* (Summer 1972), p. 357.

4. See, for example, A. B. Atkinson, *The Economics of Inequality* (Oxford University Press, 1975), and L. C. Thurow, *Generating Inequality* (Basic Books, 1975).

5. The significance of entrepreneurship in creating personal fortunes in the U.S. is described in L. C. Thurow, *The Zero Sum Society* (Basic Books, 1980), Chapter 7.

6. See D. A. Hay, D. J. Morris, *Industrial Economics* (Oxford University Press, 1979), Chapter 8, for a discussion of this point.

7. Hay and Morris, *op. cit.*, Chapter 15.

8. A lucid summary is given in J. S. Vickers, 'Strategic competition among the Few—Some Recent Developments in the Economics of Industry', *Oxford Review of Economic Policy* Vol. 1, no. 3 (1985), pp. 39–62.

9. See, for examples, W. Brown (ed.), *The Changing Contours of British Industrial Relations* (Basil Blackwell, 1981); J. T. Dunlop, W. Galenson, *Labour in the twentieth*

Century (Academic Press, New York, 1978); E. Owen Smith (ed.), *Trade Unions in the Developed Economies* (Croom Helm, London, 1981).

10. K. Midgley, R. G. Burns, *The Capital Market: its Nature and Significance* (Macmillan, 1977).

11. Two comprehensive texts are Y. K. Ng, *Welfare Economics* (Macmillan, 1979), and R. W. Boadway and N. Bruce, *Welfare Economics* (Basil Blackwell, 1984).

12. This is far from self-evident, and cannot be proved without a major excursion into economic theory. The reader who is unable to accept the statement in the text must be prepared to tackle some extremely tough reading in, for example, Ng or Boadway and Bruce, *op. cit.*

13. See, for example, E. J. Mishan, *The Costs of Economic Growth* (Penguin Books, 1979).

14. W. W. Sharkey, *The Theory of Natural Monopoly* (Cambridge University Press, 1982); J. S. Vickers and G. Yarrow, *Privatisation and the Natural Monopolies* (Public Policy Centre, London, 1985).

15. H. Demsetz, 'Information and efficiency: another viewpoint', *Journal of Law and Economics* 12 (1969), pp. 1–22.

16. The following are average annual growth rates of Gross Domestic Product reported in *World Development Report 1986* (Oxford University Press for the World Bank, 1986), Annex: World Development Indicators, Table 2:

	1965–73	*1973–84*
S. Korea	10.0	7.2
Singapore	13.0	8.2
Kenya	7.9	4.4
Liberia	5.5	0.2
Sri Lanka	4.2	5.2
India	3.9	4.1

17. J. C. H. Fei, G. Ranis, S. W. Y. Kuo, *Growth with equity: the Taiwan Case* (Oxford University Press, 1979); S. A. Morley, *Labor Markets and Inequitable Growth* (Cambridge University Press, 1982).

18. See pp.140–142.

19. F. Hirsch, *Social Limits to Growth* (Routledge and Kegan Paul, 1977), especially Part III.

20. G. A. Akerlof, 'The market for "lemons": quality, uncertainty and the market mechanism', *Quarterly Journal of Economics* 84 (1970), pp. 488–500.

21. Hirsch, *op. cit.*, Chapters 9, 10.

22. John Locke, *Of Civil Government: Book II: An Essay covering the True Original Extent and End of Civil Government.* The passages quoted are ostensibly a commentary on the mandate given to man by God in Genesis 1 and 2. Compare the restatement of the argument in R. Nozick, *Anarchy, State and Utopia* (Oxford University Press, 1974).

23. This tradition begins with Locke and J. S. Mill. Modern restatements are: F. A. von Hayek, *The Road to Serfdom* (George Routledge and Sons, London, 1944); M. Friedman, *Capitalism and Freedom* (University of Chicago Press, 1962); Ayn Rand, *Capitalism: The Unknown Ideal* (New American History, 1962); R. Nozick, *op. cit.*; C. K. Rowley, A. T. Peacock, *Welfare Economics: A Liberal Restatement* (Martin

Robertson, London, 1975). J. N. Gray has written a helpful expository essay on Hayek's views: 'F. A. Hayek and the Rebirth of Classical Liberalism', *Literature of Liberty*, Winter 1982.

24. Friedman, *op. cit.*

25. F. A. von Hayek, *Law, Legislation and Liberty* (Routledge and Kegan Paul, 1973), vol. II, especially pp. 107–132.

26. *Ibid.* p. 117.

27. B. Griffiths, *Morality and the Market Place* (Hodder and Stoughton, 1982), pp. 33–39.

28. John Locke, *op. cit.*; R. Nozick, *op. cit.*

29. It might be argued that limited liability stockholder companies exist because of the provisions of company law, and that they are not a *necessary* feature of modern capitalist economies. However the existence of similar provisions in economies all over the world supports the generalization that limited liability is an empirical feature of market capitalism, and prompts the search for an explanation. One hypothesis is that limited liability has particular characteristics (for example, in the spreading of risk) that makes it an optimal structure for market capitalism.

30. B. Griffiths, *The Creation of Wealth* (Hodder and Stoughton, 1984).

31. *Ibid.*, p. 38.

32. M. Weber, *The Protestant Ethic and the Spirit of Capitalism* (George Allen and Unwin, 1971: first published in 1905).

33. Griffiths, *op. cit.*, p. 69.

34. F. Hirsch, *op. cit.*, pp. 138–143.

35. Hirsch, *op. cit.*, p. 179.

36. B. Griffiths, *Morality and the Market Place*, pp. 113–118.

37. Griffiths, *op. cit.*, p. 121.

38. Griffiths, *op. cit.*, p. 110.

39. Griffiths, *op. cit.*, pp. 110–113.

40. See, for example, G. North, *An Introduction to Christian Economics* (Craig Press, 1974).

41. M. Moynagh, *Making Unemployment Work* (Lion, 1985), spells out a possible scheme.

42. A. W. Dilnot, J. A. Kay, C. N. Morris, *The Reform of Social Security* (Institute of Fiscal Studies, 1984).

Chapter Five: Socialism and the planned economy (pages 176–219)

1. K. Marx, F. Engels, *The Communist Manifesto* (1848), English translation in D. McLellan (ed.), *K. Marx: Selected Writings* (Oxford University Press, 1977).

2. K. Marx, *Capital* (3 vols. English translation by B. Fowkes (Penguin, 1976)).

3. These three elements of the Marxist moral critique of capitalism may be compared with our critique of capitalism in Chapter Three. Although the language in which they are stated is different, the content is not dissimilar. But the Christian basis for the critique is, of course, quite different.

4. The modification of the economic analysis is seen clearly in the work of Holland, Baran and Sweezy and to a lesser extent Sawyer and Aaronovitch. (See: S. Holland, *The Socialist Challenge* (Quartet Books, London, 1975); P. Baran, S. Sweezy, *Monopoly Capital* (Monthly Review Press, New York, 1966); M. Sawyer, S. Aaronvitch, *Big Business* (Macmillan, New York, 1975)).

5. See for instance: E. F. M. Durbin, *The Politics of Democratic Socialism* (Labour Book Service, London, 1940); C. A. R. Crosland, *The Future of Socialism* (Jonathan Cape, London, 1956); R. H. S. Crossman, 'Towards a Philosophy of Socialism' in *New Fabian Essays* (edited by Crossman) (second edition, J. M. Dent and Sons, London, 1970).

6. Crossman, *op. cit.*, p. 10.

7. R. Jenkins, 'Equality', in Crossman, *op. cit.*, p. 69.

8. Crosland, *op. cit.*, Chapter 9.

9. F. Hirsch, *Social Limits to Growth* (Routledge and Kegan Paul, for the Twentieth Century Fund, London, 1977).

10. By definition there can be only one Prime Minister, one chairman of IBM, a limited number of generals, and rather few professors. Not every aspirant to one of these positions will be able to attain it, however well he seeks to qualify himself. Similarly, the 'exclusive' tourist resort is no longer exclusive after it has been discovered by a large number of tourists. Keeping *ahead* of the Joneses is a tiring and frustrating activity.

11. Crossman, *op. cit.*, p. 12.

12. R. Niebuhr, *Moral Man and Immoral Society* (UK edition, SCM Press, 1963).

13. K. Marx, F. Engels, *The Communist Manifesto* (1848)

14. K. Marx, *Critique of the Gotha Programme* (English translation in D. McLellan, *op. cit.*).

15. S. Avineri, *The Social and Political Thought of Karl Marx* (Cambridge University Press, 1968), Chapter 8.

16. J. Wilczynski, *The Economics of Socialism* (3rd edition, G. Allen and Unwin, 1977). It is worth noting at this point that these four elements do not include direct controls on the individual in terms of direction of labour or determination of private expenditure patterns, nor is the right to hold a certain amount of 'private property' abolished.

17. S. Holland, *The Socialist Challenge* (Quartet Books, London, 1975).

18. Avineri, *op. cit.*

19. R. H. S. Crossman, 'Towards a philosophy of socialism' in Crossman (ed.), *New Fabian Essays* (J. M. Dent and Son, ²1972).

20. 'Oligopoly' exists where the supply of a good in a market is dominated by a few large firms.

21. E. F. M. Durbin, *Problems of Economic Planning* (Routledge and Kegan Paul, 1949), especially p. 44.

22. C. A. R. Crosland, *op. cit.*, Chapter 24.

23. Crosland, *op. cit.*, Chapter 20.

24. The calculation of a fair return, including a return for risk, is not, of course, a simple matter.

25. Crosland, *op. cit.*, Chapter 10.

26. Crossman, *op. cit.*

27. Crosland, *op. cit.*, Chapter 21.

28. Space precludes a discussion of the validity of the Marxist analysis of market capitalism. The introduction of *Capital* (Penguin edition), written by Ernest Mandel, gives a Marxist view of the academic debate about the validity of Marxist theory. The text of Desai is also very helpful. See E. Mandel, 'Introduction' to K. Marx, *Capital* Vols I–II (Penguin (UK), 1976); M. Desai, *Marxian Economics* (Oxford University Press, 1979).

29. Compare the warning of Samuel to the people of Israel when they asked for a king (1 Samuel 8:10–18).

30. R. Niebuhr, *op. cit.*: but the quotation in the text comes from the same author's *Children of Light Children of Darkness* (Nisbet, London, 1944), p. vi.

31. It is worth noting here that socialist planning for distributive justice might also be justified on the basis of applied welfare economics with its roots in utilitarian doctrines. Our discussion of welfare economics in Chapter Three underlined its incompatibility with Christian thought. The attempt to set social goals in terms of distributive justice, as incorporated in a social welfare function, attracts the same criticism that the social planner is trying to play God.

32. We note that this is equivalent to being a manager of a plant or subsidiary in a large capitalist enterprise.

33. A. K. Sen, 'Starvation and exchange entitlements', *Cambridge Journal of Economics* (1977) vol. 1, pp. 33–45, and *Poverty and Famines* (Clarendon Press, Oxford, 1981).

34. This is an issue to which we return in Chapter Eight.

35. L. von Mises, in F. A. von Hayek (ed.), *Collectivist Economic Planning* (George Routledge and Sons Ltd, London, 1935); F. A. von Hayek, 'Socialist Calculation: the "Capitalistic" Solution', *Economica* 7 (1940), pp. 125–149; L. Robbins, *The Great Depression* (Macmillan, 1934).

36. F. A. von Hayek, 'The use of knowledge in society', *American Economic Review* 35 (1945), pp. 519–530.

37. Lange responded to their criticisms in two articles. See O. Lange, 'On the economic theory of socialism', *Review of Economic Studies* 4 (1936–7), pp. 53–71 and 123–142.

38. M. Ellman, 'Optimal planning', in *Soviet Studies* 20 (1968); M. Ellman, *Soviet Planning Today* (Cambridge University Press, 1971); G. M. Heal, *Theory of Planning* (North Holland, 1973), Chapter 3; J. Wilczynski, *op. cit.*, Chapter 2.

39. N. Strong, M. Waterson, 'Principals, Agents and Information', in R. Clarke, T. McGuinness (eds), *The Economics of the Firm* (Blackwell, 1987), for a brief exposition and references to the literature.

40. A good summary of Liberman's views is available in English in E. G. Liberman, 'Profitability and Socialist Enterprises', in *Problems of Economics* (March 1966), pp. 3–10.

41. The problem of incentives may be overstated by the critics of socialism. The separation of ownership and control in large firms in capitalist economies has brought a parallel problem of how to give incentives for efficiency to professional managers, given that they do not usually have ownership rights over the profits.

42. F. A. von Hayek, *The Road to Serfdom* (George Routledge and Sons, 1944).

43. E. F. M. Durbin, *op. cit.*

44. *Nationalised Industries: A Review of Economic and Financial Objectives*, Cmnd 3437 (H.M.S.O., London, 1967).

45. National Economic Development Office, *A Study of UK Nationalised Industries* (H.M.S.O., 1976).

46. *The Nationalised Industries*, Cmnd 7131 (H.M.S.O., 1978).

47. R. Pryke, *Public Enterprise in Practice* (MacGibbon and Kee, 1971), and *The Nationalised Industries: Policies and Performance Since 1968* (Martin Robertson, 1981).

48. Vickers and Yarrow argue convincingly that the problem is not so much the

creation of workable control mechanisms as the instability created by political change, and the unwillingness of politicians to respect the arm's-length relationship with the industries that the control mechanisms were supposed to establish. J. Vickers, G. Yarrow, *Privatization and the Natural Monopolies* (Public Policy Centre, London, 1985).

49. F. A. von Hayek, *The Road to Serfdom*.

50. M. Friedman, *Capitalism and Freedom* (University of Chicago Press, 1962).

51. A. Solzhenitsyn, 'Misconceptions about Russia are a threat to America', *Foreign Affairs* 58 (1980); *Warning to the Western World* (Bodley Head and BBC, London, 1976).

52. Von Hayek, *op. cit.*

53. J. Vanek, *The Economics of Workers' Management* (George Allen and Unwin, 1972).

54. Department of Trade (UK), *Report of the Committee of Inquiry on Industrial Democracy* (The Bullock Report), Cmnd 6706 (H.M.S.O., 1977).

55. T. D. Wall and J. A. Lischeron, *Worker Participation* (McGraw-Hill (UK), London, 1977).

56. R. Jenkins, 'Equality', in R. H. S. Crossman (ed.), *New Fabian Essays* ((J. M. Dent and Sons, ²1972).

57. C. A. R. Crosland, *op. cit.*

Chapter Six: Macroeconomic policy (pages 220–247)

1. See A. Deaton, J. Muellbauer, *Economics and Consumer Behaviour* (Cambridge University Press, 1980), Chapter 6.

2. W. Beckerman, *National Income Analysis* (Weidenfeld and Nicholson, ³1980).

3. This is the simplest definition of the money stock, often referred to as M_1. There is much debate in monetary economics as to the most appropriate definition to use. A wider definition, including some interest-bearing bank deposits, may be a more significant indicator in some macroeconomic analyses.

4. Such large-scale macroeconomic computer models for the UK are described in K. Holden, D. A. Peel, J. K. Thompson, *Modelling the UK Economy* (Martin Robertson, 1982). For the US, see L. R. Klein, R. M. Young, *Econometric Forecasting and Forecasting Models* (Lexington Books, 1980).

5. For a perceptive practical treatment of this issue see M. Moynagh, *Making Unemployment Work* (Lion Publishing, 1985).

6. M. Friedman, *The Optimum Quantity of Money and Other Essays* (Macmillan, 1969), Chapter 1.

7. K. Cuthbertson, 'The Measurement and Behaviour of the U.K. Savings Ratio in the 1970s', *National Institute Economic Review* 99 (1982), pp. 75–84.

8. B. Griffiths, *Inflation; the Price of Prosperity* (Weidenfeld and Nicolson, 1976), Chapter 10; R. Thorp, L. Whitehead (eds.), *Inflation and Stabilization in Latin America* (Macmillan, 1979).

9. B. Griffiths, *Monetarism and morality* (Centre for Policy Studies, London, 1985).

10. Griffiths, *op. cit.*, is an example.

11. W. Beckerman and S. Clark, *Poverty and Social Security in Britain since 1961* (Oxford University Press, for Institute of Fiscal Studies, Oxford, 1982); V. Fry and P. Pashardes, 'Distributional aspects of inflation: who has suffered most?', *Fiscal Studies* 6 (1985), pp. 21–29; L. C. Thurow, *The Zero Sum Society* (Basic Books, 1980),

concludes that inflation in the US in the 1970s had minimal impact on income distribution (Chapter 3).

12. G. Justice, 'The impact of exchange rate variability on international trade flows', *Bank of England Discussion Papers: Technical Series* No. 4 (1983).

13. The balanced budget theory illustrates one aspect of the non-neutrality of taxation and government expenditure. Even when the budget is balanced, taxation displaces some consumption *and* some saving, but the government spends all the money raised. For this reason an increase in both taxation and expenditure is expansionary.

14. Organisation for Economic Cooperation and Development, *OECD Economic Studies Special Issue: The Role of the Public Sector* (OECD, Paris, 1985).

15. R. Layard, *How to Beat Unemployment* (Oxford University Press, 1986), Chapter 2.

16. A. Lindbeck, D. Snower, 'Explanations of unemployment', *Oxford Review of Economic Policy* Vol. 1, No. 2 (1985), pp. 34–59.

17. P. Minford, *Unemployment: Cause and Cure* (Blackwell, ²1985).

18. J. Muellbauer, 'Productivity and Competitiveness in British Manufacturing', *Oxford Review of Economic Policy* Vol. 2, No. 3 (1986), pp. 1–31. See also A. Lindbeck, 'The recent slowdown of productivity growth', *Economic Journal* 93 (1983), pp. 13–34, and E. Denison, *Accounting for Slower Growth: the US in the 1970s* (Brookings Institution, Washington DC, 1979).

19. Minford, *op. cit.*, Chapters 1 and 2.

20. See, for example, R. Dornbusch, S. Fischer, *Macroeconomics* (McGraw-Hill, ²1981).

21. The literature is technical and difficult. See E. Malinvaud, *The Theory of Unemployment Reconsidered* (Blackwell, 1977); J. Muellbauer, R. Portes, 'Macroeconomic models with quantity rationing', *Economic Journal* 88 (1978), pp. 788–821; P. Sinclair, *The Foundations of Macroeconomics and Monetary Theory* (Oxford University Press, 1983).

22. A textbook exposition is given in R. Jackman, C. Mulvey, J. Trevithick, *The Economics of Inflation* (Martin Robertson, ²1981), Chapter 6.

23. R. J. Barro, *Macroeconomics* (Wiley, New York, ²1987), especially Chapter 17.

24. S. M. Sheffrin, *Rational Expectations* (Cambridge University Press, 1983). A less technical treatment of the basic ideas can be found in G. K. Shaw, *Rational Expectations* (Wheatsheaf Books, 1984).

25. R. J. Barro, *op. cit.*, Chapter 14, and 'Public Debt and Taxes' in *Money, Expectations and Business Cycles* (Academic Press, New York, 1981).

26. F. A. von Hayek, *Law, Legislation and Liberty* (Routledge and Kegan Paul, 1973), Vol. II, pp. 107–132.

27. A. Leijonhufvud, *On Keynesian Economics and the Economics of Keynes* (Oxford University Press, 1968).

28. Represented in the UK particularly by the influential *National Institute Economic Review*, published quarterly by the National Institute of Economic and Social Research, London.

29. R. G. Layard, *How to Beat Unemployment* (Oxford University Press, 1986).

30. M. Friedman, 'The role of monetary policy', *American Economic Review* 58 (1968), pp. 1–17.

31. P. Minford, *op. cit.*

32. Represented in the UK by the Cambridge Economic Policy Group, whose views were disseminated through their Economic Policy Review, publication of which was discontinued in 1982. The ultra-Keynesian viewpoint is not represented in the US, but see C. Wilber, K. Jameson, *An Inquiry into the Poverty of Economics* (University of Notre Dame Press, Indiana, 1983), for an analysis which shares the same basic understanding of the economy.

33. M. Moynagh, *op. cit.*, Chapter 6.

Chapter Seven: Rich nation, poor nation (pages 248–280)

1. See R. J. Sider, *Rich Christians in an Age of Hunger*, 2nd edition (InterVarsity Press, Illinois, 1984), which probably has done more than any other single book to stimulate discussion. Sider's arguments have been vigorously countered by, among others, B. Griffiths, *Morality and the Market Place* (Hodder and Stoughton, 1982), Chapter 5.

2. The World Bank, *World Development Report 1986* (Oxford University Press, 1986). Readers wishing to update the descriptive statistics in section 2 of this Chapter will find it helpful to consult the world development indicators which are brought up to date each year in this annual publication.

3. *World Development Report 1986*, Indicators, Table 1.

4. This point has been explored in some detail by A. K. Sen, *Commodities and Capabilities* (North Holland, Amsterdam, 1985). His argument is that the satisfaction or happiness derived from a set of commodities will vary between individuals depending on their differing capacities to make use of the commodities ('utilization functions'). Culture and environmental factors will be important determinants of these capacities.

5. See S. A. Morley, *Labor markets and inequitable growth* (Cambridge University Press, 1982), Chapter 3, for a summary of evidence, and for references to the detailed discussion which the evidence provoked in the technical economics literature.

6. B. Sodersten, *International Economics* (Macmillan, ²1980; R. W. Jones, P. B. Kenen, *Handbook of International Economics* vol. I (North Holland, Amsterdam, 1984).

7. W. Leontief, 'Domestic production and foreign trade: The American Capital Position Re-examined', *Proceedings of the American Philosophical Society* 97 (1953), pp. 332–357; Sodersten, *op. cit.*, Chapter 6, gives a useful discussion of the debate which followed Leontief's seminal contribution.

8. A. V. Deardorff, 'Testing trade theories and predicting trade flows', in R. W. Jones, P. B. Kenen, *op. cit.*, pp. 467–517.

9. R. Vernon (ed.), *The Technology Factor in International Trade* (National Bureau of Economic Research, New York, 1970).

10. P. Krugman, 'Trade, accumulation and uneven development', *Journal of Development Economics* 8 (1982), pp. 149–161.

11. *World Development Report 1986*, Indicators, Table 29.

12. *World Development Report 1986*, Indicators, Table 8. The use of energy consumption as a proxy for capital per man is not without its problems. Cold countries will have a higher demand for energy than warm ones, for example. There is however a crude correlation between energy consumption and the amount of capital equipment utilized in manufacturing industry.

13. K. Griffin, *International Inequality and National Poverty* (Macmillan, London and Basingstoke, 1978).

14. J. Bhagwati, W. Dellafar, 'The Brain Drain and Income Taxation', *World Development* 1 (1973), pp. 94–101: see p. 98 table 1; J. Bhagwati (ed.), *The Brain Drain and Taxation* (North Holland, 1976).

15. M. Weber, *The Protestant Ethic and the Spirit of Capitalism* (English translation, Allen and Unwin, 1930).

16. J. K. Galbraith, *The Nature of Mass Poverty* (Penguin UK, 1980).

17. The World Bank, *World Development Report 1982* (Oxford University Press, New York), World Development Indicators, Table 2.

18. G. Fields, *Poverty, Inequality and Development* (Cambridge University Press, 1980), and 'Employment, income distribution and economic growth in seven small open economies', *Economic Journal* 94 (1984), pp. 74–83.

19. S. A. Morley, *op. cit.*

20. R. Prebisch, 'The economic development of Latin America and its principal problems', in G. Meier (ed.), *Leading Issues in Development Economics* (Oxford University Press, 1972).

21. J. Spraos, *Inequalizing Trade? A Study of North–South specialization in the context of terms of trade concepts* (Clarendon Press, Oxford, 1983); D. S. Evans, 'The long term determinants of North–South terms of trade and some recent evidence', *World Development* 15 (1987), pp. 657–671; A. Maizels, 'Commodities in crisis: an overview of the main issues', *World Development* 15 (1987), pp. 537–549.

22. A. K. Sen, *Poverty and Famines: An Essay in Entitlement and Deprivation* (Clarendon Press, 1982).

23. D. Jones, *Food and Interdependence* (ODI, London, 1976).

24. B. Sodersten, *op. cit.*, Chapter 17; International Monetary Fund, *The Rise in Protectionism* (Washington DC, 1978).

25. See, for example, G. K. Helleiner, 'Industry characteristics and the competitiveness of manufactured exports from the LDCs', *Weltwirtschaftliches Archiv.* Band 112 (1976), pp. 507–524. UNCTAD, *Review of recent trends and developments in trade in manufactures and semi-manufactures*, is a periodic publication giving details of recent changes.

26. C. I. Bradford, 'Trade and structural change: NICs and next tier NICs as transitional economies', *World Development* 15 (1987), pp. 299–316.

27. S. Page, 'The rise in protectionism since 1974', *Oxford Review of Economic Policy* vol. 3 no. 1 (1987), pp. 37–51; M. Davenport, *Trade Policy Protectionism and the Third World* (Croom Helm, London, 1986).

28. B. and C. Balassa, 'Industrial protection in the developed countries', *The World Economy* 7 (1984), pp. 179–186; I. Frank, *Trade policy issues of interest to the Third World* (Trade Policy Research Centre, Thames Essay 29, London, 1981).

29. J. Riedel, *Myths and Reality of External Constraints in Development* (Trade Policy Research Centre, Thames Essay 47, London, 1987), Chapter 5; J. Finger, A. Olechowski, *Trade Barriers: Who Does What to Whom?* (Kiel Conference Paper, June 1986: World Bank Paper, Washington DC).

30. A brief account of the Multifibre Arrangement is given in J. Pearce, J. Sutton, *Protectionism and industrial policy in Europe* (Routledge and Kegan Paul, 1985), Chapter 8.

31. The literature on agricultural protection and policies in industrialized coun-

NOTES

329

tries is extensive: the following review the main issues: *World Development Report* 1986, Chapter 6; A. Matthews, *The Common Agricultural Policy and Less Developed Countries* (Gill and Macmillan, Dublin, 1985); J. Zietz and A. Valdes, 'The cost of protectionism to the developing countries', World Bank Working Paper No. 769 (The World Bank, Washington DC, January 1986).

32. V. Cable, *Protectionism and Industrial Decline* (Hodder and Stoughton, 1983); A. O. Krueger, *Impact of LDC Exports on Employment in US Industry* (Trade Policy Research Centre, London, 1978); C. R. Frank, *Foreign Trade and Domestic Aid* (Brookings Institution, Washington DC, 1977); G. Banks, J. Tumlir, 'The political problem of adjustment', *The World Economy* 9 (1986), pp. 141–152.

33. M. Wolf *et al*, *Costs of Protecting Jobs in Textiles and Clothing* (Trade Policy Research Centre, London, 1984).

34. H. F. Lydall, *Trade and Employment* (ILO, Geneva, 1975).

35. J. Riedel, *op. cit.*, Chapter 4.

36. R. Cassen and Associates, *Does Aid Work?* (Clarendon Press, 1986); OECD, *Development Cooperation* (annual publication), gives official information and up-to-date statistics on aid.

37. R. E. Caves, *Multinational Enterprises and Economic Analysis* (Cambridge University Press, 1982), especially Chapter 9; J. H. Dunning, *International Production and the Multinational Enterprise* (Allen and Unwin, 1981).

38. I. Frank, *Foreign enterprise in developing countries* (John Hopkins University Press, Baltimore, 1980).

39. This raises the qustion of whether multinationals 'exploit' the South by earning an excessive rate of profit. R. Vernon, *Storm over the Multinationals: The Real Issues* (Macmillan, 1977), thinks that this is not proven. An analysis of the rate of return on capital to US-owned subsidiaries in the South gave a return of 20% after allowing for transfer pricing policies.

40. C. J. Allsopp, V. Joshi, 'The international debt crisis', *Oxford Review of Economic Policy* vol. 2 no. 1 (1985), pp. i–xxxiii.

41. W. R. Cline, *International Debt and the Stability of the World Economy* (Institute for International Economics, Washington DC, 1983).

42. S. Griffith-Jones, 'Ways forward from the debt crisis', *Oxford Review of Economic Policy* vol. 2 no. 1 (1985), pp. 39–61.

43. G. K. Helleiner, *International Economic Disorder* (Macmillan, 1980); G. K. Helleiner (ed.), *For Good or Evil: Economic Theory and North–South Negotiations* (University of Toronto Press, 1982); W. M. Corden, *The NIEO Proposals: A Cool Look* (Trade Policy Research Centre, London, 1979); Brandt Commission, *North–South: A Programme for Survival* (Pan Books, London and Sydney, 1979); J. Bhagwati (ed.), *The New International Economic Order: The North–South Debate* (MIT Press, Cambridge, Mass., 1977).

44. A. Maizels, 'Commodities in crisis: an overview of the main issues', *World Development* 15 (1987), pp. 537–549. This whole issue of *World Development* is edited by Maizels with the general title *Primary Commodities in the World Economy: Problems and Policies.*

45. C. Gilbert, 'International commodity agreements: design and performance', *World Development* 15 (1987), pp. 591–616; D. M. G. Newbery, J. E. Stiglitz, *Theory of Commodity Price Stabilization: A Study in the Economics of Risk* (Clarendon Press, 1981).

46. A. P. Hewitt, 'Stabex and commodity export compensation schemes: prospects

for globalization', *World Development* 15 (1987), pp. 617–631.

47. J. Williamson, 'The economics of IMF conditionality' in G. K. Helleiner (ed.), *op. cit.*; J. Williamson (ed.), *IMF Conditionality* (Institute for International Economics, Washington DC, 1983); T. Killick *et al*, *The quest for economic stabilization: the IMF and the Third World* (Heinemann, London, 1984).

48. See, for example, the symposium *The Evolving International Monetary System*, *World Development* 15 (1987), no. 12.

49. This section draws on the critique by P. D. Henderson, 'Survival, Development and the Report of the Brandt commission', *The World Economy* 3 (1980), pp. 87–117.

50. O. M. T. O'Donovan, *In Pursuit of a Christian View of War* (Grove Books on Ethics, Nottingham, 1977).

Chapter Eight: Economic growth (pages 281–308)

1. Most advanced undergraduate macroeconomic texts include a section on growth theory: for examples see R. Dornbusch, S. Fischer, *Macroeconomics* (McGraw-Hill, ²1981), Chapter 17; R. Levacic and A. Rebmann, *Macroeconomics* (Macmillan, ²1982), Chapter 15.

2. E. F. Denison, *Accounting for US Economic Growth 1929–1969* (Brookings Institution, 1974); *Accounting for Slower Growth: the US in the 1970s* (Brookings Institution, 1979); R. C. O. Matthews, C. H. Feinstein, J. C. Odling-Smee, *British Economic Growth, 1856–1973* (Cambridge University Press, 1982); E. F. Denison, J-P. Pouillier, *Why Growth Rates Differ* (Brookings Institution, 1967).

3. A comprehensive technical analysis of this problem is to be found in *The Global 2000 Report to the President: Entering the Twenty-First Century*, 3 vols. (Government Printing Office, Washington DC, 1980). A useful description of the main problem areas is given in L. Wilkinson (ed.), *Earthkeeping: Christian Stewardship of Natural Resources* (Eerdmans, 1980), Section 1. Issues relating to agriculture are summarized in C. D. Freudenberger, *Food for Tomorrow* (Augsburg Publishing House, 1984).

4. L. G. Thurow, *The Zero Sum Society* (Basic Books, 1980); E. J. Mishan, *The Costs of Economic Growth* (Pelican Books, 1969); T. Scitovsky, *The Joyless Economy* (Oxford University Press, New York, 1976); F. Hirsch, *The Social Limits to Growth* (Routledge and Kegan Paul, 1977).

5. J. Seabrook, *What went wrong? Why hasn't having more made people happier?* (Pantheon Books, 1978).

6. R. A. Easterlin, 'Does economic growth improve the human lot?', in P. A. David, M. W. Reder (eds.), *Nations and Households in Economic Growth* (Academic Press, 1974).

7. J. L. Simon, 'Interpersonal welfare comparisons can be made—and used for redistribution decisions', *Kyklos* 27 (1974), pp. 63–98.

8. W. Nordhaus, J. Tobin, 'Is growth obsolete?', in *Economic Growth* (National Bureau of Economic Research, 1972).

9. L. G. Thurow, *op. cit.*

10. Thurow, *op. cit.*, Chapters 6–8.

11. E. J. Mishan, *op. cit.* A previous hardback edition, published by Staples Press, appeared in 1967.

12. A. C. Pigou, *The Economics of Welfare* (Macmillan, ⁴1932).

13. W. Beckerman, *In Defence of Economic Growth* (Jonathan Cape, 1974).

14. F. Hirsch, *op. cit.*

15. F. Hirsch, *op. cit.*, p. 52.

16. F. Hirsch, *op. cit.*, Part III.

17. S. B. Linder, *The Harried Leisure Class* (Columbia University Press, 1970).

18. T. Scitovsky, *op. cit.*

19. An excellent survey of applications to fisheries and forestry is J. M. Hartwick, N. D. Olewiler, *The Economics of Natural Resource Use* (Harper and Row, 1986), Chapters 8–11.

20. Note that the inverted curve gives an *average* relationship. In practice, such biological relationships are stochastic depending on chance factors in the natural environment in a particular year. Introducing uncertainty complicates the analysis without, however, affecting the substantive conclusions.

21. The reader will note that this application of the model to cropping is somewhat strained. A more straightforward description would involve some aspect of the biological system, *e.g.* the quantity and quality of the soil. Given the environmental conditions, it is possible to define a sustainable crop yield which can be taken in the long run (possibly with a suitable rotation of crops) without damaging the soil. Though the biological dynamics are considerably more complex in this case, the principles to be applied are fundamentally the same.

22. Hartwick, Olewiler, *op. cit.*, Chapters 3–6; P. S. Dasgupta, G. M. Heal, *Economic Theory and Exhaustible Resources* (Cambridge University Press, 1979), Chapters 6–7.

23. W. Granberg-Michaelson, *A Worldly Spirituality: The Call to Redeem Life on Earth* (Harper and Row, 1984), especially Part II. See also K. Bockmuehl, *Conservation and Lifestyle* (Grove Books, Nottingham, 1977), translated from German by B. N. Kaye; L. Wilkinson (ed.), *op. cit.*, Section III. H. P. Santmire, *The Travail of Nature* (Fortress Press, 1985), traces the ambiguous responses to nature in Christian theology from the Fathers to the present day, and concludes with a reconsideration of the biblical material.

24. This ignores the stochastic element. If environmental conditions are adverse, for example, then the take in a particular season will need to be adjusted downwards appropriately, if the stock is not to be harmed.

25. The possibility of a high yield, but sustainable, agriculture is well documented in W. Jackson, *New Roots for Agriculture* (Brick, Andover Mass., 1980). See also C. D. Freudenberger, *Food for tomorrow?*, *op. cit.*, Parts 2 and 3.

26. This section and the next rely heavily on Hartwick and Olewiler, *op. cit.*, and Dasgupta and Heal, *op. cit.* For detailed analysis and applications the text by Hartwick and Olewiler is particularly interesting.

27. The phrase is the title of a seminal book on 'simple lifestyle': J. V. Taylor, *Enough is Enough* (SCM, 1975).

28. See R. Sider, *Rich Christians in an Age of Hunger* (IVP, Downers Grove, Ill., ²1984), pp. 137–151.

29. Radical proposals for an economy in steady state with no growth are too complex to be treated here. See H. Daly, *Steady State Economics* (W. H. Freeman and Co., 1977), and H. Daly (ed.), *Towards a Steady State Economy* ((W. H. Freeman and Co., 1983).

Index